SUPERMAN: THE JOURNEY

ERHEIDEN WRITER ED BENES THOMAS DERENICK JOE PRADO IVAN REIS ELTON RAMALHO PENCILLERS

S WAYNE FAUCHER MARIAH BENES ALEX LEI ROB LEA JOE PRADO MARC CAMPOS OCLAIR ALBERT INKERS

S COLORIST PAT BROSSEAU JARED K. FLETCHER ROB LEIGH KEN LOPEZ NICK J. NAPOLITANO LETTERERS

RO/ZOOM RACE SEQUENCE GAIL SIMONE WRITER JOHN BYRNE PENCILLER NELSON DeCASTRO INKER

SSEAU LETTERER GUY MAJOR COLORIST SUPERMAN CREATED BY JERRY SIEGEL & JOE SHUSTER

W9-AGG-009

OUR STORY SO FAR

Faster than a speeding bullet, more powerful than a locomotive, able to leap the tallest buildings with a single bound... **Superman** is known to all as the world's greatest superhero. While he has faced many challenges that have tested his heroic abilities — including his own death and resurrection — the Man of Steel finds his life in a downward spiral...

Clark Kent and his *Daily Planet* editor Perry White faked Clark's firing, thus allowing him to go undercover to look for proof that President Lex Luthor was engaged in criminal activities. In the meantime, White hired Clark's professional rival Jack Ryder to fill his investigative reporting slot. When Clark was finally ready to return to work, he had to settle for something lower on the newspaper food chain.

Clark's wife, Lois Lane, had known about the demotion for some time, but was sworn to secrecy by White. Once Clark found this out, he was naturally upset. But before he had a chance to react to the news, he was needed again as Superman.

In his hometown of Smallville, he had to deal with the wrathful time traveler Gog, who was seeking to kill Superman to prevent a particular future from coming to pass. The Man of Steel was badly wounded, and he needed allies — including Steel, Wonder Woman, and the Teen Titans — to help him.

Rushed home to heal from his wounds, Superman would have to endure one final stab...this time to the heart. Lana Lang — his boyhood sweetheart — confronted Clark, confessing her love for him and accusing Lois of treating him unfairly. In part, her words rang true.

The Man of Steel had to put his marital woes on hold when a new threat — named Ruin — arrived on the scene. For unknown reasons, Ruin made his attacks personal, and he was aided by twins with parasitic powers. During all this, Lois was embedded with the U.S. armed forces, sent by the *Planet* to cover a Middle East conflict. Her assignment was interrupted when a sniper shot her, nearly killing her. Superman extracted Lois from the battlefield, and it took all of Dr. Mid-Nite's skills to save her life.

Soon thereafter, Superman was led to believe that he had created a true paradise, a better world that existed beyond ours, in the Kryptonian Phantom Zone. One million people — including Lois — were whisked there during the phenomenon known as "the vanishing." But paradise was quickly lost, superseded by the madness of the Kryptonian criminal Zod, becoming a living hell only Superman could undo.

Back in the real world, the Man of Steel found himself the victim of a deadly conspiracy, and at odds with several of his fellow heroes, even coming to blows with his dearest friends.

In this series of events, Superman and Wonder Woman fought, and their battle destroyed his Arctic home, the Fortress of Solitude. Thus Superman was forced to search for a new location for his personal refuge.

Dan DiDio Senior VP-Executive Editor   **Eddie Berganza** Editor-original series
Tom Palmer Jr. Associate Editor-original series   **Jeanine Schaefer** Assistant Editor-original series
Robert Greenberger Senior Editor-collected edition   **Robbin Brosterman** Senior Art Director
Louis Prandi Art Director   **Paul Levitz** President & Publisher   **Georg Brewer** VP-Design & DC Direct Creative
Richard Bruning Senior VP-Creative Director   **Patrick Caldon** Executive VP-Finance & Operations
Chris Caramalis VP-Finance   **John Cunningham** VP-Marketing   **Terri Cunningham** VP-Managing Editor
Stephanie Fierman Senior VP-Sales & Marketing   **Alison Gill** VP-Manufacturing   **Rich Johnson** VP-Book Trade Sales
Hank Kanalz VP-General Manager, WildStorm   **Lillian Laserson** Senior VP & General Counsel
Jim Lee Editorial Director-WildStorm   **Paula Lowitt** Senior VP-Business & Legal Affairs
David McKillips VP-Advertising & Custom Publishing   **John Nee** VP-Business Development
Gregory Noveck Senior VP-Creative Affairs   **Cheryl Rubin** Senior VP-Brand Management
Jeff Trojan VP-Business Development, DC Direct   **Bob Wayne** VP-Sales

SUPERMAN: THE JOURNEY Published by DC Comics. Cover, introduction, and compilation copyright © 2006
DC Comics. All Rights Reserved. Originally published in single magazine form in ACTION COMICS 831, SUPERMAN 217,
221-225. Copyright © 2005 DC Comics. All Rights Reserved. All characters, their distinctive likenesses and related
elements featured in this publication are trademarks of DC Comics. The stories, characters and incidents featured in this
publication are entirely fictional. DC Comics does not read or accept unsolicited submissions of ideas, stories or artwork.
DC Comics, 1700 Broadway, New York, NY 10019. A Warner Bros. Entertainment Company.
Printed in Canada. First Printing. ISBN: 1-4012-0918-1. ISBN 13: 978-1-4012-0918-6
Cover illustration by Ed Benes and Mariah Benes. Cover color by Rod Reis.
Special thanks to Ricardo Riamonde and Ronaldo Barata.

OH MY GOD.

WASHINGTON, D.C., THE NATIONAL PHOTOGRAPHIC INTERPRETATION CENTER, PRESENT DAY.

CLEAR THE HALL! MOVE IT!

WHEN THE HELL DID THIS COME IN?

LATE LAST NIGHT. I WAS DOING THE PRELIMINARY WORK-UPS WHEN I SPOTTED IT.

ARE YOU SAYING WE DISCOVERED THIS BY CHANCE?

NOT QUITE.

LAST WEEK ONE OF OUR INFRARED SATELLITES PICKED UP A HEAT-BLOOM EMANATING FROM THE CORDILLERA DEL CONDOR MOUNTAINS, ON THE BORDER OF ECUADOR AND PERU.

SINCE FOREST FIRES DON'T GENE[RATE] NUCLEAR-LEVEL HE[AT], WE RETASKED ONE [OF] OUR KH-11'S TO GE[T A] CLOSER LOOK...

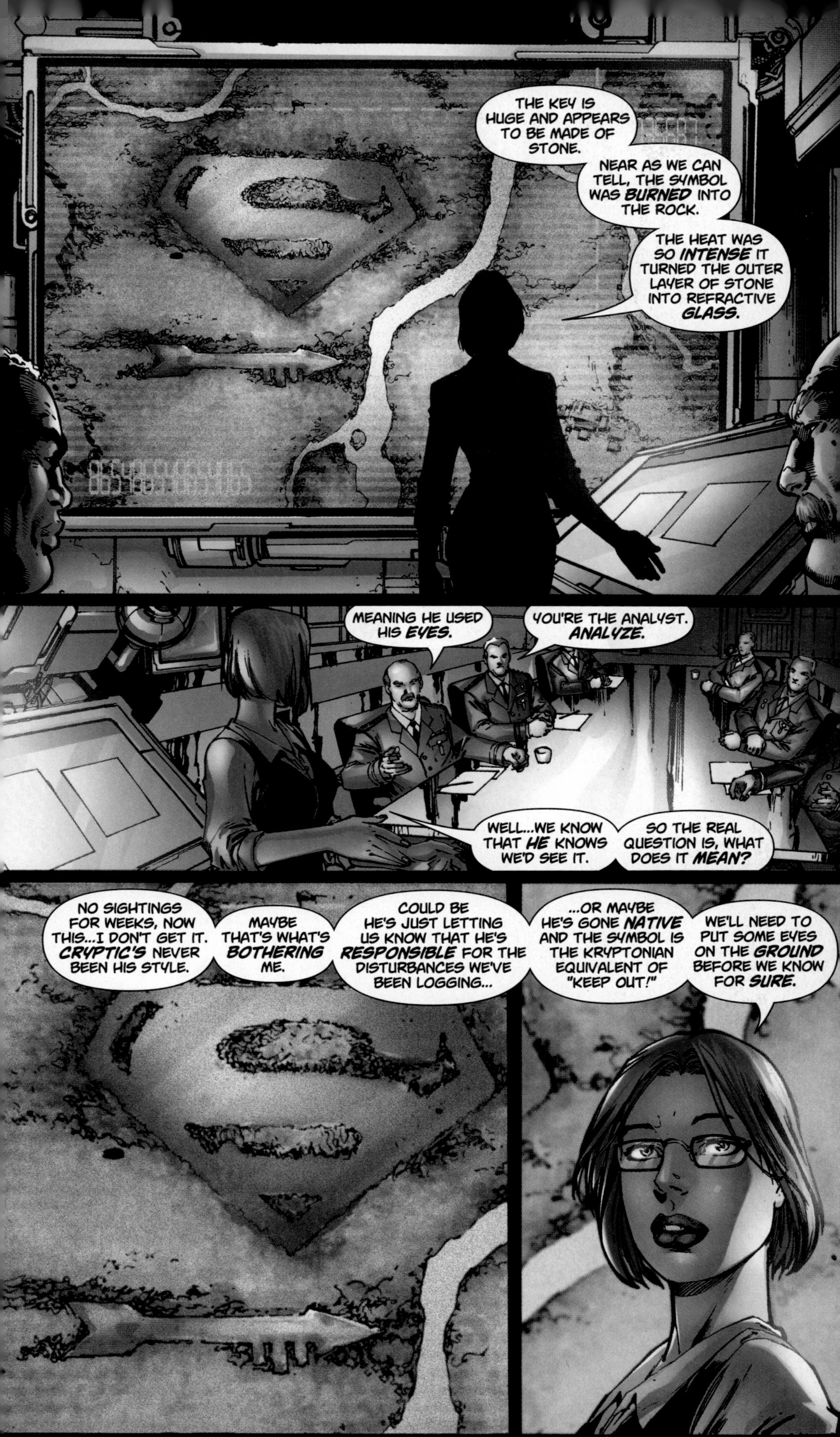
THE KEY IS HUGE AND APPEARS TO BE MADE OF STONE.
NEAR AS WE CAN TELL, THE SYMBOL WAS BURNED INTO THE ROCK.
THE HEAT WAS SO INTENSE IT TURNED THE OUTER LAYER OF STONE INTO REFRACTIVE GLASS.
MEANING HE USED HIS EYES.
YOU'RE THE ANALYST. ANALYZE.
WELL...WE KNOW THAT HE KNOWS WE'D SEE IT.
SO THE REAL QUESTION IS, WHAT DOES IT MEAN?
NO SIGHTINGS FOR WEEKS, NOW THIS...I DON'T GET IT. CRYPTIC'S NEVER BEEN HIS STYLE.
MAYBE THAT'S WHAT'S BOTHERING ME.
COULD BE HE'S JUST LETTING US KNOW THAT HE'S RESPONSIBLE FOR THE DISTURBANCES WE'VE BEEN LOGGING...
...OR MAYBE HE'S GONE NATIVE AND THE SYMBOL IS THE KRYPTONIAN EQUIVALENT OF "KEEP OUT!"
WE'LL NEED TO PUT SOME EYES ON THE GROUND BEFORE WE KNOW FOR SURE.

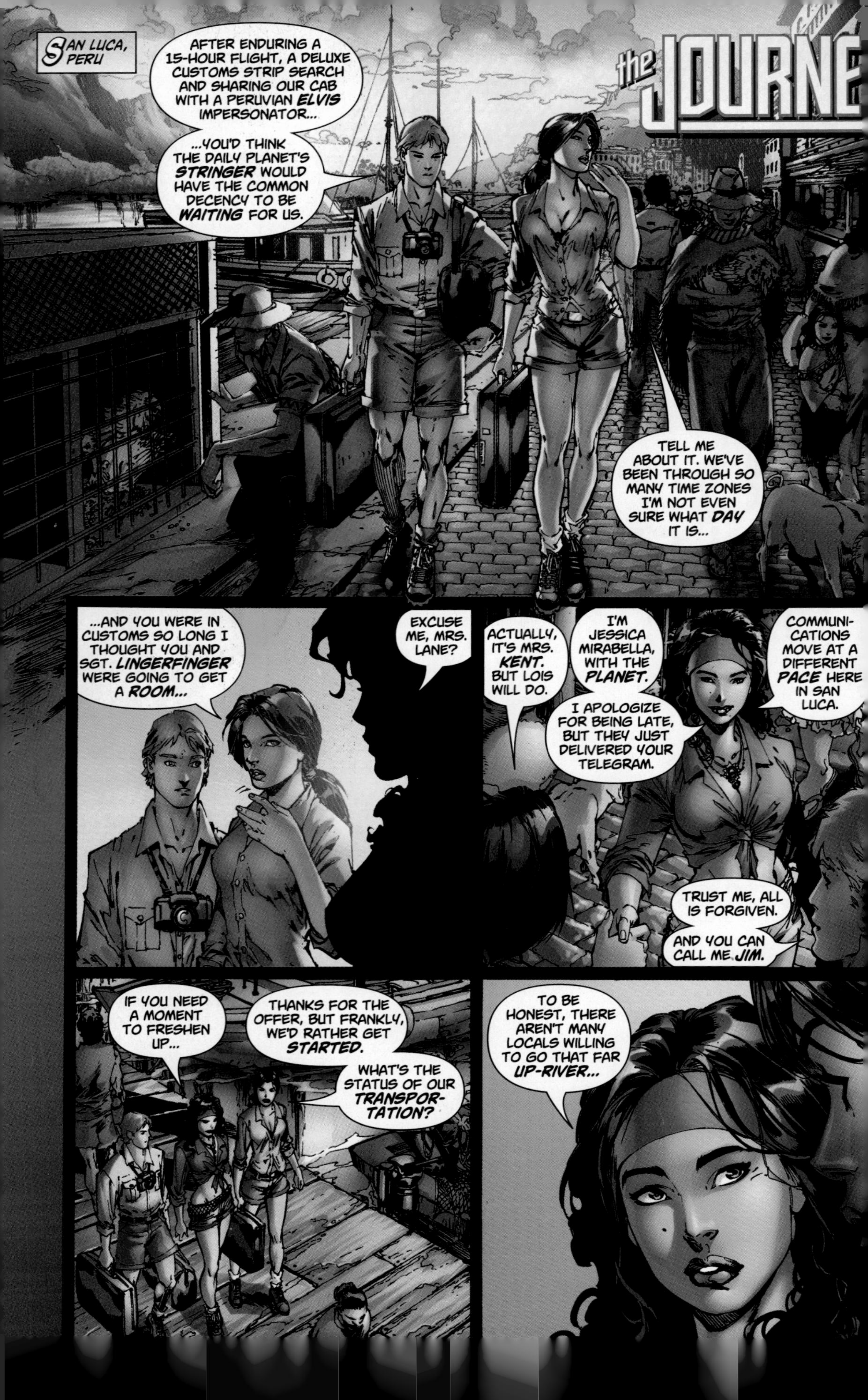
SAN LUCA, PERU
the JOURNE
AFTER ENDURING A 15-HOUR FLIGHT, A DELUXE CUSTOMS STRIP SEARCH AND SHARING OUR CAB WITH A PERUVIAN ELVIS IMPERSONATOR...
...YOU'D THINK THE DAILY PLANET'S STRINGER WOULD HAVE THE COMMON DECENCY TO BE WAITING FOR US.
TELL ME ABOUT IT. WE'VE BEEN THROUGH SO MANY TIME ZONES I'M NOT EVEN SURE WHAT DAY IT IS...
...AND YOU WERE IN CUSTOMS SO LONG I THOUGHT YOU AND SGT. LINGERFINGER WERE GOING TO GET A ROOM...
EXCUSE ME, MRS. LANE?
ACTUALLY, IT'S MRS. KENT. BUT LOIS WILL DO.
I'M JESSICA MIRABELLA, WITH THE PLANET.
I APOLOGIZE FOR BEING LATE, BUT THEY JUST DELIVERED YOUR TELEGRAM.
COMMUNICATIONS MOVE AT A DIFFERENT PACE HERE IN SAN LUCA.
TRUST ME, ALL IS FORGIVEN.
AND YOU CAN CALL ME JIM.
IF YOU NEED A MOMENT TO FRESHEN UP...
THANKS FOR THE OFFER, BUT FRANKLY, WE'D RATHER GET STARTED.
WHAT'S THE STATUS OF OUR TRANSPORTATION?
TO BE HONEST, THERE AREN'T MANY LOCALS WILLING TO GO THAT FAR UP-RIVER...

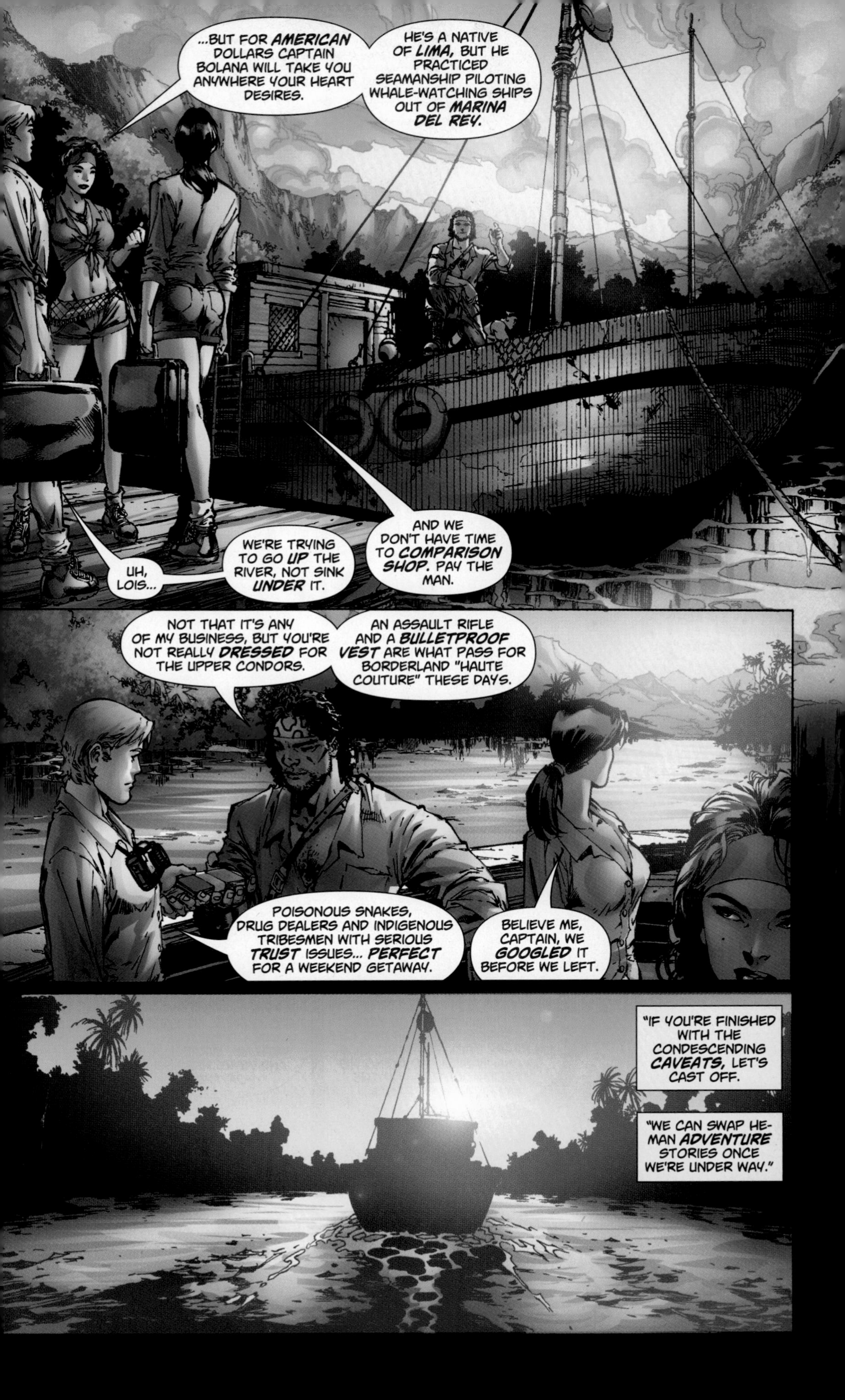
...BUT FOR AMERICAN DOLLARS CAPTAIN BOLANA WILL TAKE YOU ANYWHERE YOUR HEART DESIRES.
HE'S A NATIVE OF LIMA, BUT HE PRACTICED SEAMANSHIP PILOTING WHALE-WATCHING SHIPS OUT OF MARINA DEL REY.
UH, LOIS...
WE'RE TRYING TO GO UP THE RIVER, NOT SINK UNDER IT.
AND WE DON'T HAVE TIME TO COMPARISON SHOP. PAY THE MAN.
NOT THAT IT'S ANY OF MY BUSINESS, BUT YOU'RE NOT REALLY DRESSED FOR THE UPPER CONDORS.
AN ASSAULT RIFLE AND A BULLETPROOF VEST ARE WHAT PASS FOR BORDERLAND "HAUTE COUTURE" THESE DAYS.
POISONOUS SNAKES, DRUG DEALERS AND INDIGENOUS TRIBESMEN WITH SERIOUS TRUST ISSUES... PERFECT FOR A WEEKEND GETAWAY.
BELIEVE ME, CAPTAIN, WE GOOGLED IT BEFORE WE LEFT.
"IF YOU'RE FINISHED WITH THE CONDESCENDING CAVEATS, LET'S CAST OFF.
"WE CAN SWAP HE-MAN ADVENTURE STORIES ONCE WE'RE UNDER WAY."

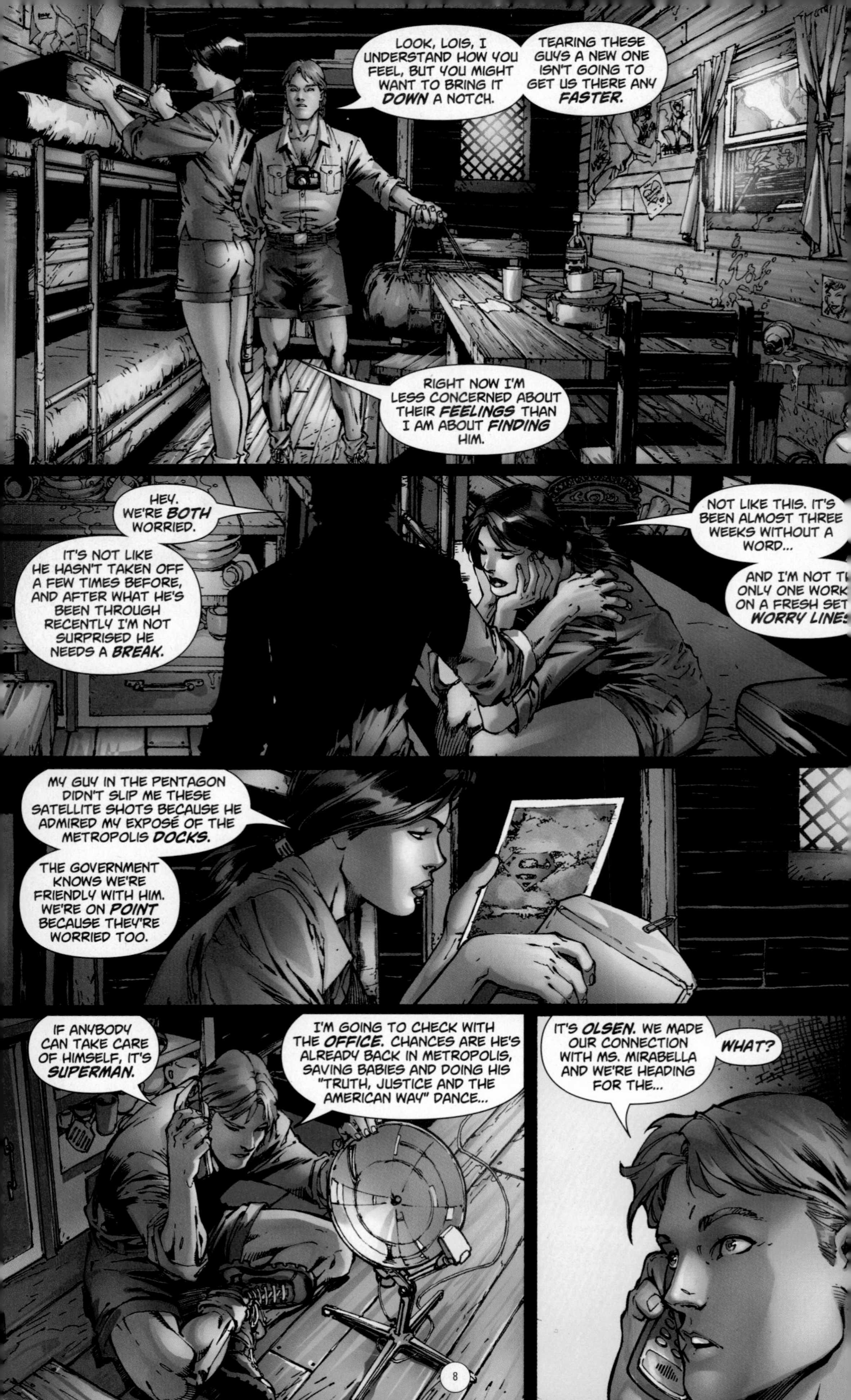
LOOK, LOIS, I UNDERSTAND HOW YOU FEEL, BUT YOU MIGHT WANT TO BRING IT DOWN A NOTCH.
TEARING THESE GUYS A NEW ONE ISN'T GOING TO GET US THERE ANY FASTER.
RIGHT NOW I'M LESS CONCERNED ABOUT THEIR FEELINGS THAN I AM ABOUT FINDING HIM.
HEY. WE'RE BOTH WORRIED.
IT'S NOT LIKE HE HASN'T TAKEN OFF A FEW TIMES BEFORE, AND AFTER WHAT HE'S BEEN THROUGH RECENTLY I'M NOT SURPRISED HE NEEDS A BREAK.
NOT LIKE THIS. IT'S BEEN ALMOST THREE WEEKS WITHOUT A WORD...
AND I'M NOT T ONLY ONE WORK ON A FRESH SET WORRY LINES
MY GUY IN THE PENTAGON DIDN'T SLIP ME THESE SATELLITE SHOTS BECAUSE HE ADMIRED MY EXPOSÉ OF THE METROPOLIS DOCKS.
THE GOVERNMENT KNOWS WE'RE FRIENDLY WITH HIM. WE'RE ON POINT BECAUSE THEY'RE WORRIED TOO.
IF ANYBODY CAN TAKE CARE OF HIMSELF, IT'S SUPERMAN.
I'M GOING TO CHECK WITH THE OFFICE. CHANCES ARE HE'S ALREADY BACK IN METROPOLIS, SAVING BABIES AND DOING HIS "TRUTH, JUSTICE AND THE AMERICAN WAY" DANCE...
IT'S OLSEN. WE MADE OUR CONNECTION WITH MS. MIRABELLA AND WE'RE HEADING FOR THE...
WHAT?

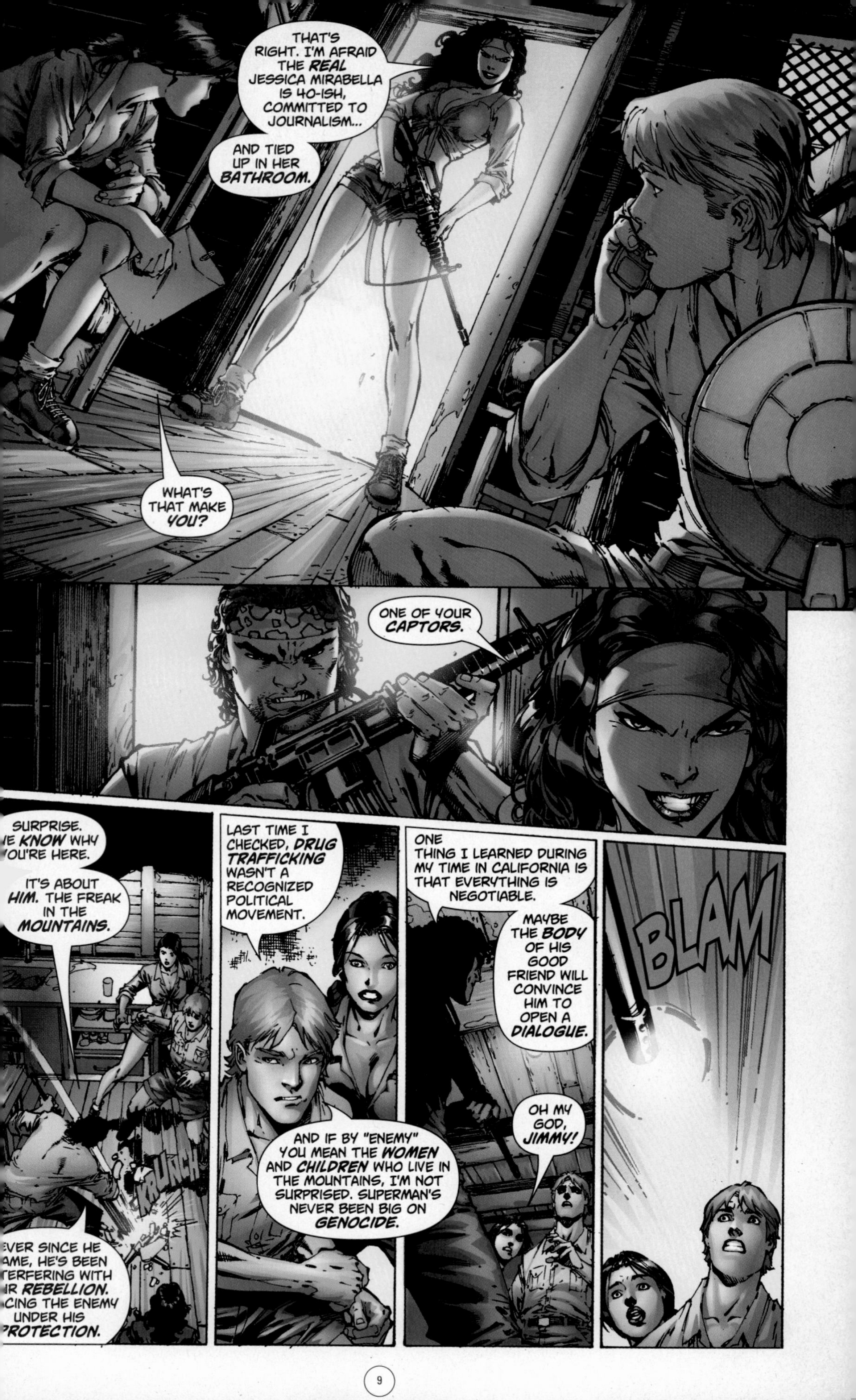

THAT'S RIGHT. I'M AFRAID THE REAL JESSICA MIRABELLA IS 40-ISH, COMMITTED TO JOURNALISM...
AND TIED UP IN HER BATHROOM.
WHAT'S THAT MAKE YOU?
ONE OF YOUR CAPTORS.
SURPRISE. E KNOW WHY OU'RE HERE.
IT'S ABOUT HIM. THE FREAK IN THE MOUNTAINS.
KRUNCH
EVER SINCE HE AME, HE'S BEEN TERFERING WITH R REBELLION. CING THE ENEMY UNDER HIS ROTECTION.
LAST TIME I CHECKED, DRUG TRAFFICKING WASN'T A RECOGNIZED POLITICAL MOVEMENT.
AND IF BY "ENEMY" YOU MEAN THE WOMEN AND CHILDREN WHO LIVE IN THE MOUNTAINS, I'M NOT SURPRISED. SUPERMAN'S NEVER BEEN BIG ON GENOCIDE.
ONE THING I LEARNED DURING MY TIME IN CALIFORNIA IS THAT EVERYTHING IS NEGOTIABLE.
MAYBE THE BODY OF HIS GOOD FRIEND WILL CONVINCE HIM TO OPEN A DIALOGUE.
OH MY GOD, JIMMY!
BLAM

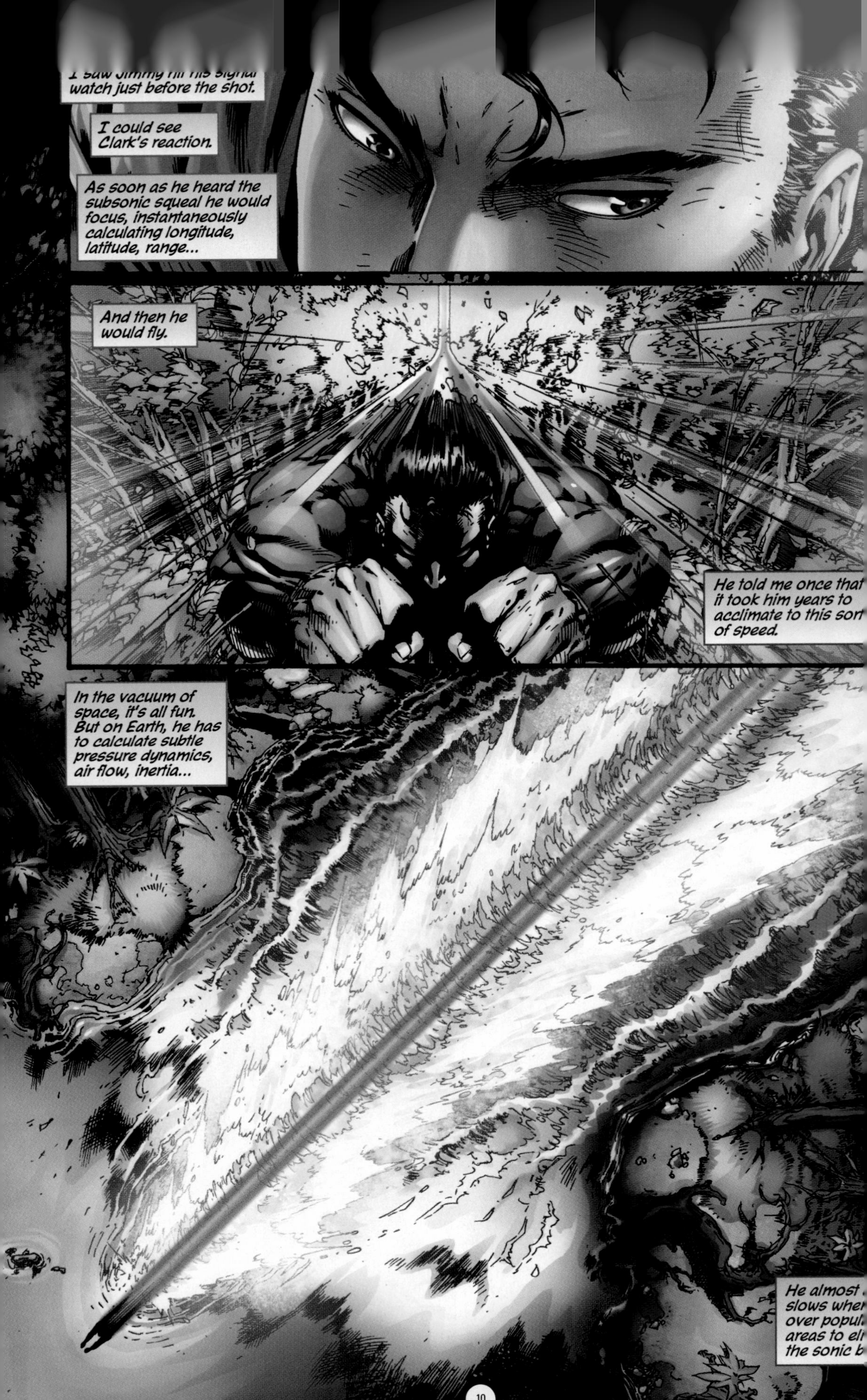
I saw Jimmy hit his signal watch just before the shot.
I could see Clark's reaction.
As soon as he heard the subsonic squeal he would focus, instantaneously calculating longitude, latitude, range...
And then he would fly.
He told me once that it took him years to acclimate to this sort of speed.
In the vacuum of space, it's all fun. But on Earth, he has to calculate subtle pressure dynamics, air flow, inertia...
He almost slows whe over popul areas to eli the sonic b

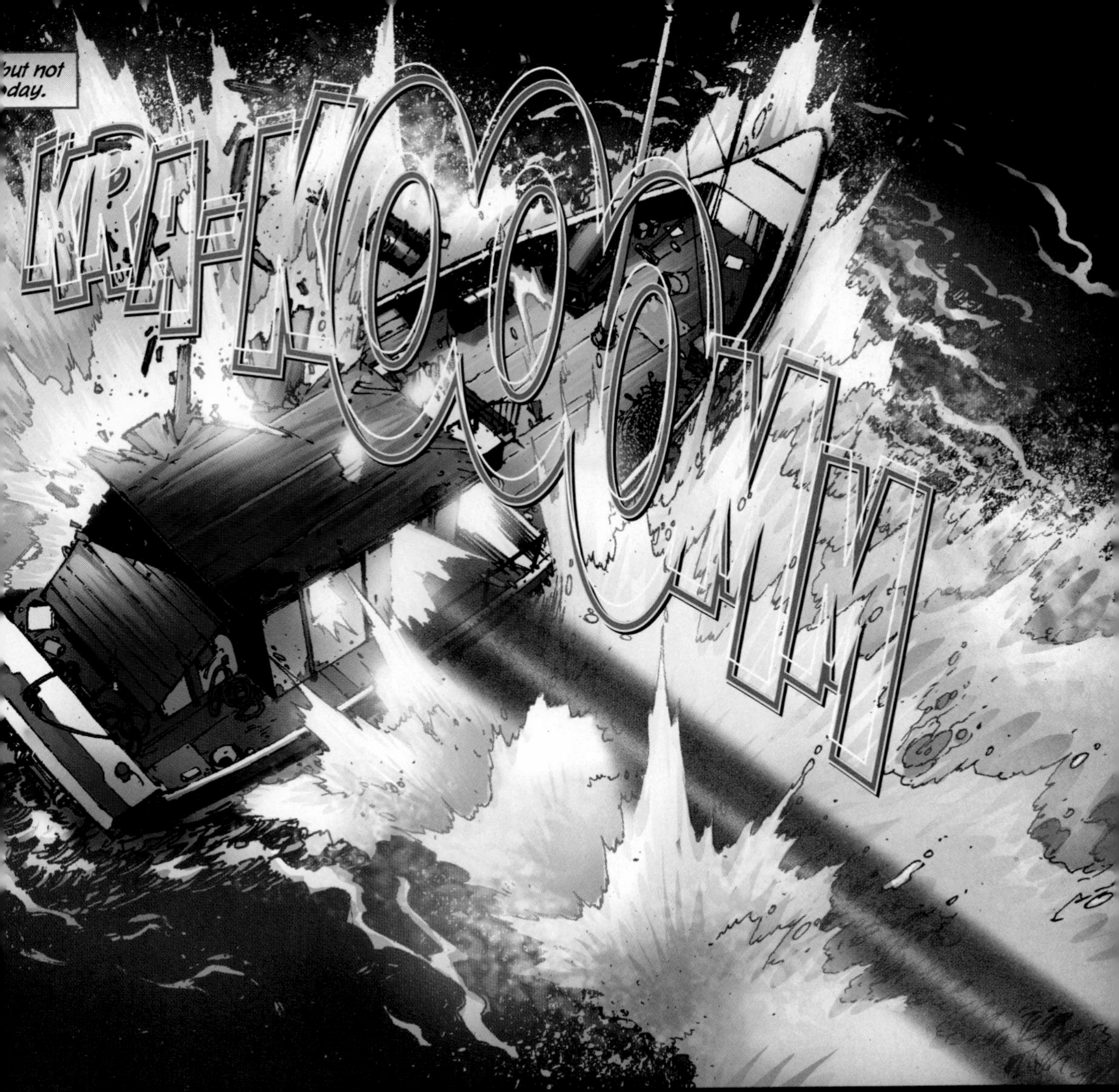
ut not
day.
KRA-KOOOOOM

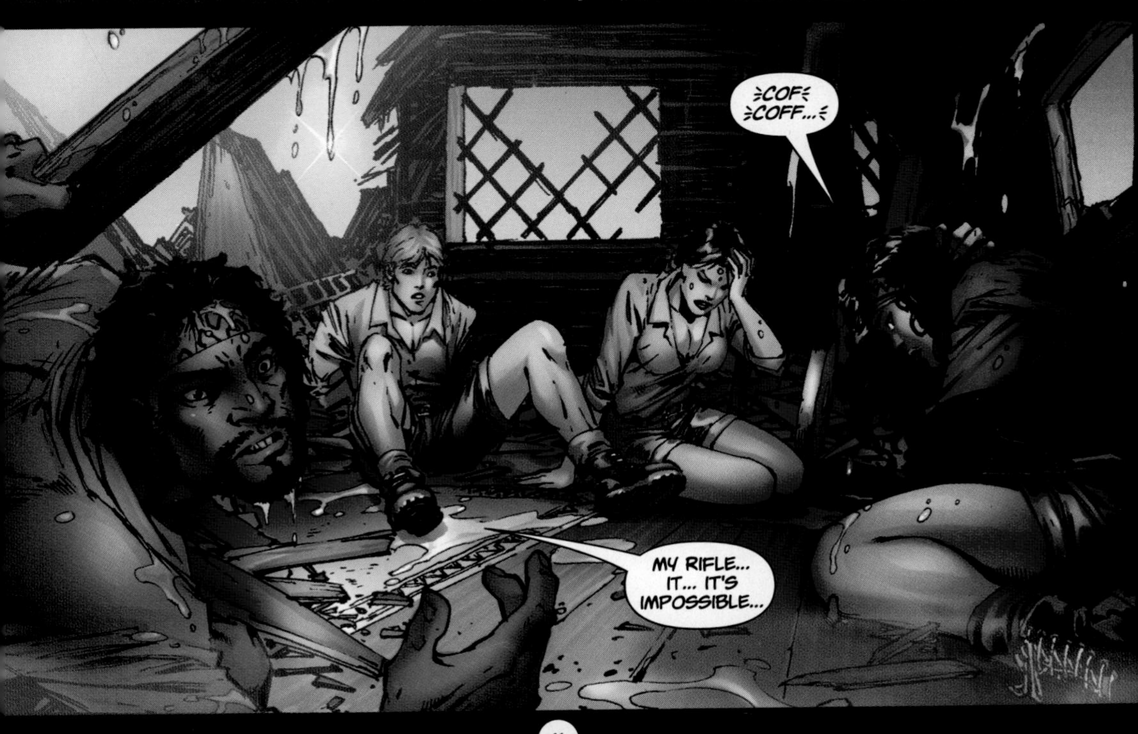
COF COFF...
MY RIFLE... IT... IT'S IMPOSSIBLE...

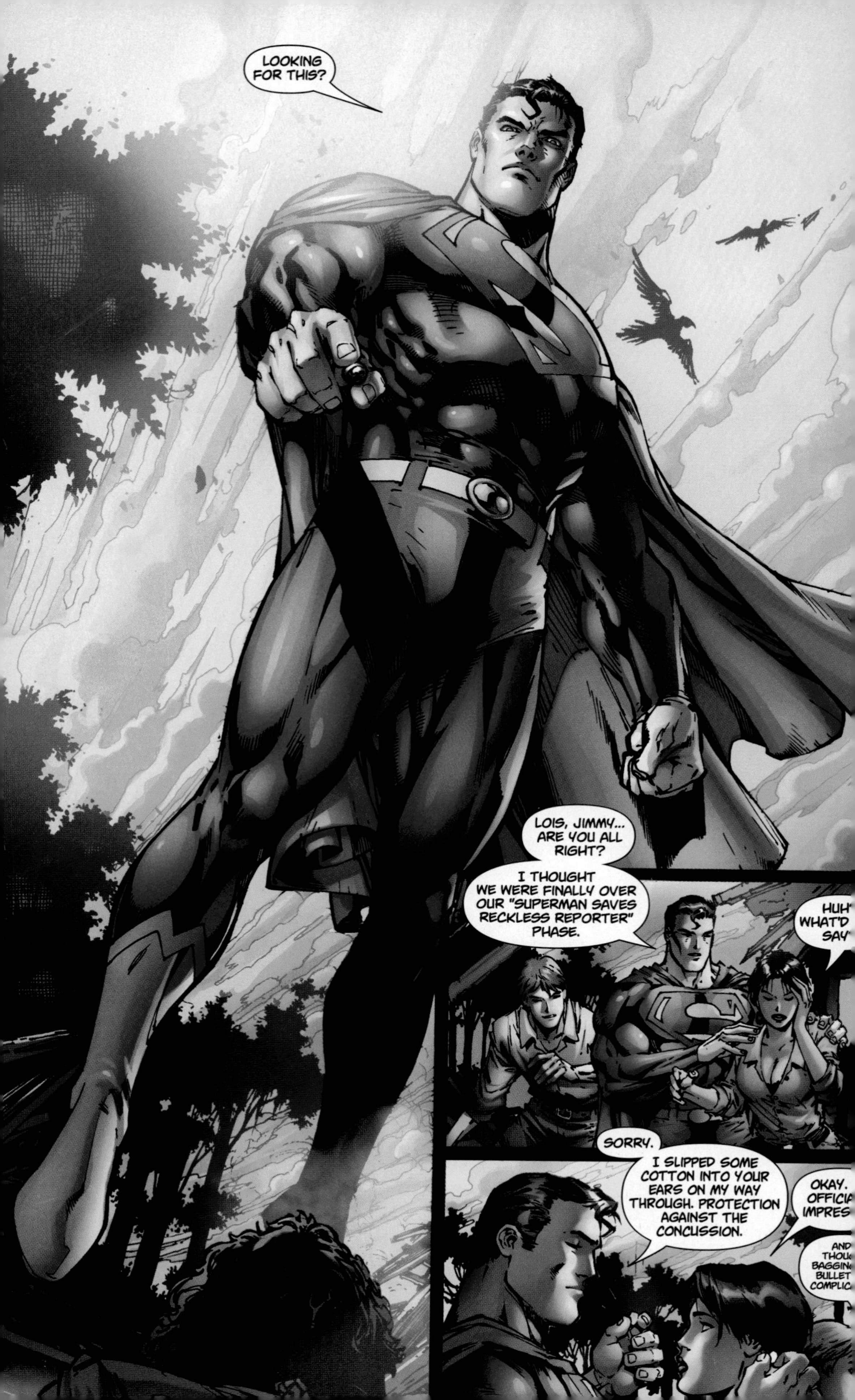
LOOKING FOR THIS?
LOIS, JIMMY... ARE YOU ALL RIGHT?
I THOUGHT WE WERE FINALLY OVER OUR "SUPERMAN SAVES RECKLESS REPORTER" PHASE.
SORRY.
I SLIPPED SOME COTTON INTO YOUR EARS ON MY WAY THROUGH. PROTECTION AGAINST THE CONCUSSION.

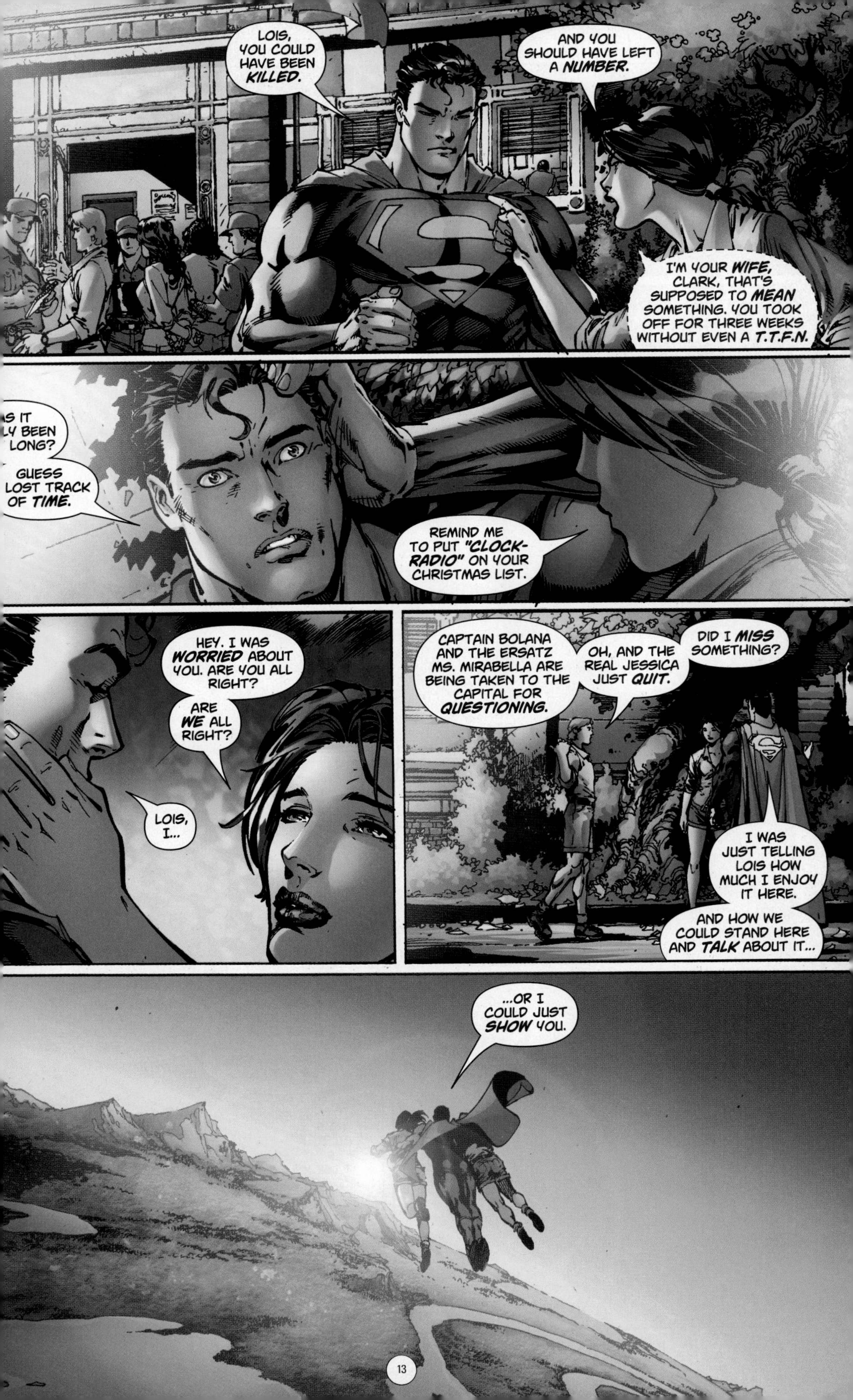
LOIS, YOU COULD HAVE BEEN KILLED.
AND YOU SHOULD HAVE LEFT A NUMBER.
I'M YOUR WIFE, CLARK, THAT'S SUPPOSED TO MEAN SOMETHING. YOU TOOK OFF FOR THREE WEEKS WITHOUT EVEN A T.T.F.N.
S IT LY BEEN LONG?
GUESS LOST TRACK OF TIME.
REMIND ME TO PUT "CLOCK-RADIO" ON YOUR CHRISTMAS LIST.
HEY. I WAS WORRIED ABOUT YOU. ARE YOU ALL RIGHT?
ARE WE ALL RIGHT?
LOIS, I...
CAPTAIN BOLANA AND THE ERSATZ MS. MIRABELLA ARE BEING TAKEN TO THE CAPITAL FOR QUESTIONING.
OH, AND THE REAL JESSICA JUST QUIT.
DID I MISS SOMETHING?
I WAS JUST TELLING LOIS HOW MUCH I ENJOY IT HERE.
AND HOW WE COULD STAND HERE AND TALK ABOUT IT...
...OR I COULD JUST SHOW YOU.

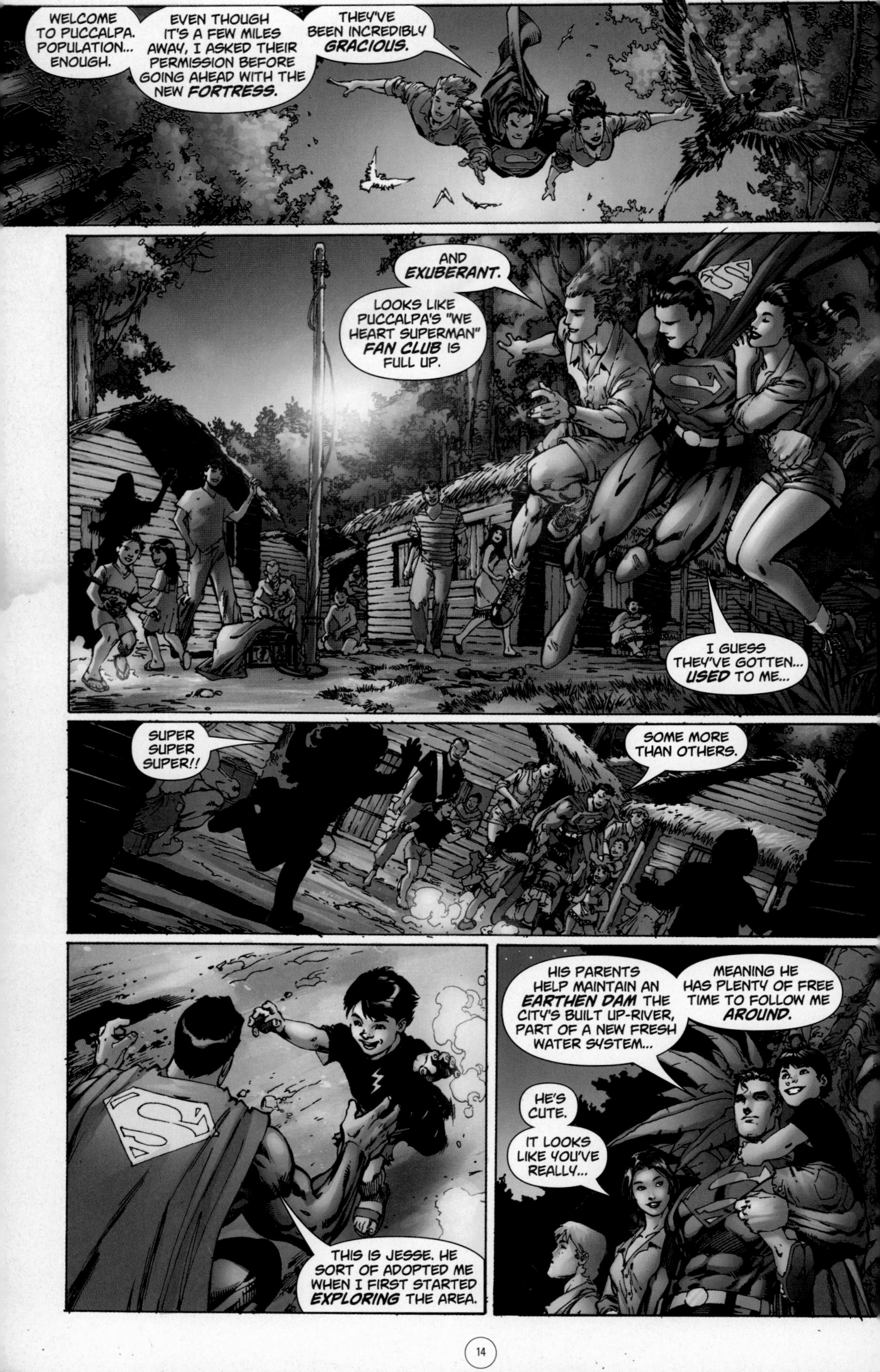
WELCOME TO PUCCALPA. POPULATION... ENOUGH.
EVEN THOUGH IT'S A FEW MILES AWAY, I ASKED THEIR PERMISSION BEFORE GOING AHEAD WITH THE NEW **FORTRESS**.
THEY'VE BEEN INCREDIBLY **GRACIOUS**.
AND **EXUBERANT**.
LOOKS LIKE PUCCALPA'S "WE HEART SUPERMAN" **FAN CLUB** IS FULL UP.
I GUESS THEY'VE GOTTEN... **USED** TO ME...
SUPER SUPER SUPER!!
SOME MORE THAN OTHERS.
THIS IS JESSE. HE SORT OF ADOPTED ME WHEN I FIRST STARTED **EXPLORING** THE AREA.
HIS PARENTS HELP MAINTAIN AN **EARTHEN DAM** THE CITY'S BUILT UP-RIVER, PART OF A NEW FRESH WATER SYSTEM...
MEANING HE HAS PLENTY OF FREE TIME TO FOLLOW ME **AROUND**.
HE'S CUTE.
IT LOOKS LIKE YOU'VE REALLY...

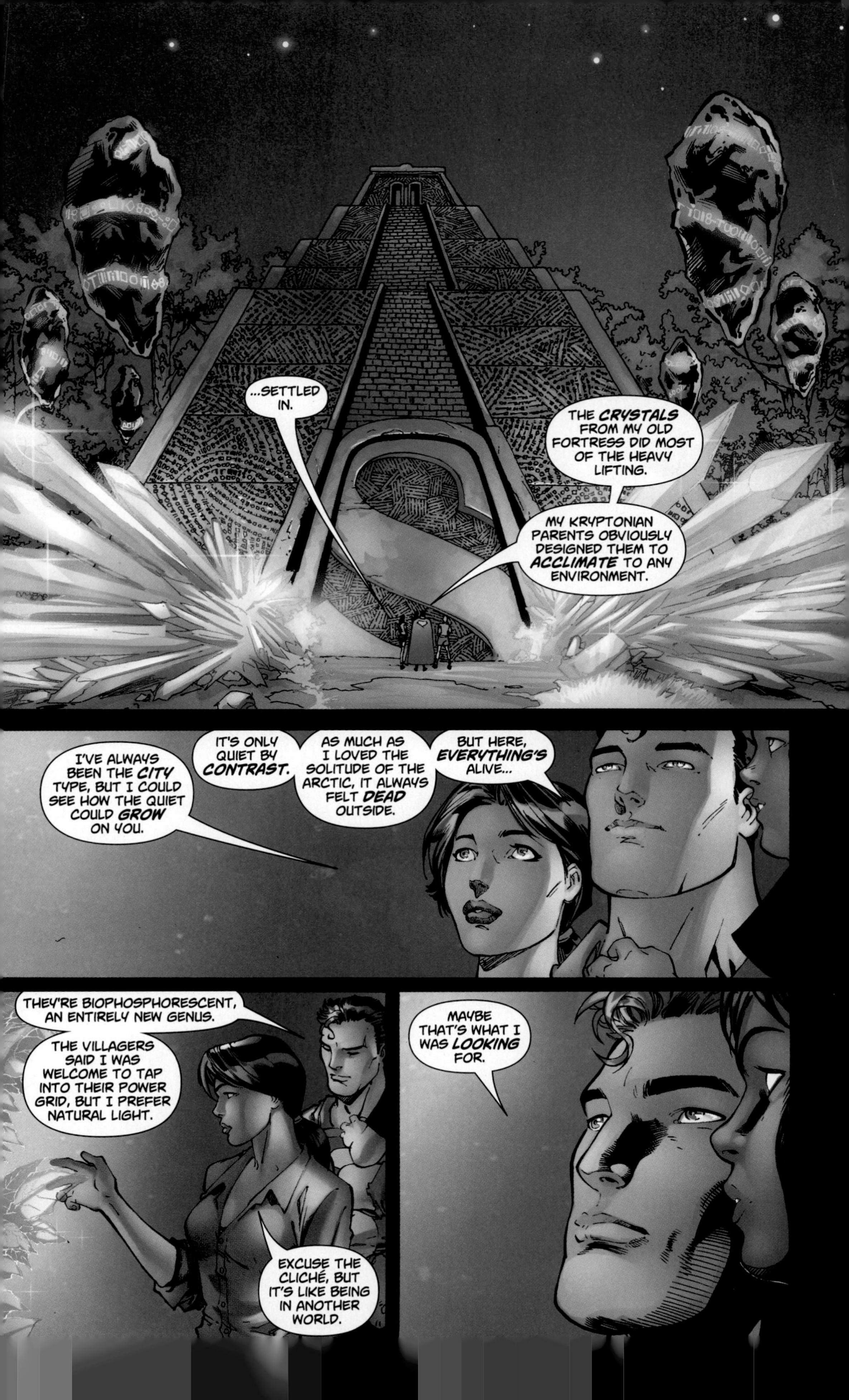
...SETTLED IN.
THE CRYSTALS FROM MY OLD FORTRESS DID MOST OF THE HEAVY LIFTING.
MY KRYPTONIAN PARENTS OBVIOUSLY DESIGNED THEM TO ACCLIMATE TO ANY ENVIRONMENT.
I'VE ALWAYS BEEN THE CITY TYPE, BUT I COULD SEE HOW THE QUIET COULD GROW ON YOU.
IT'S ONLY QUIET BY CONTRAST.
AS MUCH AS I LOVED THE SOLITUDE OF THE ARCTIC, IT ALWAYS FELT DEAD OUTSIDE.
BUT HERE, EVERYTHING'S ALIVE...
THEY'RE BIOPHOSPHORESCENT, AN ENTIRELY NEW GENUS.
THE VILLAGERS SAID I WAS WELCOME TO TAP INTO THEIR POWER GRID, BUT I PREFER NATURAL LIGHT.
EXCUSE THE CLICHÉ, BUT IT'S LIKE BEING IN ANOTHER WORLD.
MAYBE THAT'S WHAT I WAS LOOKING FOR.

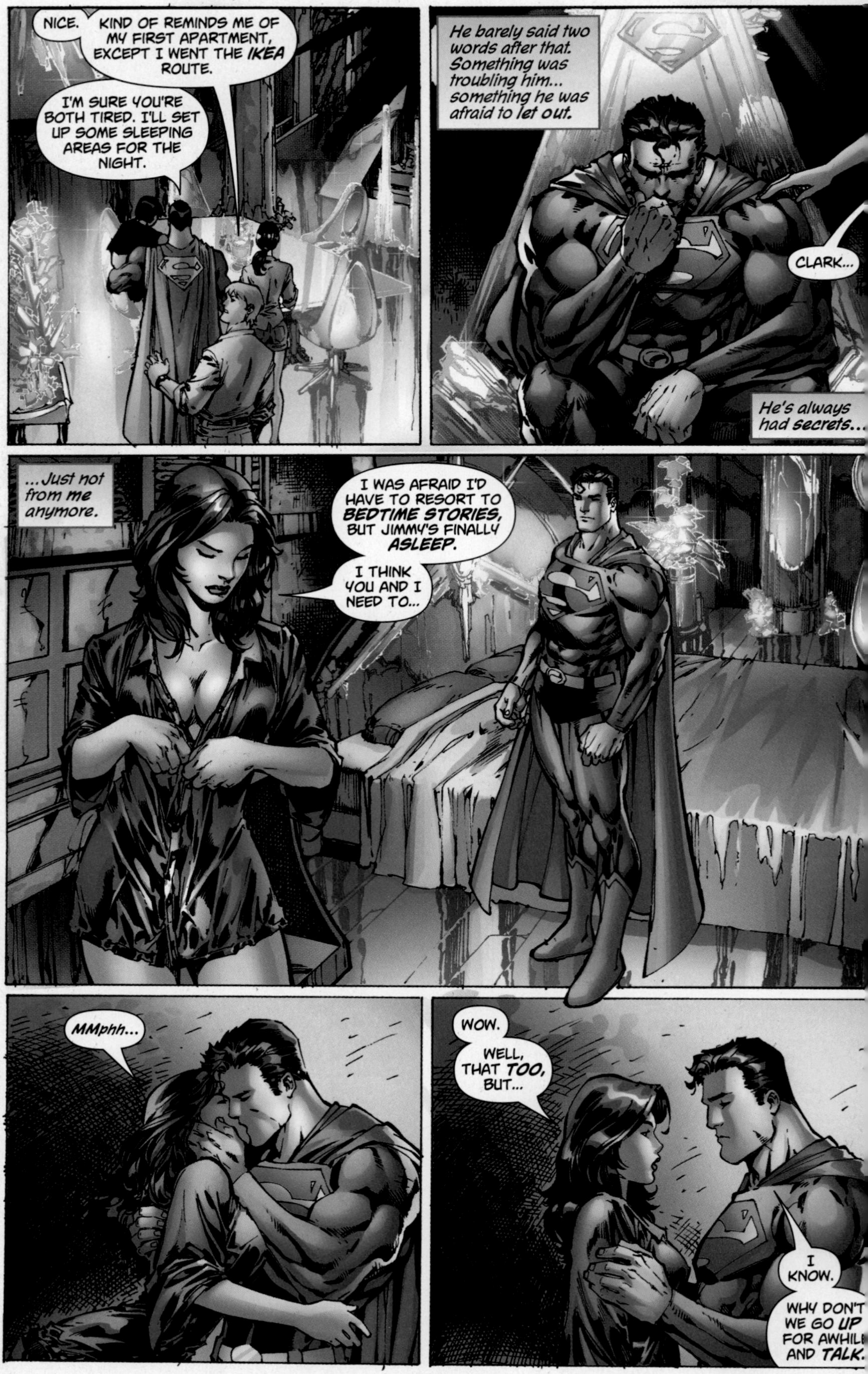

NICE.
KIND OF REMINDS ME OF MY FIRST APARTMENT, EXCEPT I WENT THE IKEA ROUTE.
I'M SURE YOU'RE BOTH TIRED. I'LL SET UP SOME SLEEPING AREAS FOR THE NIGHT.
He barely said two words after that. Something was troubling him... something he was afraid to let out.
CLARK...
He's always had secrets...
...Just not from me anymore.
I WAS AFRAID I'D HAVE TO RESORT TO BEDTIME STORIES, BUT JIMMY'S FINALLY ASLEEP.
I THINK YOU AND I NEED TO...
MMphh...
WOW.
WELL, THAT TOO, BUT...
I KNOW.
WHY DON'T WE GO UP FOR AWHILE AND TALK.

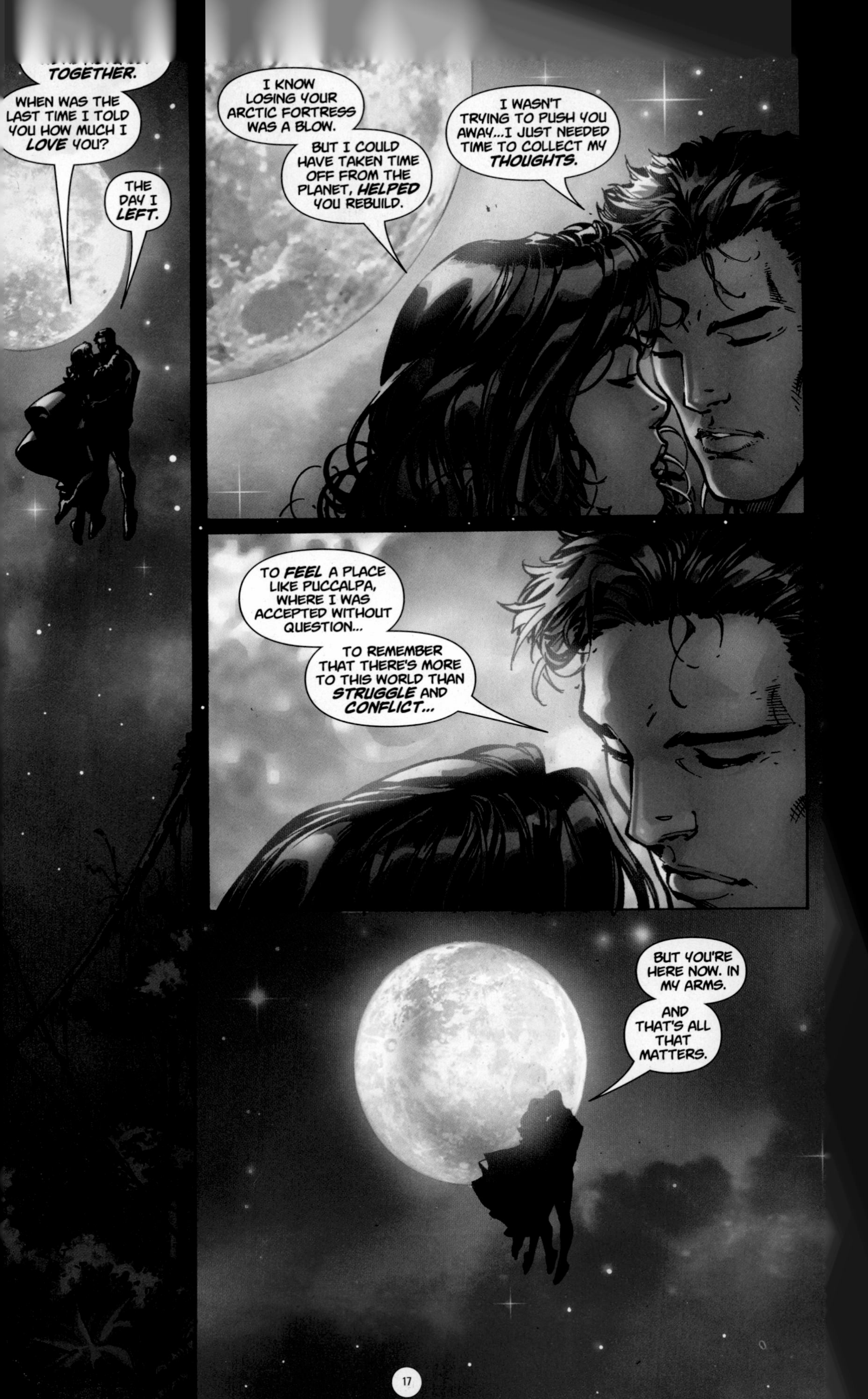
TOGETHER.
WHEN WAS THE LAST TIME I TOLD YOU HOW MUCH I LOVE YOU?
THE DAY I LEFT.
I KNOW LOSING YOUR ARCTIC FORTRESS WAS A BLOW.
BUT I COULD HAVE TAKEN TIME OFF FROM THE PLANET, HELPED YOU REBUILD.
I WASN'T TRYING TO PUSH YOU AWAY...I JUST NEEDED TIME TO COLLECT MY THOUGHTS.
TO FEEL A PLACE LIKE PUCCALPA, WHERE I WAS ACCEPTED WITHOUT QUESTION...
TO REMEMBER THAT THERE'S MORE TO THIS WORLD THAN STRUGGLE AND CONFLICT...
BUT YOU'RE HERE NOW. IN MY ARMS.
AND THAT'S ALL THAT MATTERS.

HEY! WHERE IS EVERYBODY?

JIMMY.

CLARK?

LOIS!?

WHAT?

WE HAVE A PROBLEM. HAVE YOU SEEN SUPER...

JIM, WHAT'S WRONG?

I'M NOT SURE, BUT WHOEVER'S ON THE OTHER END OF YOUR SHORTWAVE SOUNDS AWFULLY EXCITED.

DO YOU KNOW WHAT "MALECON" MEANS?

I GAVE A RADIO TO THE VILLAGE ELDER IN CASE OF TROUBLE... AND "MALECON" IS THEIR WORD FOR "DAM."

SOMETHING MUST HAVE GONE WRONG AT THE WATER PROJECT.

SUPERMAN...

WAIT...?

18

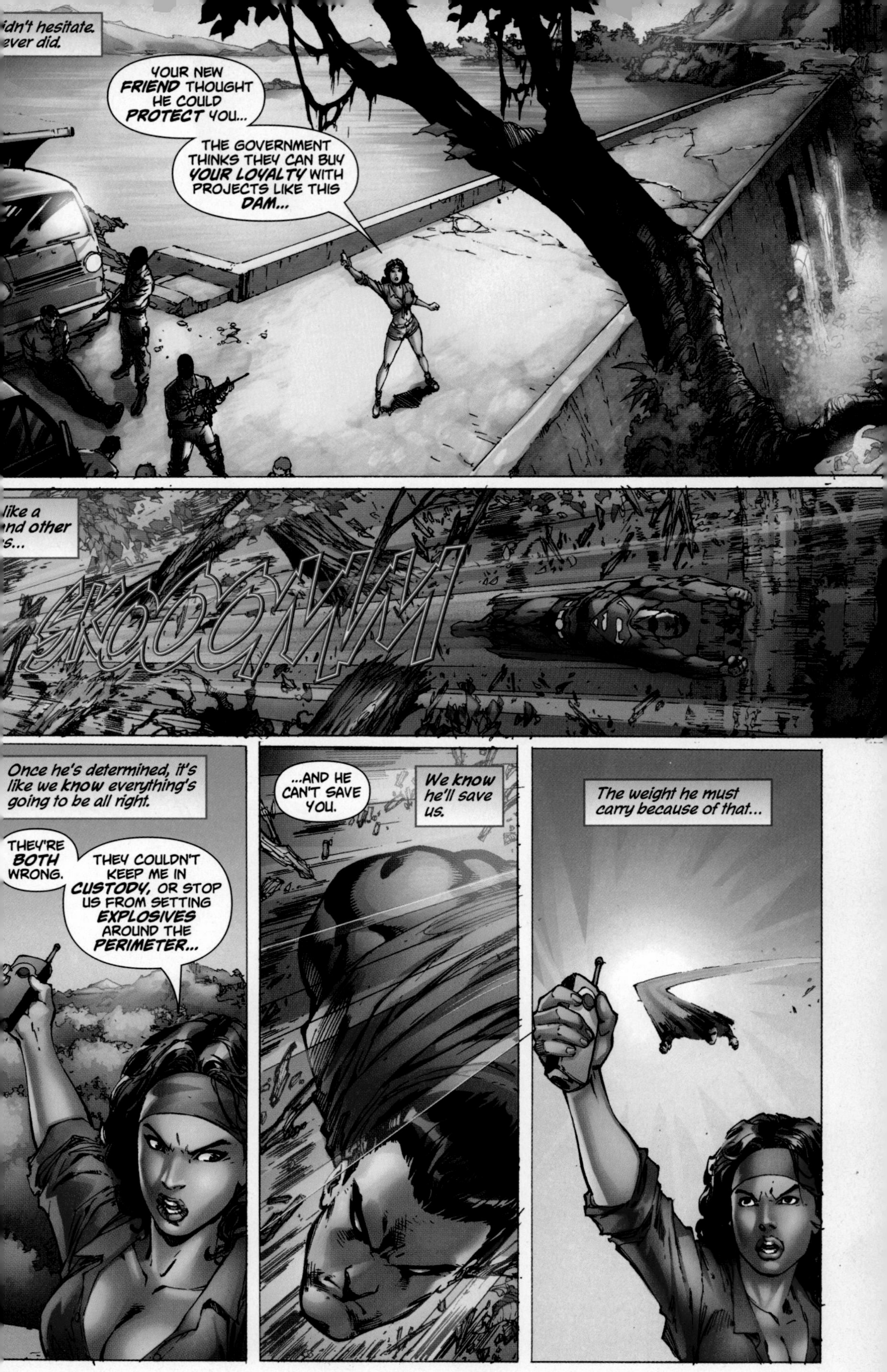

idn't hesitate.
ever did.
YOUR NEW FRIEND THOUGHT HE COULD PROTECT YOU...
THE GOVERNMENT THINKS THEY CAN BUY YOUR LOYALTY WITH PROJECTS LIKE THIS DAM...
like a
nd other
s...
SKOOOWWW
Once he's determined, it's like we know everything's going to be all right.
THEY'RE BOTH WRONG.
THEY COULDN'T KEEP ME IN CUSTODY, OR STOP US FROM SETTING EXPLOSIVES AROUND THE PERIMETER...
...AND HE CAN'T SAVE YOU.
We know he'll save us.
The weight he must carry because of that...

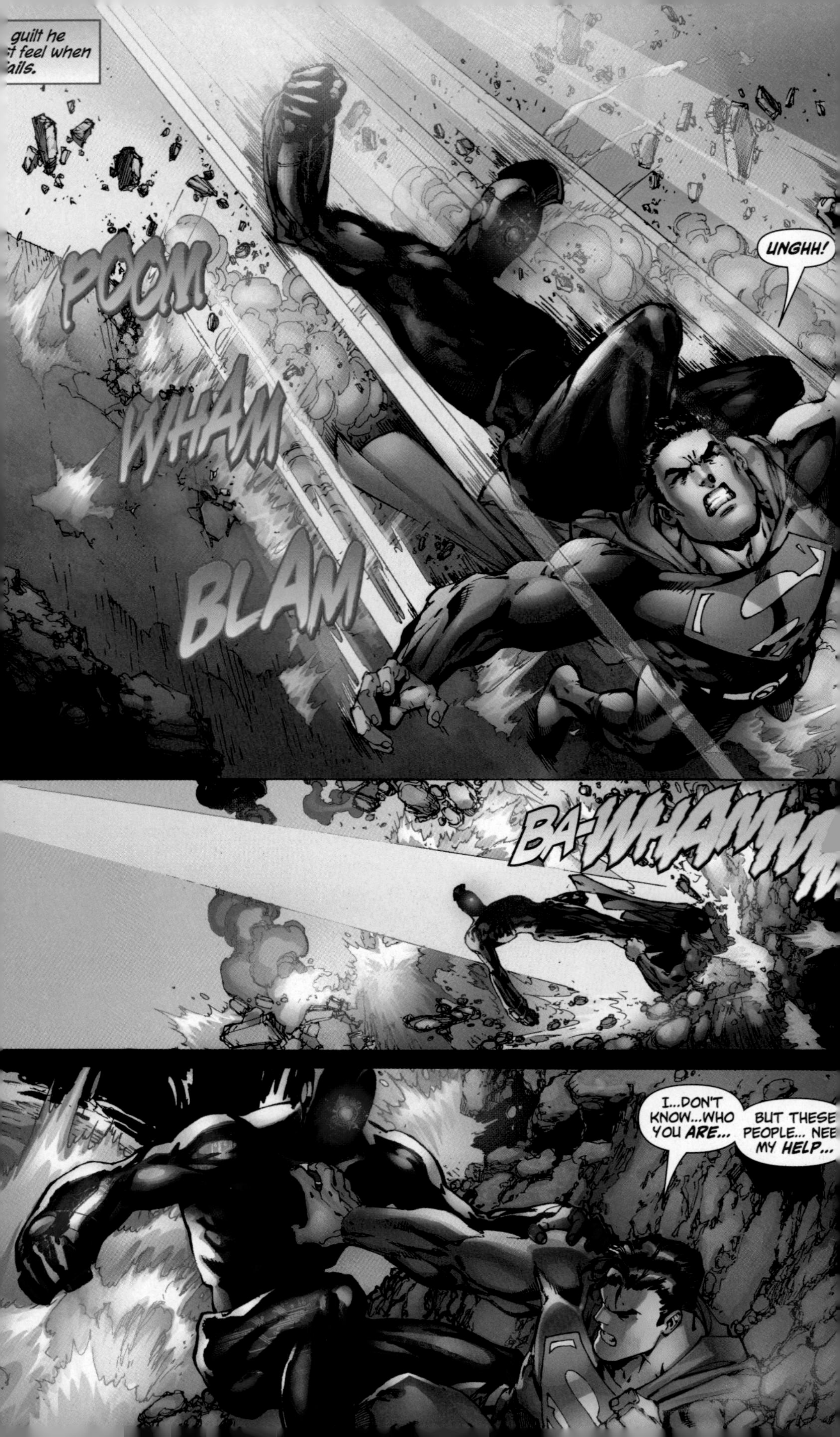
guilt he
t feel when
ails.
POOM
WHAM
BLAM
UNGHH!
BA-WHAMM
I...DON'T KNOW...WHO YOU ARE...
BUT THESE PEOPLE... NEE MY HELP...

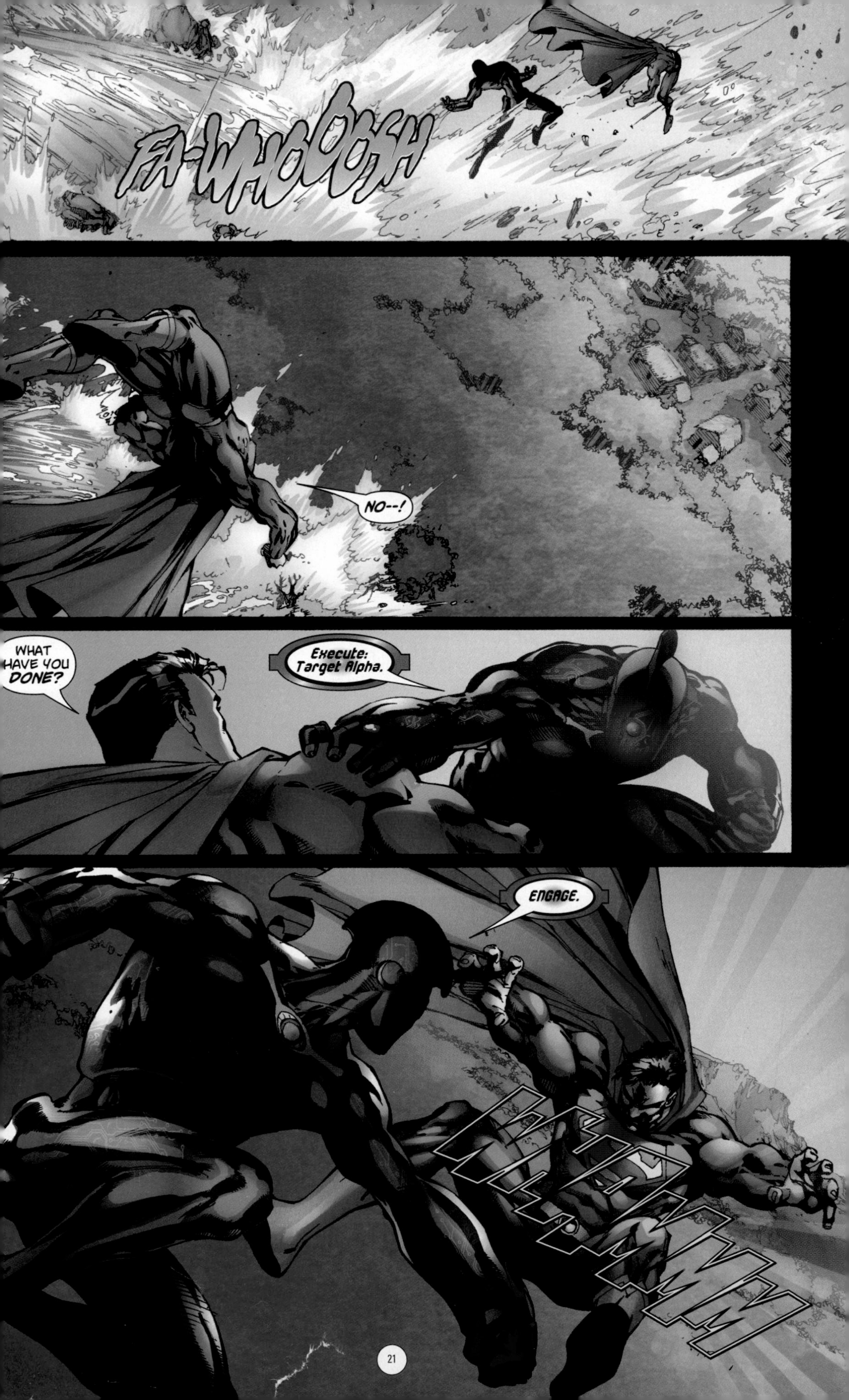
FA-WHOOOSH
NO--!
WHAT HAVE YOU DONE?
Execute: Target Alpha.
ENGAGE.

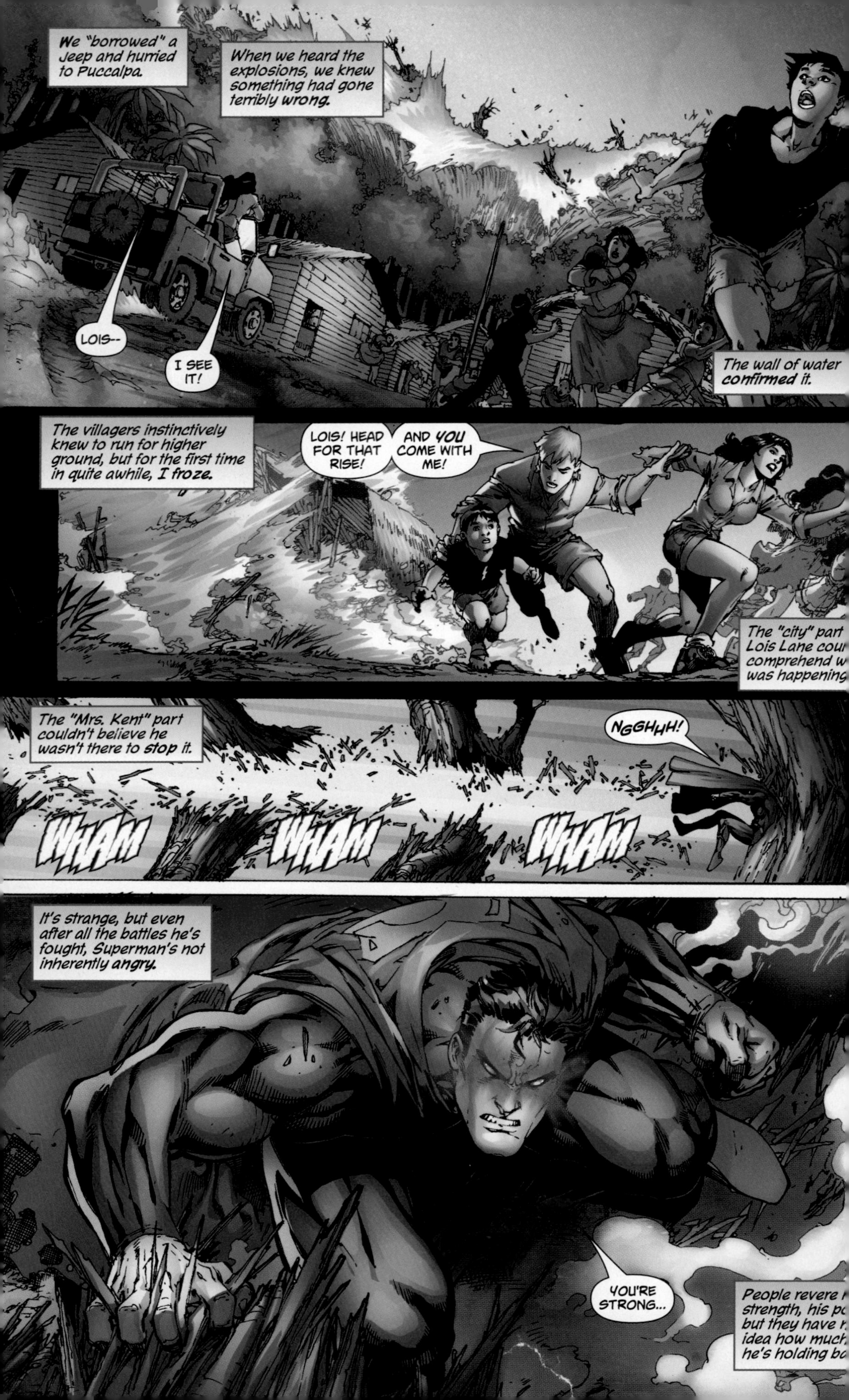
We "borrowed" a Jeep and hurried to Puccalpa.
When we heard the explosions, we knew something had gone terribly wrong.
LOIS--
I SEE IT!
The wall of water confirmed it.
The villagers instinctively knew to run for higher ground, but for the first time in quite awhile, I froze.
LOIS! HEAD FOR THAT RISE!
AND YOU COME WITH ME!
The "city" part
Lois Lane cou
comprehend w
was happening
The "Mrs. Kent" part couldn't believe he wasn't there to stop it.
NGGHHH!
WHAM
WHAM
WHAM
It's strange, but even after all the battles he's fought, Superman's not inherently angry.
YOU'RE STRONG...
People revere
strength, his p
but they have
idea how much
he's holding b

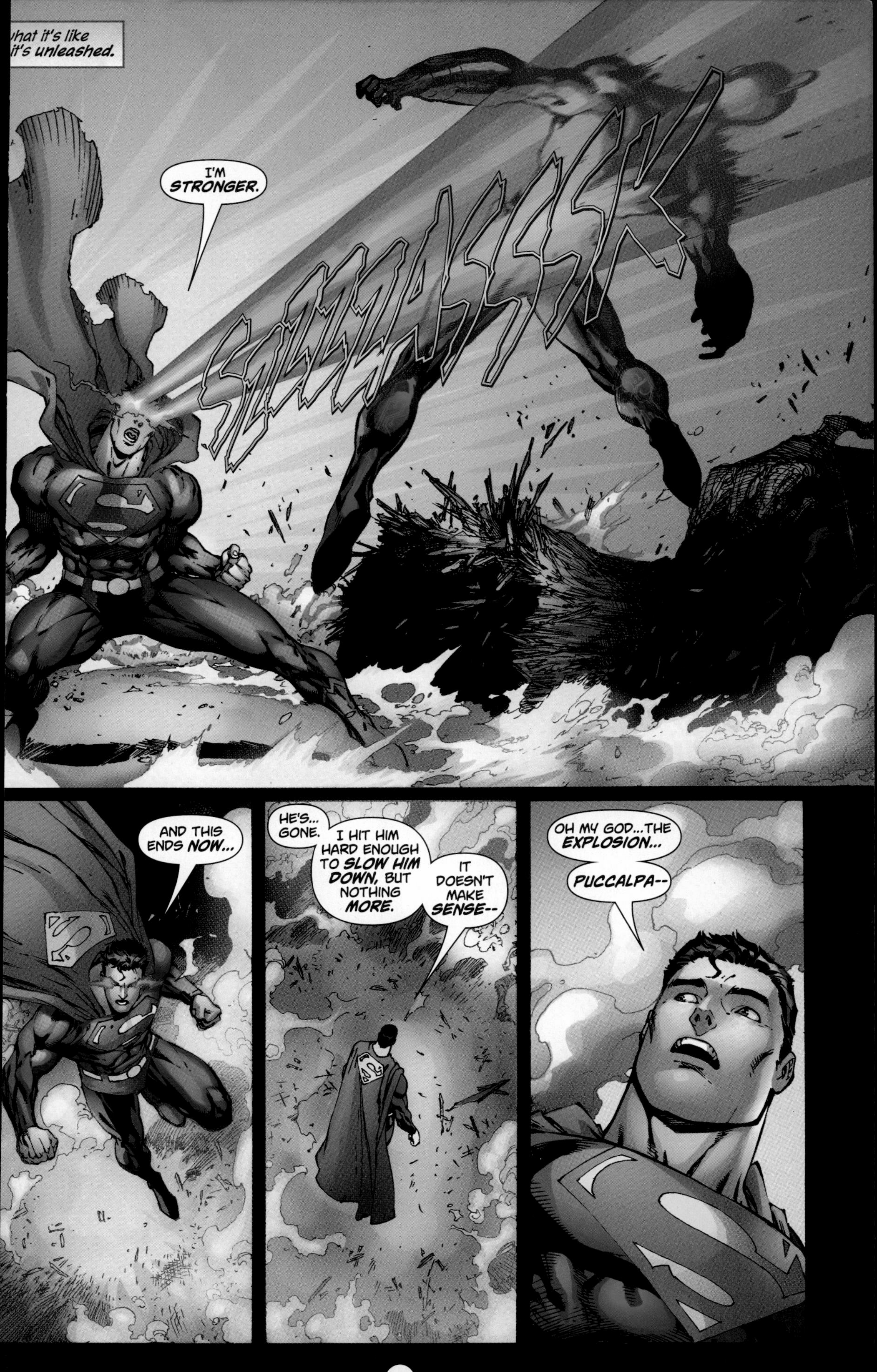
what it's like
it's unleashed.
I'M STRONGER.
SZZZZASSSSK!
AND THIS ENDS NOW...
HE'S... GONE.
I HIT HIM HARD ENOUGH TO SLOW HIM DOWN, BUT NOTHING MORE.
IT DOESN'T MAKE SENSE--
OH MY GOD...THE EXPLOSION...
PUCCALPA--

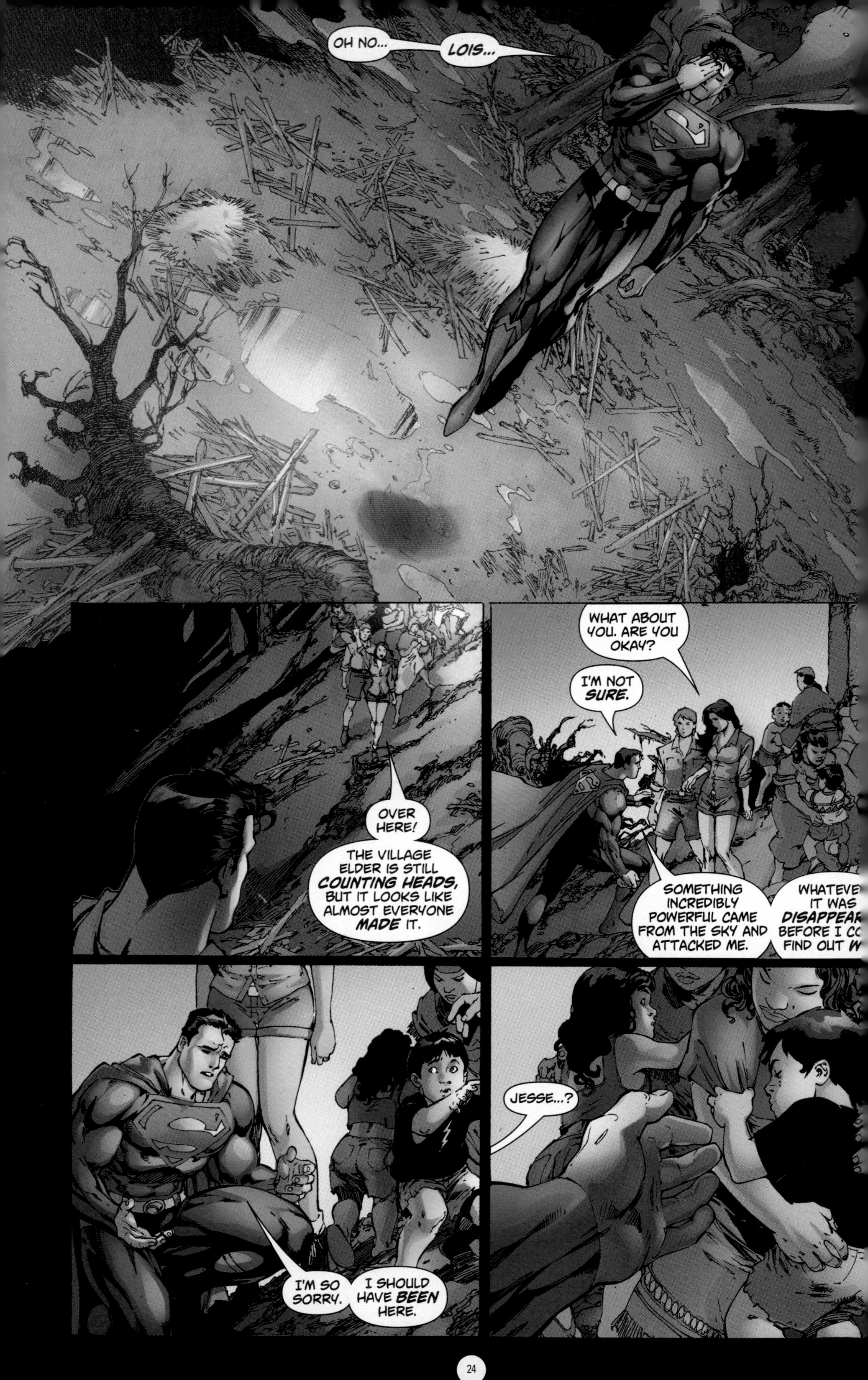

OH NO... LOIS...
OVER HERE!
THE VILLAGE ELDER IS STILL COUNTING HEADS, BUT IT LOOKS LIKE ALMOST EVERYONE MADE IT.
WHAT ABOUT YOU. ARE YOU OKAY?
I'M NOT SURE.
SOMETHING INCREDIBLY POWERFUL CAME FROM THE SKY AND ATTACKED ME.
I'M SO SORRY.
I SHOULD HAVE BEEN HERE.
JESSE...?

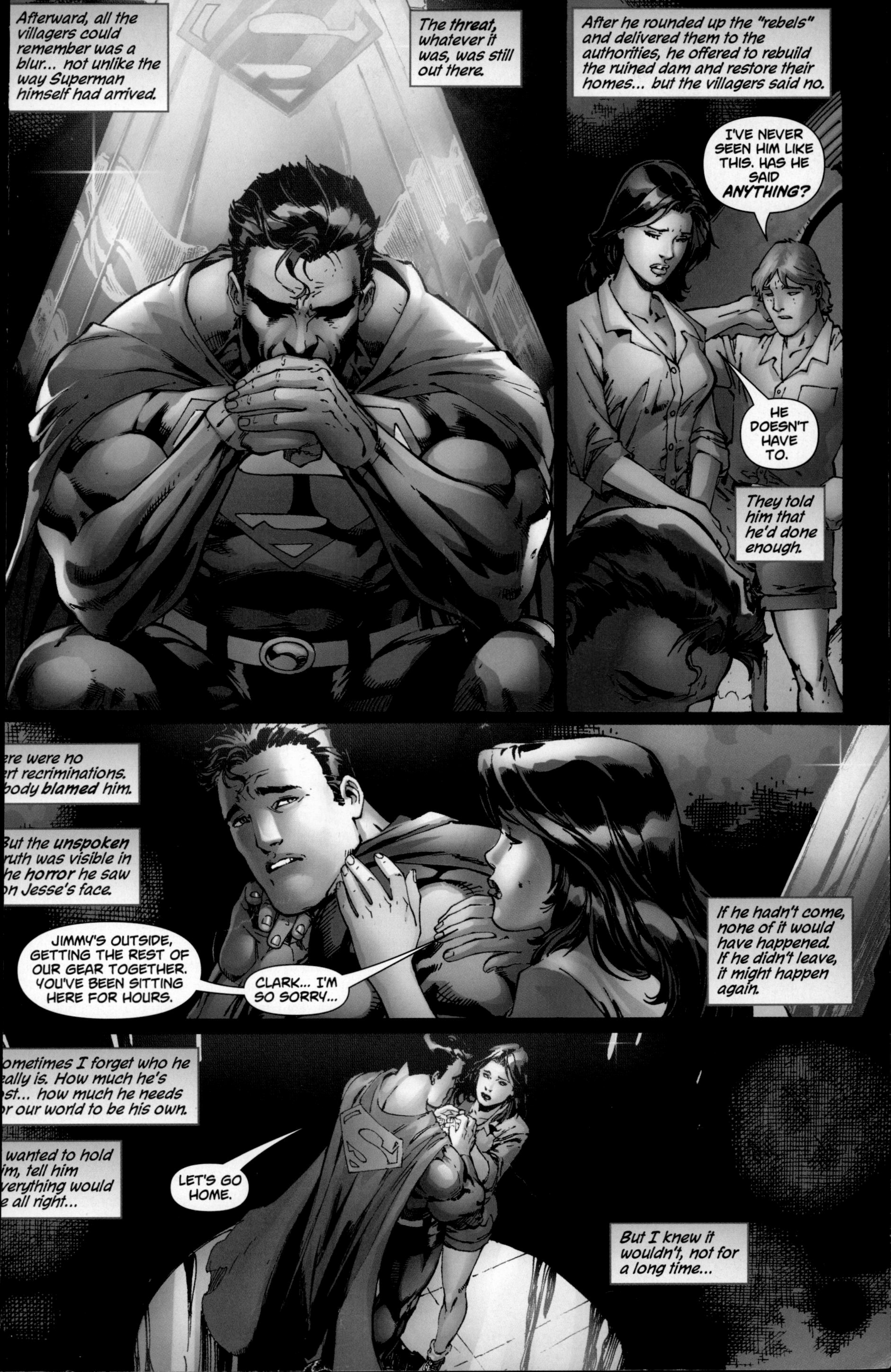

Afterward, all the villagers could remember was a blur... not unlike the way Superman himself had arrived.
The threat, whatever it was, was still out there.
After he rounded up the "rebels" and delivered them to the authorities, he offered to rebuild the ruined dam and restore their homes... but the villagers said no.
I'VE NEVER SEEN HIM LIKE THIS. HAS HE SAID ANYTHING?
HE DOESN'T HAVE TO.
They told him that he'd done enough.
ere were no
ert recriminations.
body blamed him.
But the unspoken
ruth was visible in
he horror he saw
on Jesse's face.
JIMMY'S OUTSIDE, GETTING THE REST OF OUR GEAR TOGETHER. YOU'VE BEEN SITTING HERE FOR HOURS.
CLARK... I'M SO SORRY...
If he hadn't come, none of it would have happened. If he didn't leave, it might happen again.
ometimes I forget who he
eally is. How much he's
ost... how much he needs
or our world to be his own.
wanted to hold
im, tell him
verything would
e all right...
LET'S GO HOME.
But I knew it wouldn't, not for a long time...

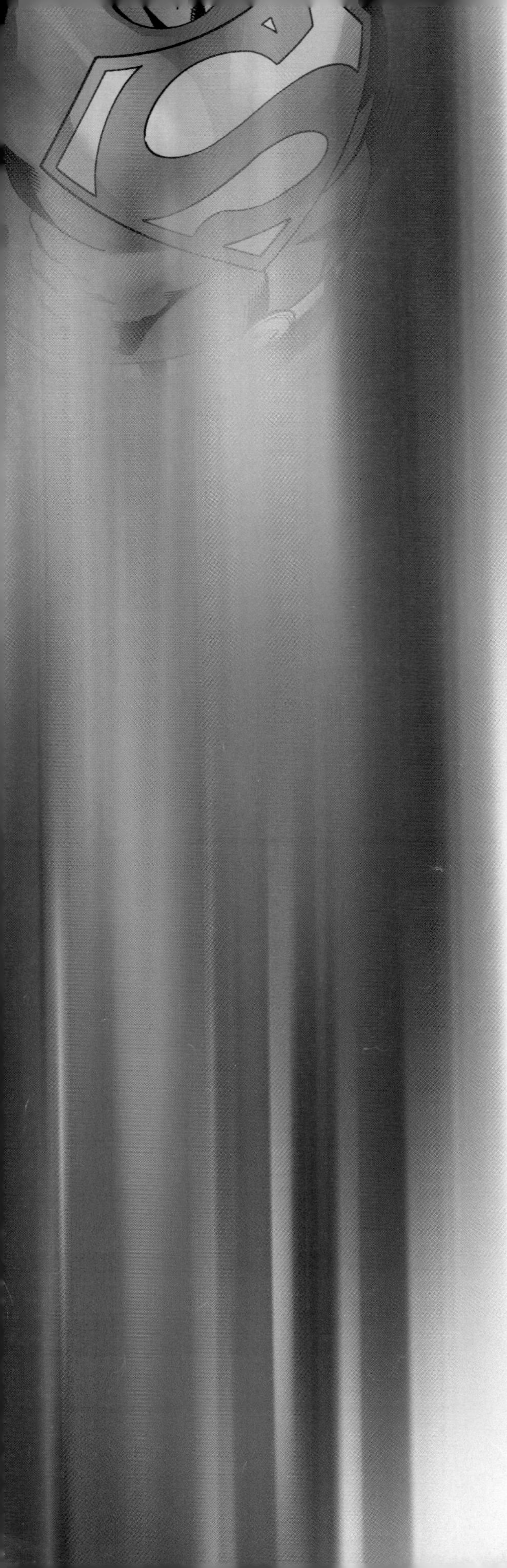

OUR STORY CONTINUES

The cybernetic OMAC's attack was just a hint of terror to come, one that would grip every man, woman a child living on Earth.

Superman and his peers have had to cope with violent death of several comrades, including the Blue Bee and Sue Dibny, wife of the Elongated Man, a burd compounded by a grim discovery. Various heroes have co spired to alter the memories — and even the personalities of their criminal opponents, and this knowledge is spreadi through the ranks of the costumed champions and th deadliest foes. The resulting rift among the members of JLA has led to physical conflict, and the gap is growing.

As a result of this stunning revelation, the villains ha begun working together to see to it that such affronts ne occur again. Several of Superman's foes have joined newly christened Society, but not all. Those who declin include the reincarnation of a minor villain named Blackro who has reappeared more powerful than ever.

As events unfolded, the telepathic Maxwell Lo slowly began exercising influence over Superman's mir Lord, having taken control of the clandestine organizati known as Checkmate, also acquired access to Brother Ey the artificial intelligence satellite that controls the OMAC Under Lord's influence, Superman nearly killed Batman b was opposed by Wonder Woman, and their confrontation, t second in a short span of time, was bloody.

When Lord refused to relinquish his control over t Man of Steel, the Amazon Princess saw no other choice than snap Lord's neck, killing him, an act that was recorded a subsequently broadcast worldwide by Brother Eye.

While recovering from his battle with the Amazo Superman felt a warning buzzing in the back of his mind – a gift from his old nuisance Mr. Mxyzptlk. It spoke of a tir of darkness that is coming, during which he will find himse at the center of a great crisis. Yet with all that has happene to him and his loved ones, Superman cannot fathom wh could possibly get worse. And that thought chills him the core.

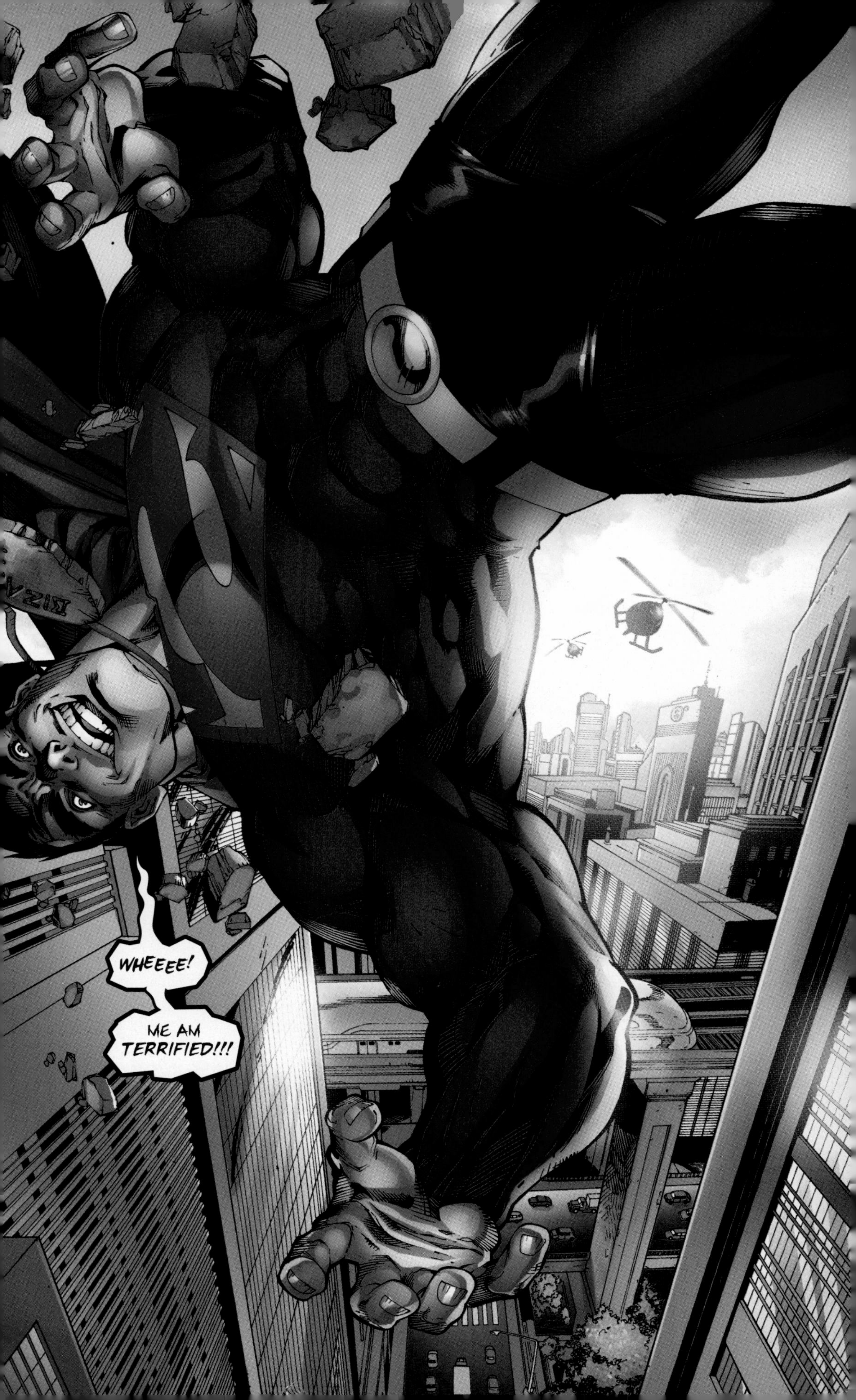
WHEEEE!
ME AM TERRIFIED!!!

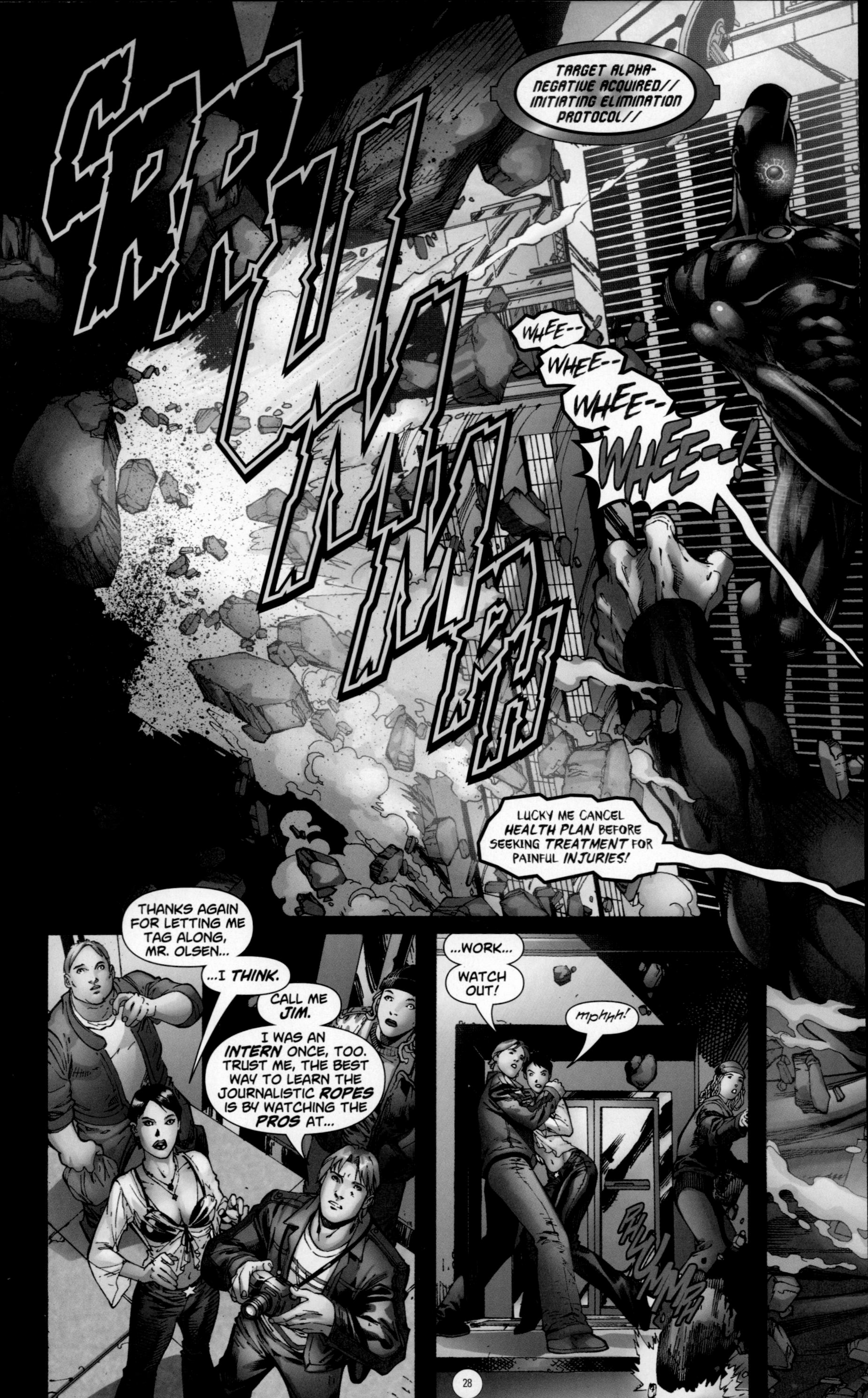
CRUMMMBB
TARGET ALPHA-NEGATIVE ACQUIRED// INITIATING ELIMINATION PROTOCOL//
WHEE--
WHEE--
WHEE--
WHEE--!
LUCKY ME CANCEL HEALTH PLAN BEFORE SEEKING TREATMENT FOR PAINFUL INJURIES!
THANKS AGAIN FOR LETTING ME TAG ALONG, MR. OLSEN...
...I THINK.
CALL ME JIM.
I WAS AN INTERN ONCE, TOO. TRUST ME, THE BEST WAY TO LEARN THE JOURNALISTIC ROPES IS BY WATCHING THE PROS AT...
...WORK...
WATCH OUT!
mphhh!

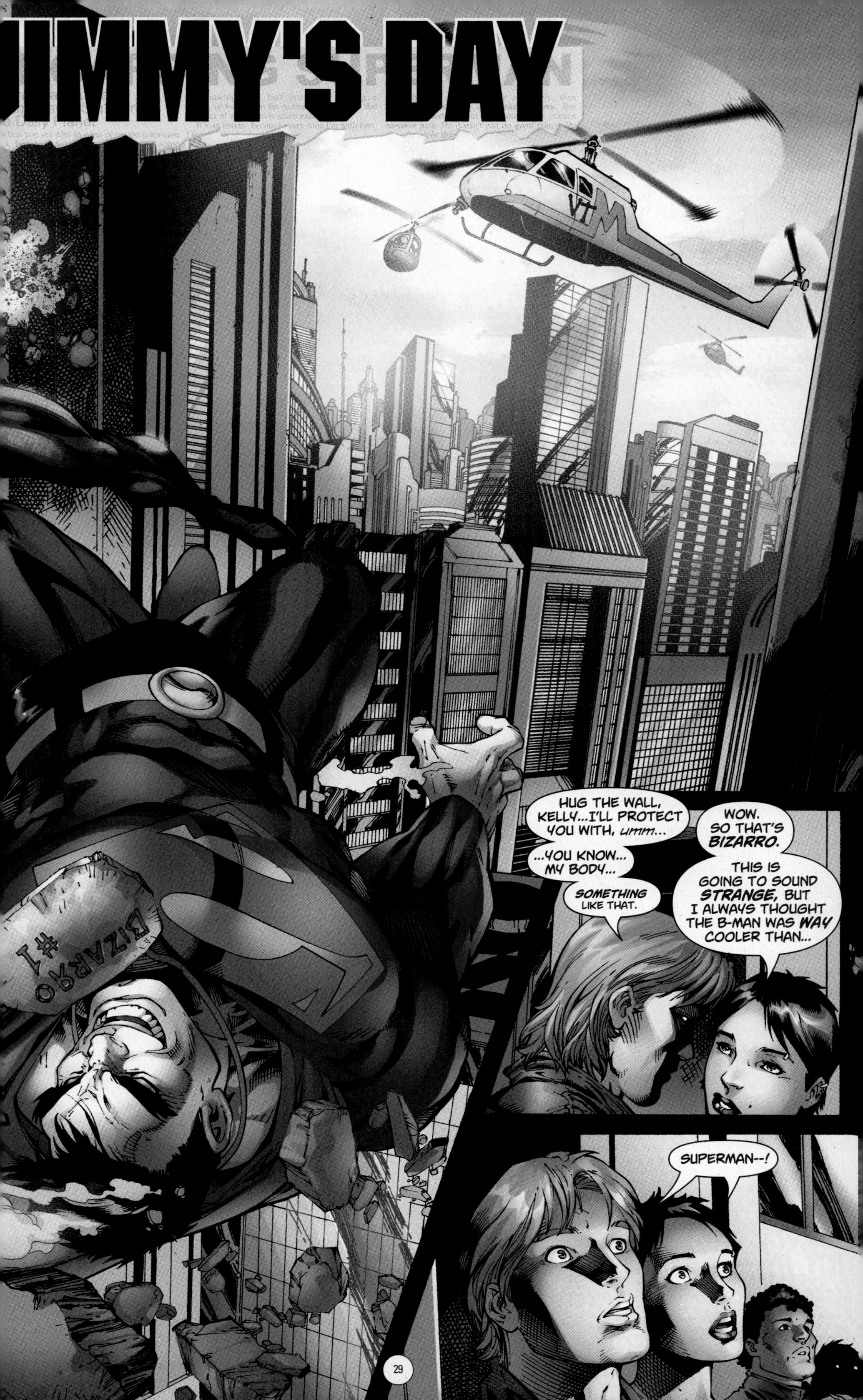
IMMY'S DAY
BIZARRO #1
HUG THE WALL, KELLY...I'LL PROTECT YOU WITH, *umm*...
...YOU KNOW... MY BODY...
SOMETHING LIKE THAT.
WOW. SO THAT'S *BIZARRO.*
THIS IS GOING TO SOUND *STRANGE,* BUT I ALWAYS THOUGHT THE B-MAN WAS *WAY* COOLER THAN...
SUPERMAN--!

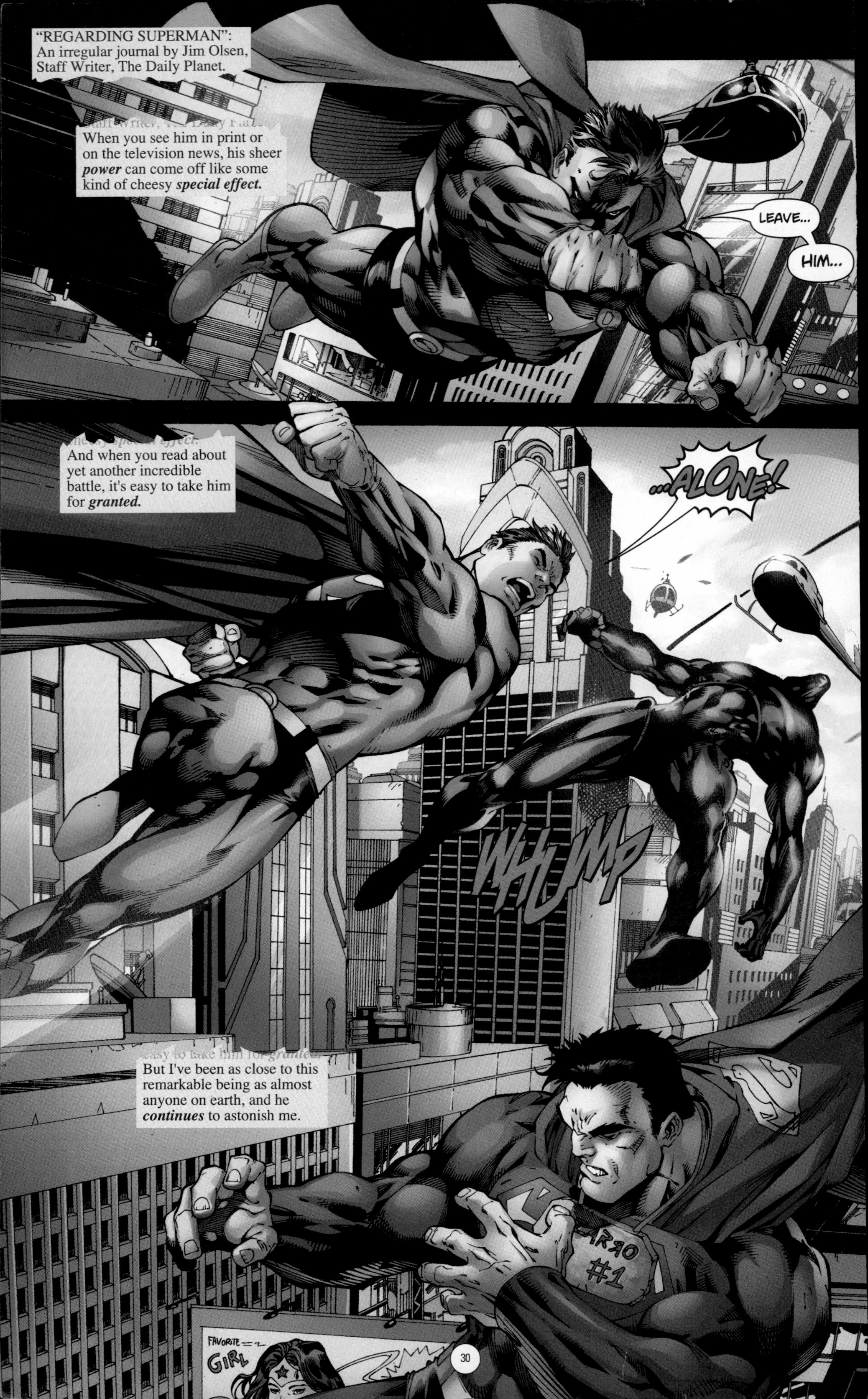
"REGARDING SUPERMAN": An irregular journal by Jim Olsen, Staff Writer, The Daily Planet.
When you see him in print or on the television news, his sheer *power* can come off like some kind of cheesy *special effect.*
LEAVE...
HIM...
And when you read about yet another incredible battle, it's easy to take him for *granted.*
...ALONE!
WHUMP
But I've been as close to this remarkable being as almost anyone on earth, and he *continues* to astonish me.
FAVORITE GIRL

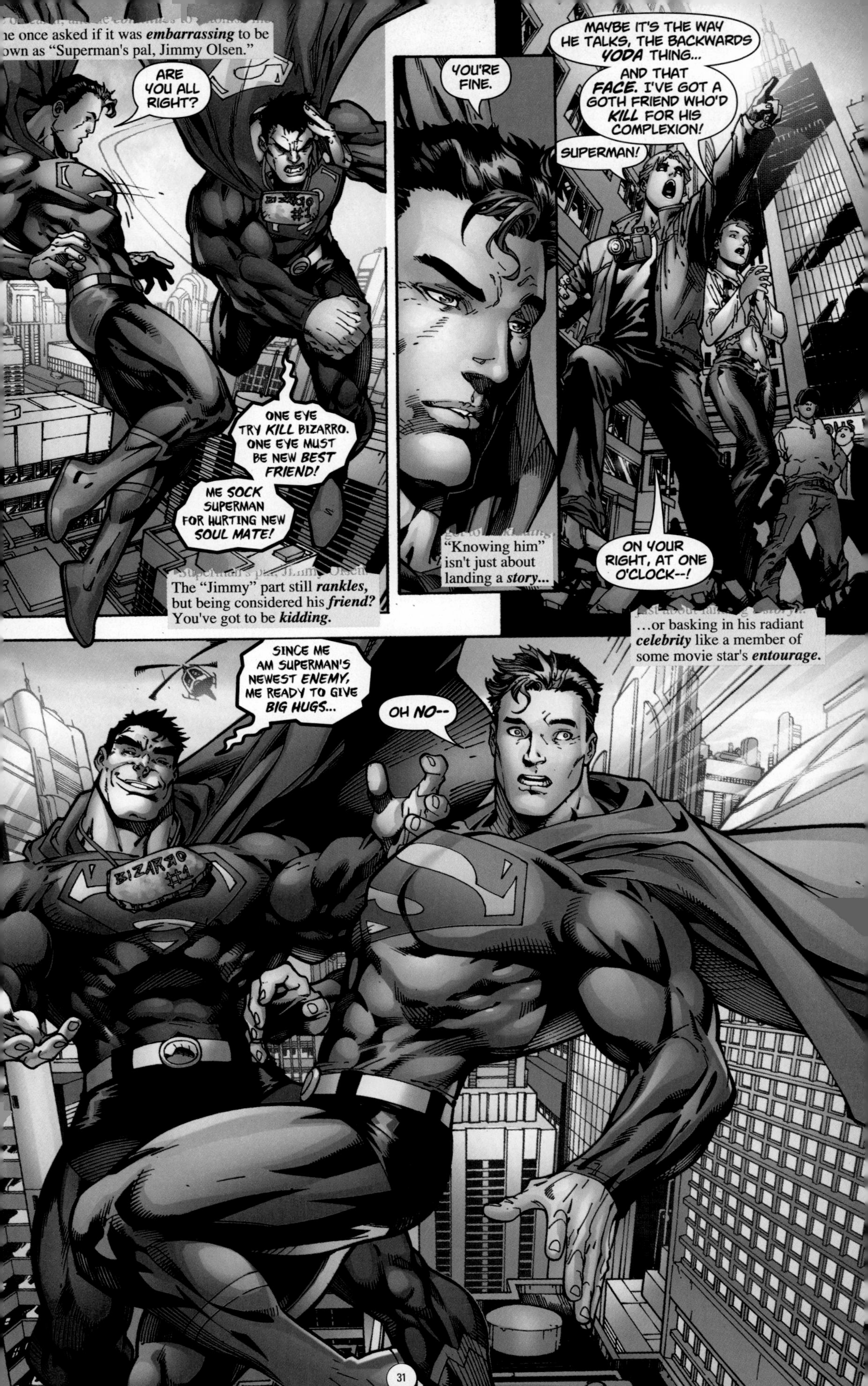

...he once asked if it was *embarrassing* to be known as "Superman's pal, Jimmy Olsen."
ARE YOU ALL RIGHT?
ONE EYE TRY KILL BIZARRO. ONE EYE MUST BE NEW BEST FRIEND!
ME SOCK SUPERMAN FOR HURTING NEW SOUL MATE!
The "Jimmy" part still *rankles,* but being considered his *friend?* You've got to be *kidding*.
YOU'RE FINE.
"Knowing him" isn't just about landing a *story*...
MAYBE IT'S THE WAY HE TALKS, THE BACKWARDS YODA THING...
AND THAT FACE. I'VE GOT A GOTH FRIEND WHO'D KILL FOR HIS COMPLEXION!
SUPERMAN!
ON YOUR RIGHT, AT ONE O'CLOCK--!
...or basking in his radiant *celebrity* like a member of some movie star's *entourage*.
SINCE ME AM SUPERMAN'S NEWEST ENEMY, ME READY TO GIVE BIG HUGS...
OH NO--

CRUMMPH

movie-star's *entourage*. It's an honor. Because every time I'm with him, I *learn* something.

something
I learn about *selflessness*...

SSSSK...

UMPHH--!

selflessness
decency...

THIS IS SO DISASTER-MOVIE--!

BETTER GRAB A QUICK--

the sometimes *unfortunate* laws of *physics*...

...SHOT...

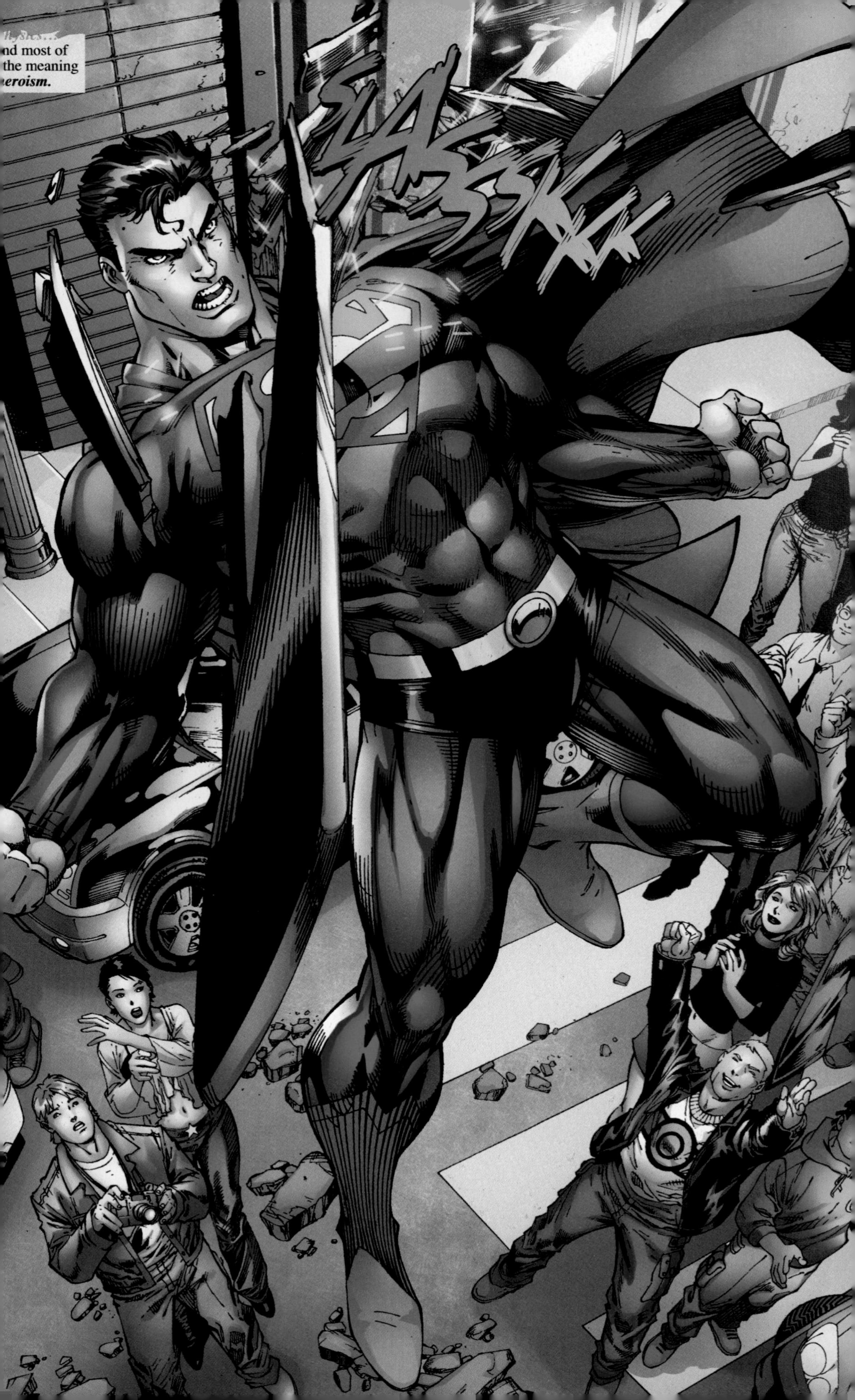

nd most of
the meaning
eroism.

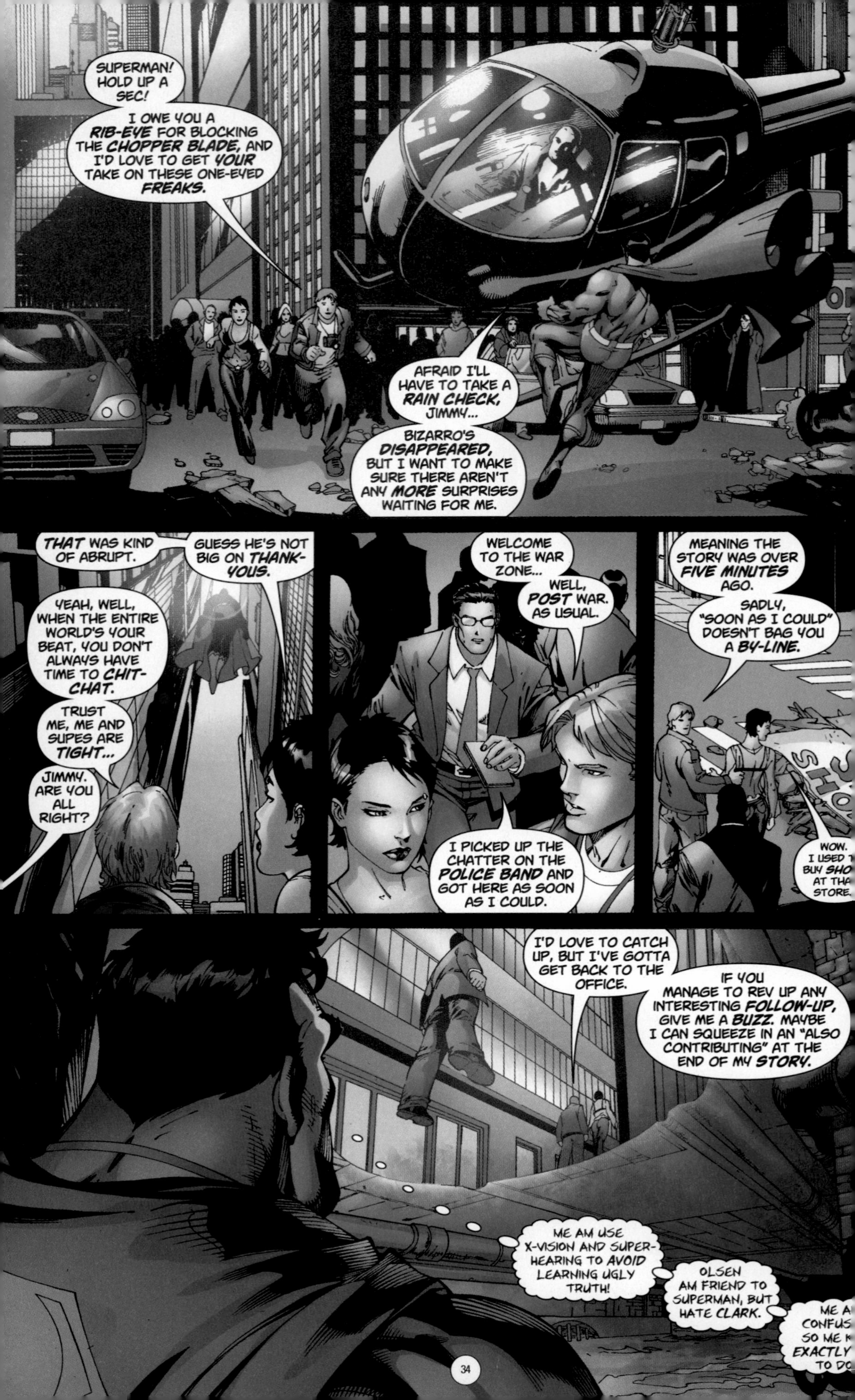
SUPERMAN! HOLD UP A SEC!
I OWE YOU A RIB-EYE FOR BLOCKING THE CHOPPER BLADE, AND I'D LOVE TO GET YOUR TAKE ON THESE ONE-EYED FREAKS.
AFRAID I'LL HAVE TO TAKE A RAIN CHECK, JIMMY...
BIZARRO'S DISAPPEARED, BUT I WANT TO MAKE SURE THERE AREN'T ANY MORE SURPRISES WAITING FOR ME.
THAT WAS KIND OF ABRUPT.
GUESS HE'S NOT BIG ON THANK-YOUS.
YEAH, WELL, WHEN THE ENTIRE WORLD'S YOUR BEAT, YOU DON'T ALWAYS HAVE TIME TO CHIT-CHAT.
TRUST ME, ME AND SUPES ARE TIGHT...
JIMMY. ARE YOU ALL RIGHT?
WELCOME TO THE WAR ZONE...
WELL, POST WAR. AS USUAL.
I PICKED UP THE CHATTER ON THE POLICE BAND AND GOT HERE AS SOON AS I COULD.
MEANING THE STORY WAS OVER FIVE MINUTES AGO.
SADLY, "SOON AS I COULD" DOESN'T BAG YOU A BY-LINE.
SHO
WOW. I USED T BUY SHO AT THA STORE.
I'D LOVE TO CATCH UP, BUT I'VE GOTTA GET BACK TO THE OFFICE.
IF YOU MANAGE TO REV UP ANY INTERESTING FOLLOW-UP, GIVE ME A BUZZ. MAYBE I CAN SQUEEZE IN AN "ALSO CONTRIBUTING" AT THE END OF MY STORY.
ME AM USE X-VISION AND SUPER-HEARING TO AVOID LEARNING UGLY TRUTH!
OLSEN AM FRIEND TO SUPERMAN, BUT HATE CLARK.
ME A CONFUS SO ME K EXACTLY TO DO

...Superman has taught me ...ng a reporter is about more ...recitation of dry *fact.*

...recitation of dry *fact.* It's about finding the human truth **behind** the story.

TRUST ME, KELLY, REPORTING'S NOT ALWAYS **THAT** EXCITING.

BUT IF YOU'RE STILL **INTERESTED** IN THE PROFESSION, MAYBE WE COULD TALK ABOUT IT OVER **DRINKS** SOME EVENING...

SURE, MR. OLSEN, WHATEVER.

HERE ARE YOUR MESSAGES... OH, AND MR. WHITE NEEDS YOUR STORY ON TODAY'S **BIZARRO BATTLE** ASAP.

...H, RIGHT, AFTER ...H THE FIFTY OTHER ...PRIORITY" ITEMS ON ...Y "TO-DO" LIST.

HOW THE HELL WAS **CLARK** ABLE TO JUGGLE SO MANY STORIES AT ONCE?

EVER THINK THAT MAYBE HE WAS **GOOD**?

LOIS. DIDN'T SEE YOU THERE.

YOU CAUGHT ME IN A RARE MOMENT OF, *umm,* "INTROSPECTION."

YEAH, I NOTICED YOU "INTROSPECTING" THE NEW INTERN'S **BUTT** ALL THE WAY ACROSS THE BULLPEN.

AND I HEARD ABOUT THE WAY YOU DISSED **CLARK** TODAY.

LOOK, I KNOW YOU DON'T LIKE THE WAY I WAS **PROMOTED.**

BUT THERE'S A REASON WHY CLARK WAS SENT DOWN TO THE **MINORS.**

AND EVEN THOUGH IT HURT CLARK **DEEPLY,** I TRIED TO GIVE YOU THE BENEFIT OF THE **DOUBT.**

ACTUALLY **COVERED** FOR YOU A COUPLE OF TIMES WHEN YOU WERE SLIDING ON A **DEADLINE.**

BUT THAT WAS **THEN.** THIS IS **NOW.**

IF I CATCH YOU PUTTING DOWN MY **HUSBAND** ONE MORE TIME, YOU AND I ARE GOING TO HAVE A **PROBLEM.**

ARE WE UNDER-STANDING ONE ANOTHER, "JAMES"?

YES. MA'AM.

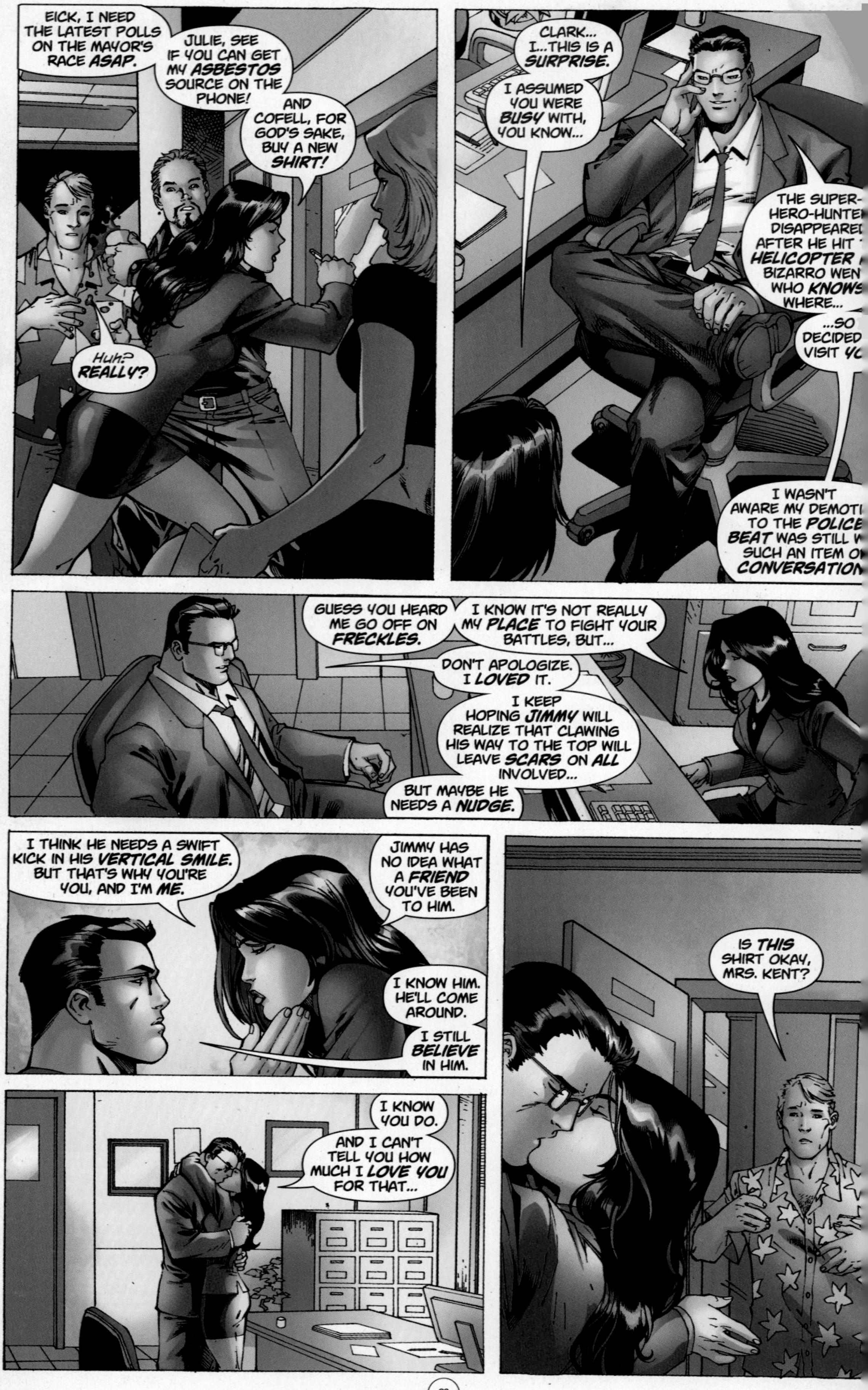

EICK, I NEED THE LATEST POLLS ON THE MAYOR'S RACE ASAP.
JULIE, SEE IF YOU CAN GET MY ASBESTOS SOURCE ON THE PHONE!
AND COFELL, FOR GOD'S SAKE, BUY A NEW SHIRT!
Huh? REALLY?
CLARK... I...THIS IS A SURPRISE.
I ASSUMED YOU WERE BUSY WITH, YOU KNOW...
THE SUPER-HERO-HUNTE DISAPPEARED AFTER HE HIT HELICOPTER BIZARRO WEN WHO KNOWS WHERE...
...SO DECIDED VISIT
I WASN'T AWARE MY DEMOT TO THE POLICE BEAT WAS STILL SUCH AN ITEM O CONVERSATION
GUESS YOU HEARD ME GO OFF ON FRECKLES.
I KNOW IT'S NOT REALLY MY PLACE TO FIGHT YOUR BATTLES, BUT...
DON'T APOLOGIZE. I LOVED IT.
I KEEP HOPING JIMMY WILL REALIZE THAT CLAWING HIS WAY TO THE TOP WILL LEAVE SCARS ON ALL INVOLVED...
BUT MAYBE HE NEEDS A NUDGE.
I THINK HE NEEDS A SWIFT KICK IN HIS VERTICAL SMILE. BUT THAT'S WHY YOU'RE YOU, AND I'M ME.
JIMMY HAS NO IDEA WHAT A FRIEND YOU'VE BEEN TO HIM.
I KNOW HIM. HE'LL COME AROUND.
I STILL BELIEVE IN HIM.
I KNOW YOU DO.
AND I CAN'T TELL YOU HOW MUCH I LOVE YOU FOR THAT...
IS THIS SHIRT OKAY, MRS. KENT?

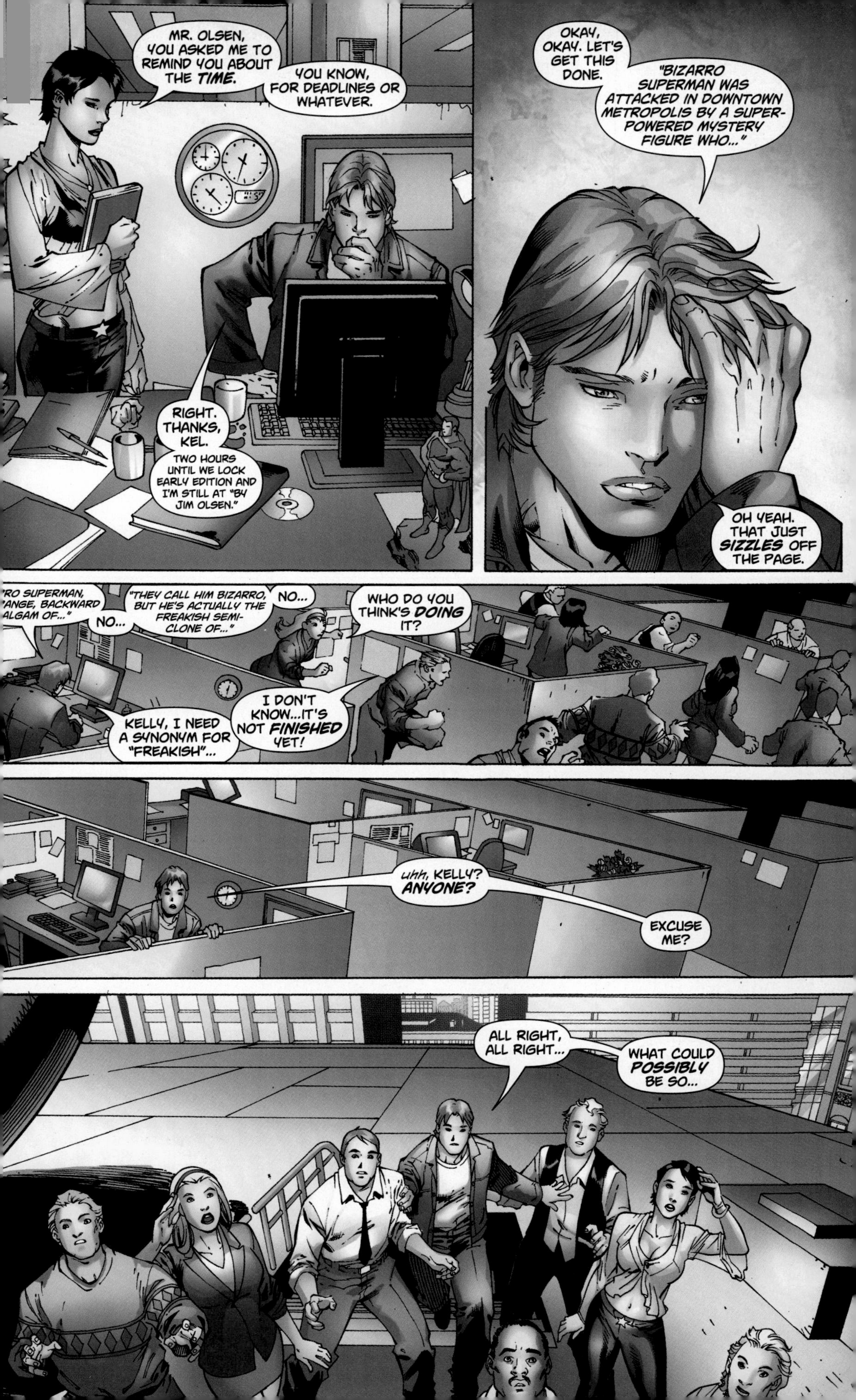
MR. OLSEN, YOU ASKED ME TO REMIND YOU ABOUT THE TIME.
YOU KNOW, FOR DEADLINES OR WHATEVER.
RIGHT. THANKS, KEL.
TWO HOURS UNTIL WE LOCK EARLY EDITION AND I'M STILL AT "BY JIM OLSEN."
OKAY, OKAY. LET'S GET THIS DONE.
"BIZARRO SUPERMAN WAS ATTACKED IN DOWNTOWN METROPOLIS BY A SUPER-POWERED MYSTERY FIGURE WHO..."
OH YEAH. THAT JUST SIZZLES OFF THE PAGE.
"RO SUPERMAN, ANGE, BACKWARD ALGAM OF..."
NO...
"THEY CALL HIM BIZARRO, BUT HE'S ACTUALLY THE FREAKISH SEMI-CLONE OF..."
NO...
KELLY, I NEED A SYNONYM FOR "FREAKISH"...
WHO DO YOU THINK'S DOING IT?
I DON'T KNOW...IT'S NOT FINISHED YET!
uhh, KELLY? ANYONE?
EXCUSE ME?
ALL RIGHT, ALL RIGHT...
WHAT COULD POSSIBLY BE SO...

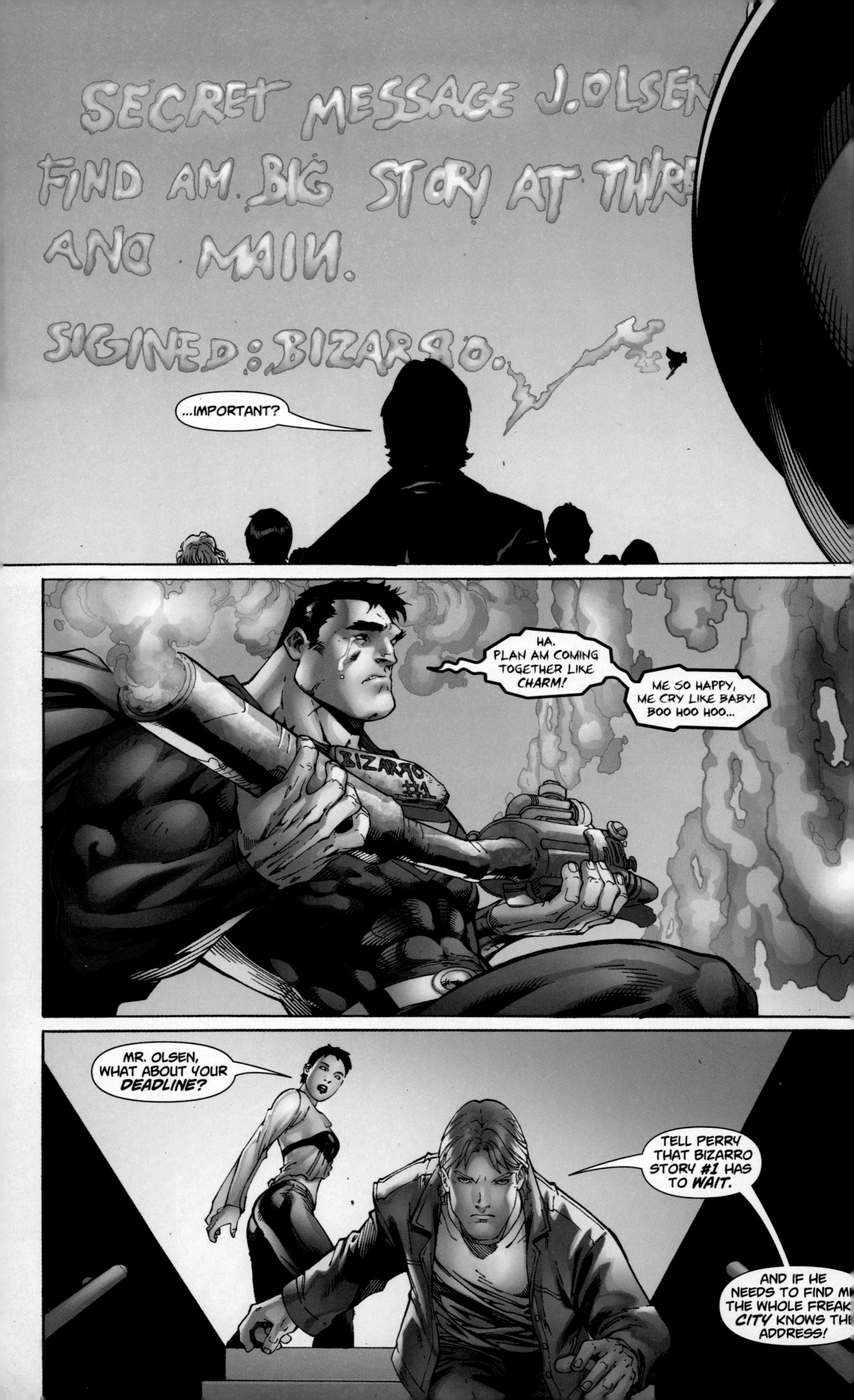
SECRET MESSAGE J.OLSEN
FIND AM BIG STORY AT THIR
AND MAIN.
SIGINED: BIZARRO.
...IMPORTANT?
HA. PLAN AM COMING TOGETHER LIKE CHARM!
ME SO HAPPY, ME CRY LIKE BABY! BOO HOO HOO...
BIZARRO #1
MR. OLSEN, WHAT ABOUT YOUR DEADLINE?
TELL PERRY THAT BIZARRO STORY #1 HAS TO WAIT.
AND IF HE NEEDS TO FIND M THE WHOLE FREAK CITY KNOWS TH ADDRESS!

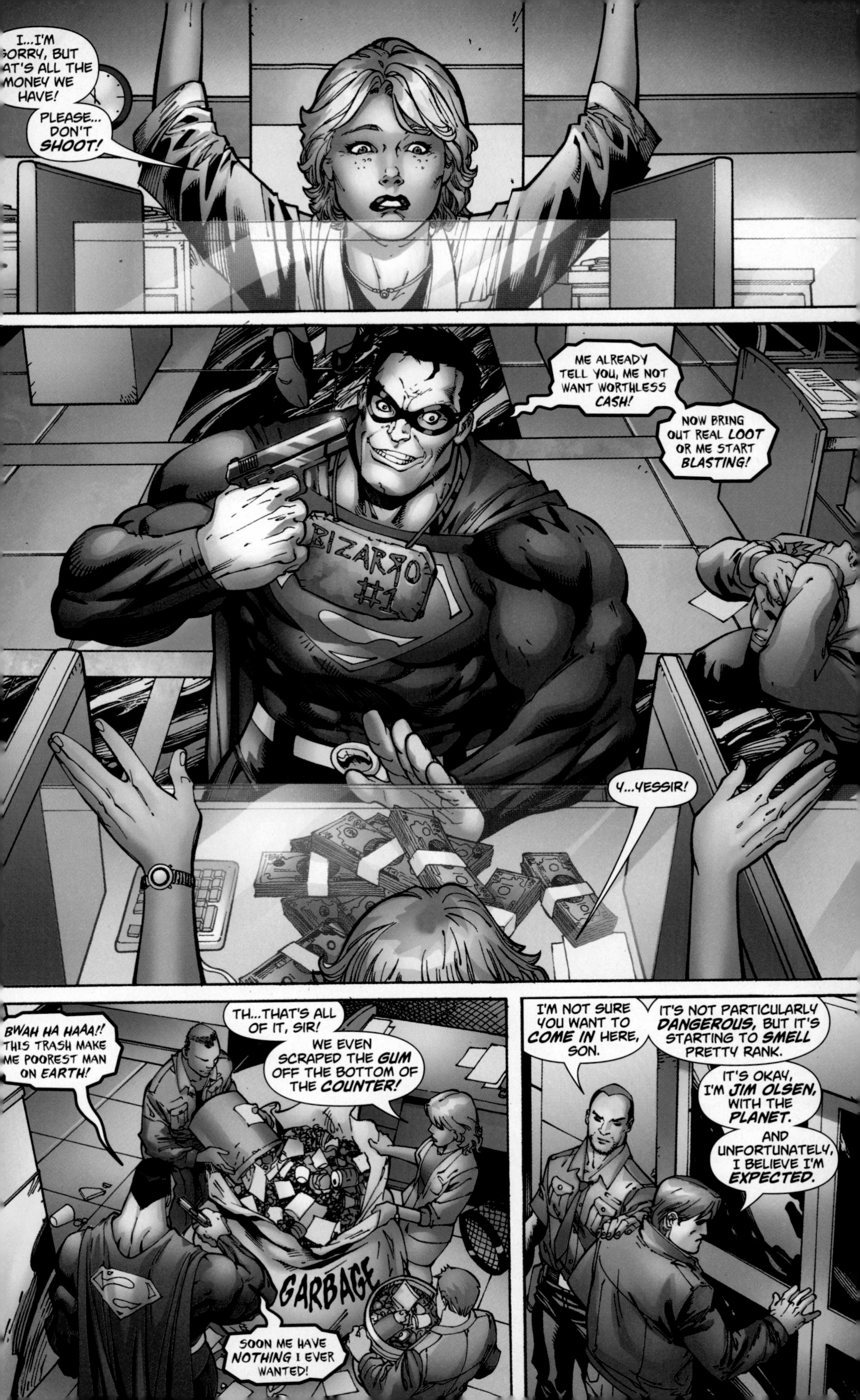
I...I'M SORRY, BUT THAT'S ALL THE MONEY WE HAVE!
PLEASE... DON'T SHOOT!
ME ALREADY TELL YOU, ME NOT WANT WORTHLESS CASH!
NOW BRING OUT REAL LOOT OR ME START BLASTING!
BIZARRO #1
Y...YESSIR!
BWAH HA HAAA!! THIS TRASH MAKE ME POOREST MAN ON EARTH!
TH...THAT'S ALL OF IT, SIR!
WE EVEN SCRAPED THE GUM OFF THE BOTTOM OF THE COUNTER!
GARBAGE
SOON ME HAVE NOTHING I EVER WANTED!
I'M NOT SURE YOU WANT TO COME IN HERE, SON.
IT'S NOT PARTICULARLY DANGEROUS, BUT IT'S STARTING TO SMELL PRETTY RANK.
IT'S OKAY, I'M JIM OLSEN, WITH THE PLANET.
AND UNFORTUNATELY, I BELIEVE I'M EXPECTED.

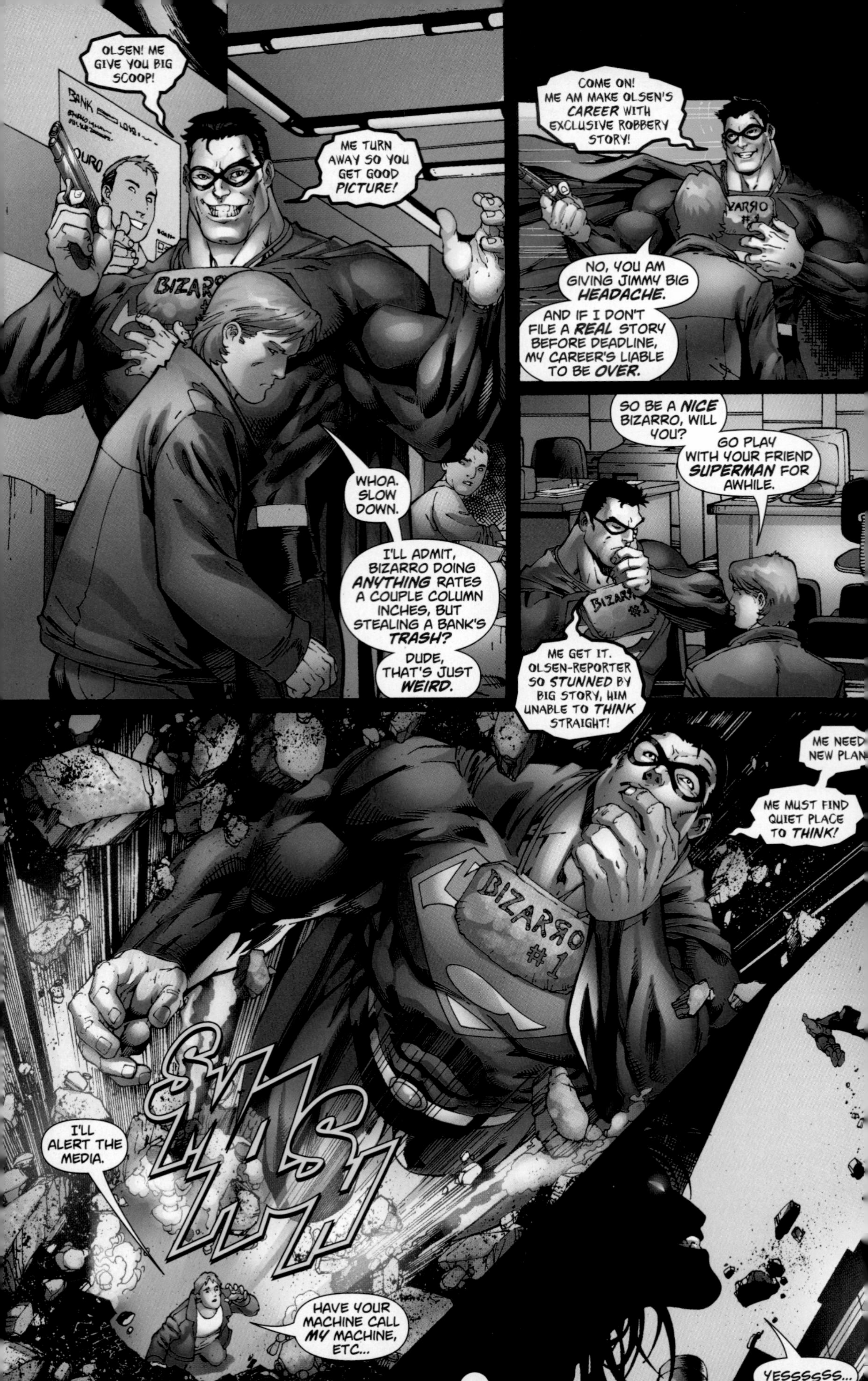
OLSEN! ME GIVE YOU BIG SCOOP!
ME TURN AWAY SO YOU GET GOOD PICTURE!
WHOA. SLOW DOWN.
I'LL ADMIT, BIZARRO DOING ANYTHING RATES A COUPLE COLUMN INCHES, BUT STEALING A BANK'S TRASH?
DUDE, THAT'S JUST WEIRD.
COME ON! ME AM MAKE OLSEN'S CAREER WITH EXCLUSIVE ROBBERY STORY!
NO, YOU AM GIVING JIMMY BIG HEADACHE.
AND IF I DON'T FILE A REAL STORY BEFORE DEADLINE, MY CAREER'S LIABLE TO BE OVER.
SO BE A NICE BIZARRO, WILL YOU?
GO PLAY WITH YOUR FRIEND SUPERMAN FOR AWHILE.
ME GET IT. OLSEN-REPORTER SO STUNNED BY BIG STORY, HIM UNABLE TO THINK STRAIGHT!
ME NEED NEW PLAN
ME MUST FIND QUIET PLACE TO THINK!
I'LL ALERT THE MEDIA.
HAVE YOUR MACHINE CALL MY MACHINE, ETC...
YESSSSSS...

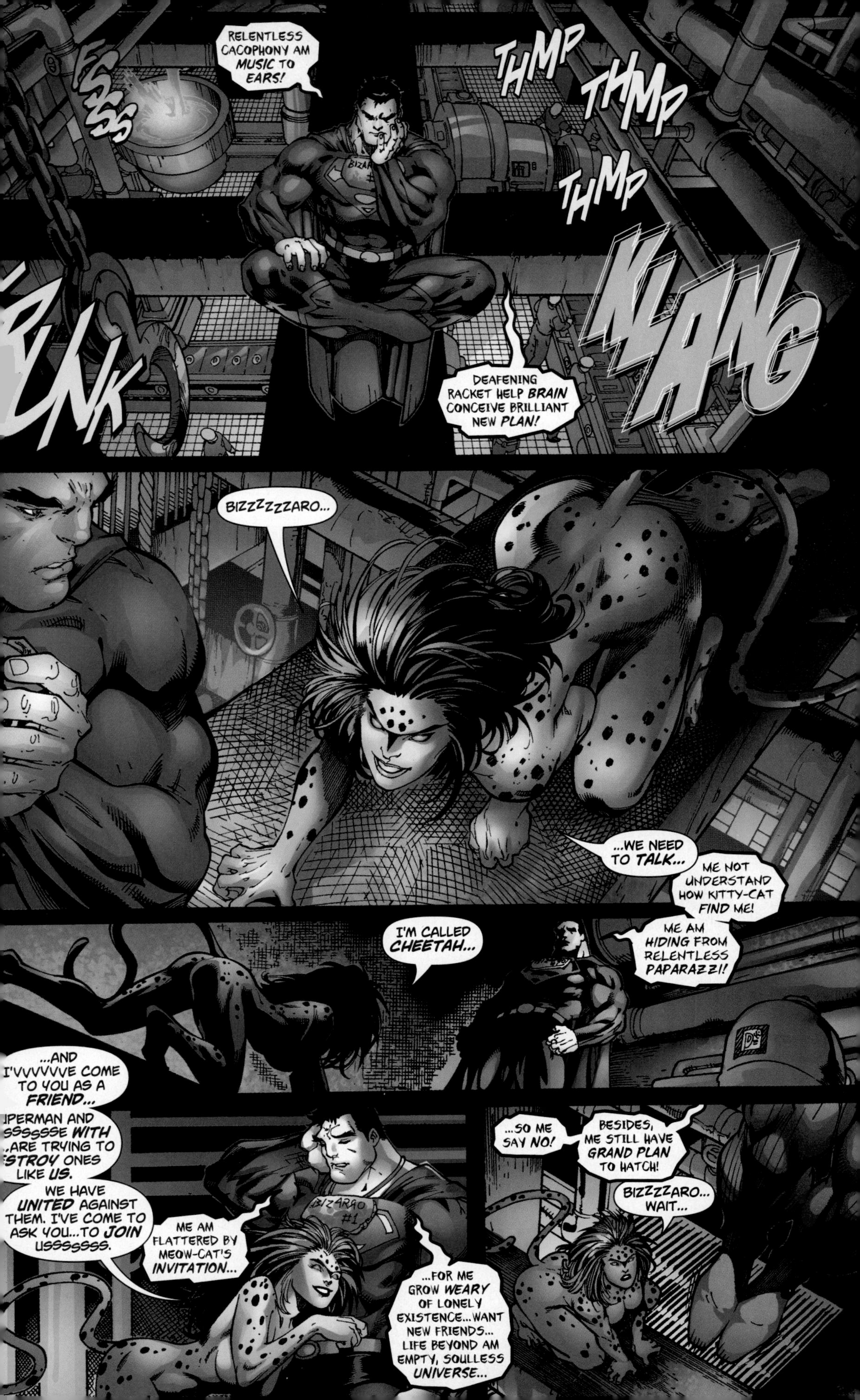
FSSSS
RELENTLESS CACOPHONY AM MUSIC TO EARS!
THMP THMP THMP
KLANG
DEAFENING RACKET HELP BRAIN CONCEIVE BRILLIANT NEW PLAN!
BIZZZZZZARO...
...WE NEED TO TALK...
ME NOT UNDERSTAND HOW KITTY-CAT FIND ME!
ME AM HIDING FROM RELENTLESS PAPARAZZI!
I'M CALLED CHEETAH...
...AND I'VVVVVVE COME TO YOU AS A FRIEND...
WE HAVE UNITED AGAINST THEM. I'VE COME TO ASK YOU...TO JOIN USSSSSSS.
ME AM FLATTERED BY MEOW-CAT'S INVITATION...
...FOR ME GROW WEARY OF LONELY EXISTENCE...WANT NEW FRIENDS... LIFE BEYOND AM EMPTY, SOULLESS UNIVERSE...
...SO ME SAY NO!
BESIDES, ME STILL HAVE GRAND PLAN TO HATCH!
BIZZZZARO... WAIT...

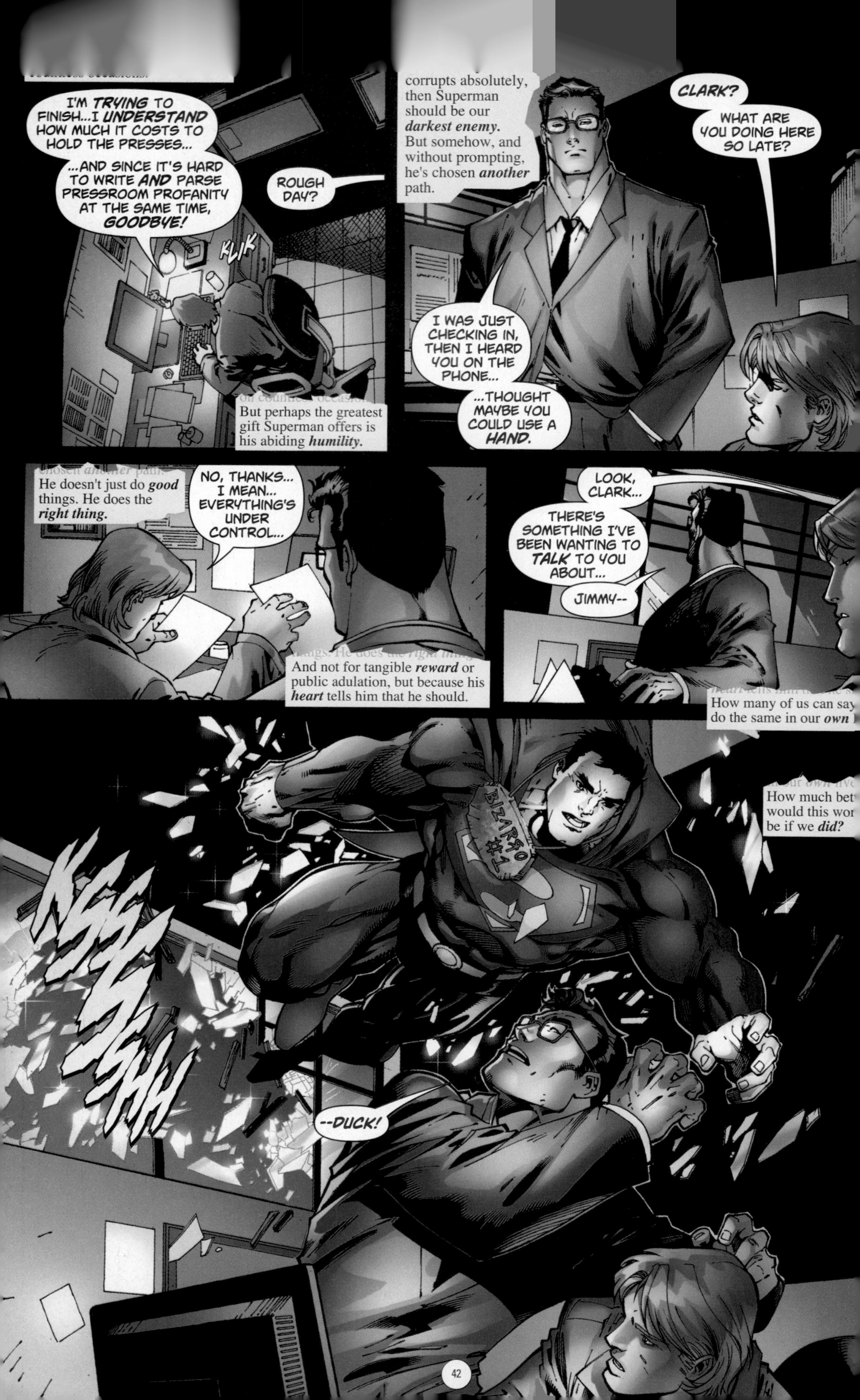
I'M TRYING TO FINISH...I UNDERSTAND HOW MUCH IT COSTS TO HOLD THE PRESSES...
...AND SINCE IT'S HARD TO WRITE AND PARSE PRESSROOM PROFANITY AT THE SAME TIME, GOODBYE!
KLIK
ROUGH DAY?
But perhaps the greatest gift Superman offers is his abiding humility.
corrupts absolutely, then Superman should be our darkest enemy. But somehow, and without prompting, he's chosen another path.
CLARK?
WHAT ARE YOU DOING HERE SO LATE?
I WAS JUST CHECKING IN, THEN I HEARD YOU ON THE PHONE...
...THOUGHT MAYBE YOU COULD USE A HAND.
He doesn't just do good things. He does the right thing.
NO, THANKS... I MEAN... EVERYTHING'S UNDER CONTROL...
And not for tangible reward or public adulation, but because his heart tells him that he should.
LOOK, CLARK...
THERE'S SOMETHING I'VE BEEN WANTING TO TALK TO YOU ABOUT...
JIMMY--
How many of us can say
do the same in our own
How much bet
would this wor
be if we did?
BIZARRO #1
--DUCK!

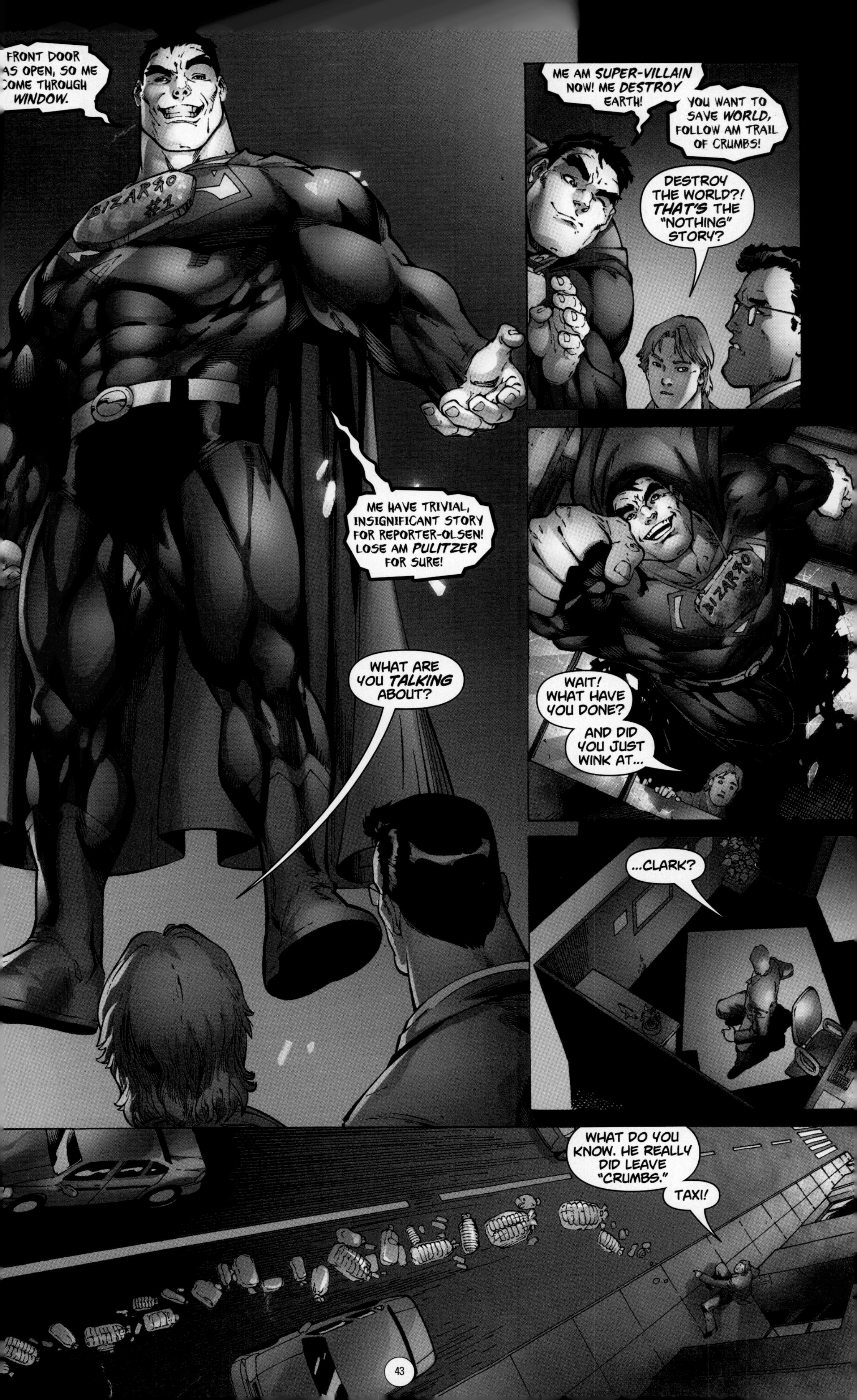

FRONT DOOR AS OPEN, SO ME COME THROUGH WINDOW.
ME HAVE TRIVIAL, INSIGNIFICANT STORY FOR REPORTER-OLSEN! LOSE AM PULITZER FOR SURE!
WHAT ARE YOU TALKING ABOUT?
ME AM SUPER-VILLAIN NOW! ME DESTROY EARTH!
YOU WANT TO SAVE WORLD, FOLLOW AM TRAIL OF CRUMBS!
DESTROY THE WORLD?! THAT'S THE "NOTHING" STORY?
WAIT! WHAT HAVE YOU DONE?
AND DID YOU JUST WINK AT...
...CLARK?
WHAT DO YOU KNOW. HE REALLY DID LEAVE "CRUMBS."
TAXI!

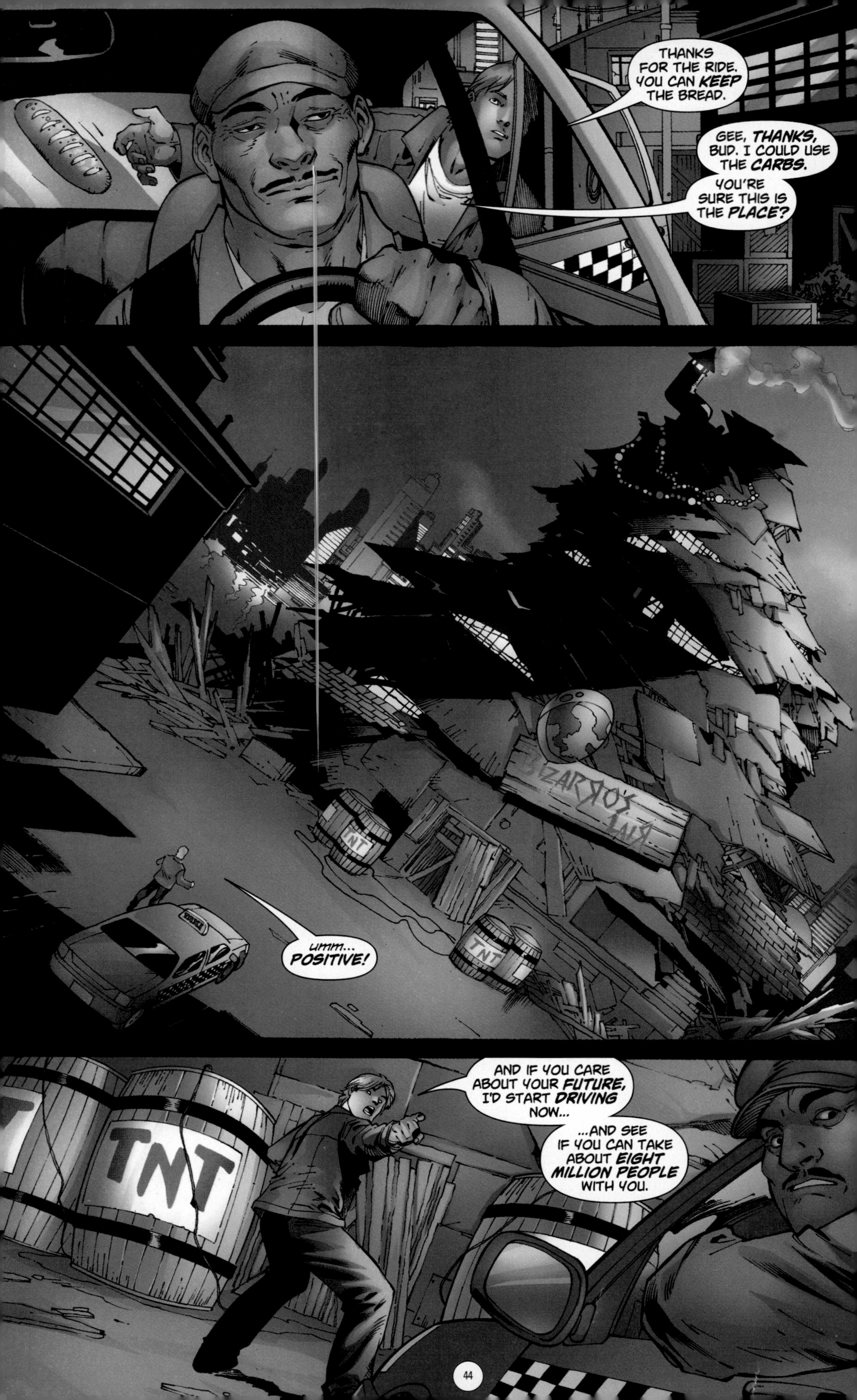
THANKS FOR THE RIDE. YOU CAN KEEP THE BREAD.
GEE, THANKS, BUD. I COULD USE THE CARBS.
YOU'RE SURE THIS IS THE PLACE?
umm... POSITIVE!
AND IF YOU CARE ABOUT YOUR FUTURE, I'D START DRIVING NOW...
...AND SEE IF YOU CAN TAKE ABOUT EIGHT MILLION PEOPLE WITH YOU.

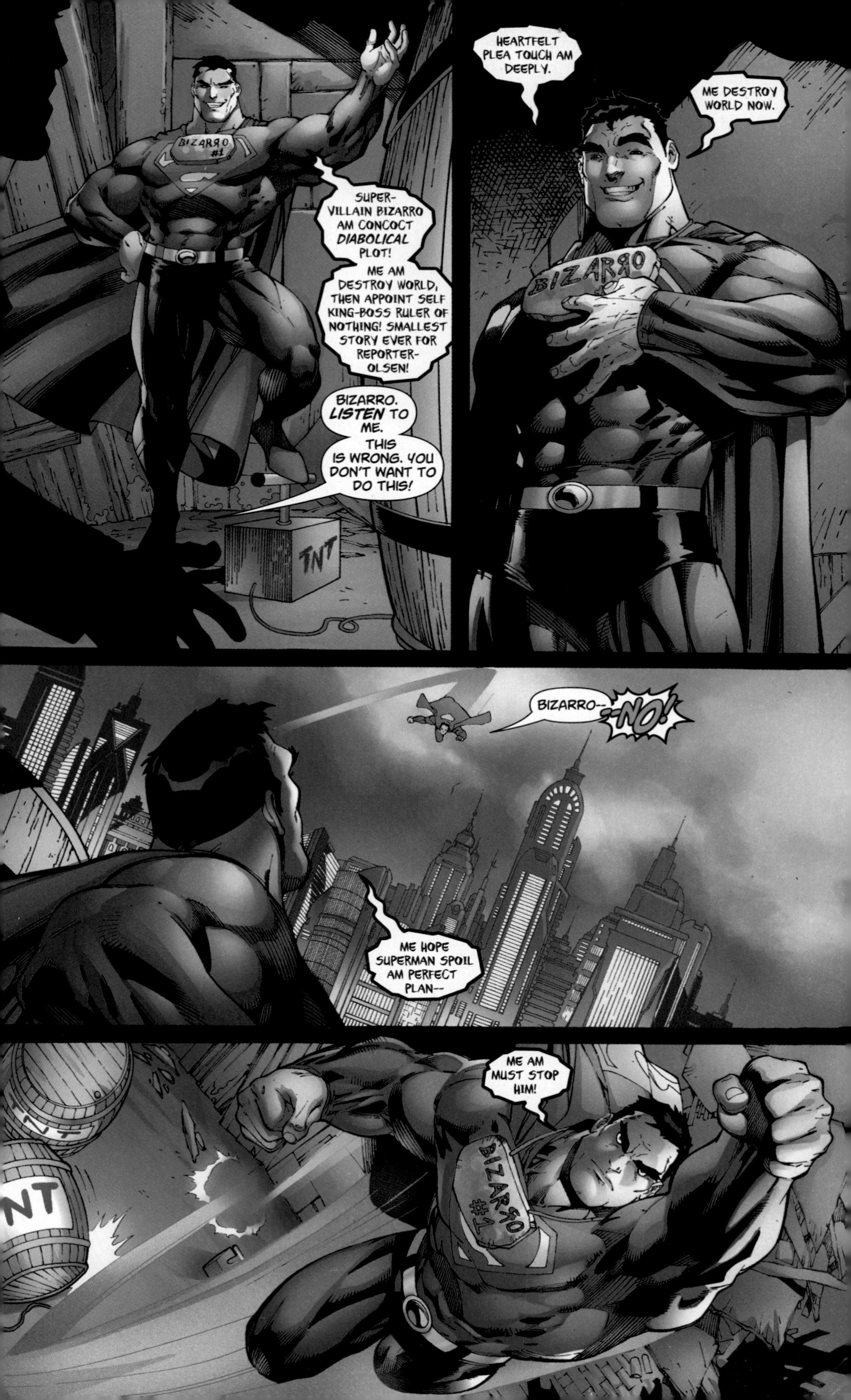
BIZARRO #1
SUPER-VILLAIN BIZARRO AM CONCOCT DIABOLICAL PLOT!
ME AM DESTROY WORLD, THEN APPOINT SELF KING-BOSS RULER OF NOTHING! SMALLEST STORY EVER FOR REPORTER-OLSEN!
BIZARRO. LISTEN TO ME.
THIS IS WRONG. YOU DON'T WANT TO DO THIS!
TNT
HEARTFELT PLEA TOUCH AM DEEPLY.
ME DESTROY WORLD NOW.
BIZARRO
BIZARRO--
--NO!
ME HOPE SUPERMAN SPOIL AM PERFECT PLAN--
ME AM MUST STOP HIM!
TNT
BIZARRO #1

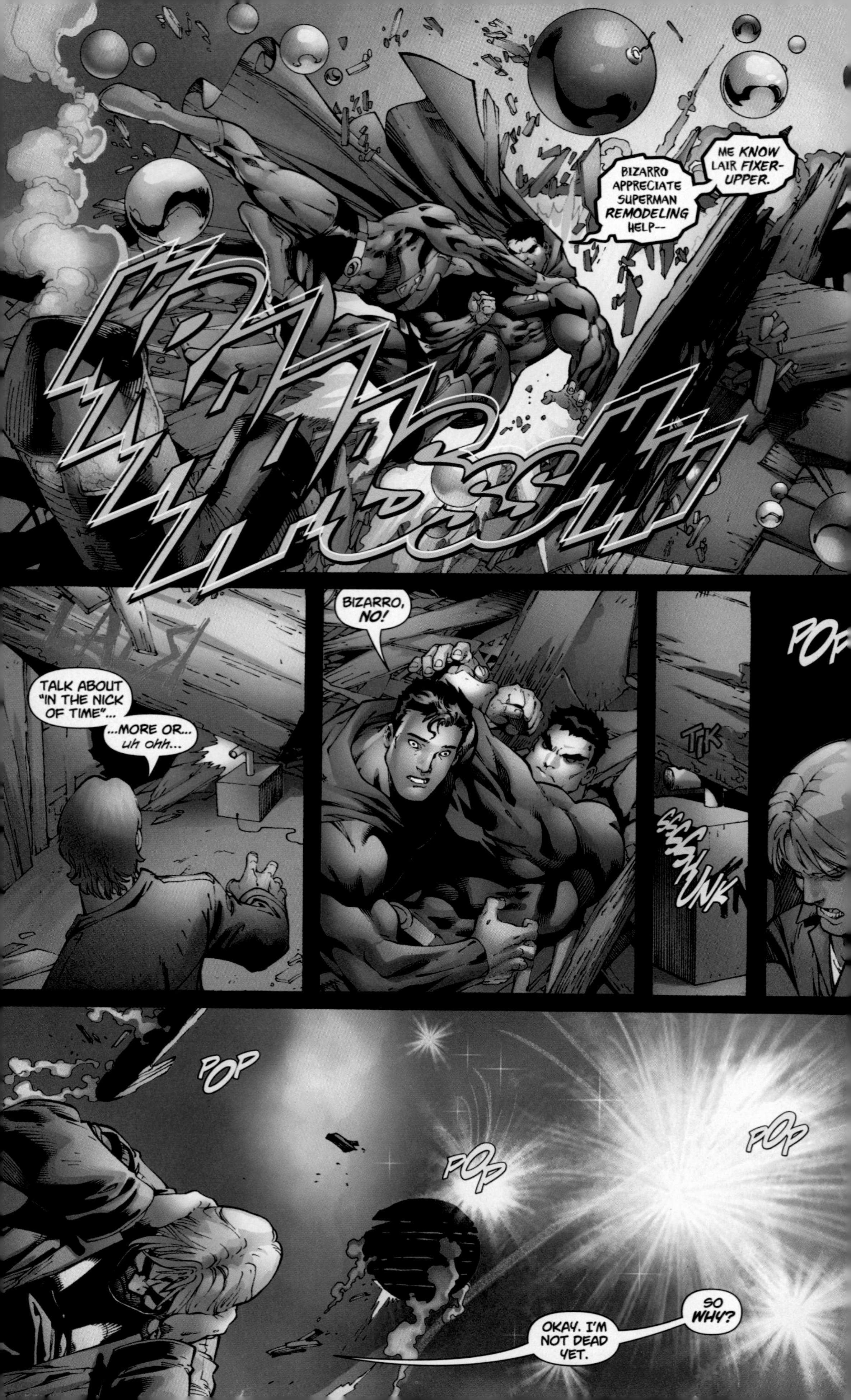
BIZARRO APPRECIATE SUPERMAN REMODELING HELP--
ME KNOW LAIR FIXER-UPPER.
TALK ABOUT "IN THE NICK OF TIME"...
...MORE OR... uh ohh...
BIZARRO, NO!
POP
TIK
POP
POP
POP
OKAY. I'M NOT DEAD YET.
SO WHY?

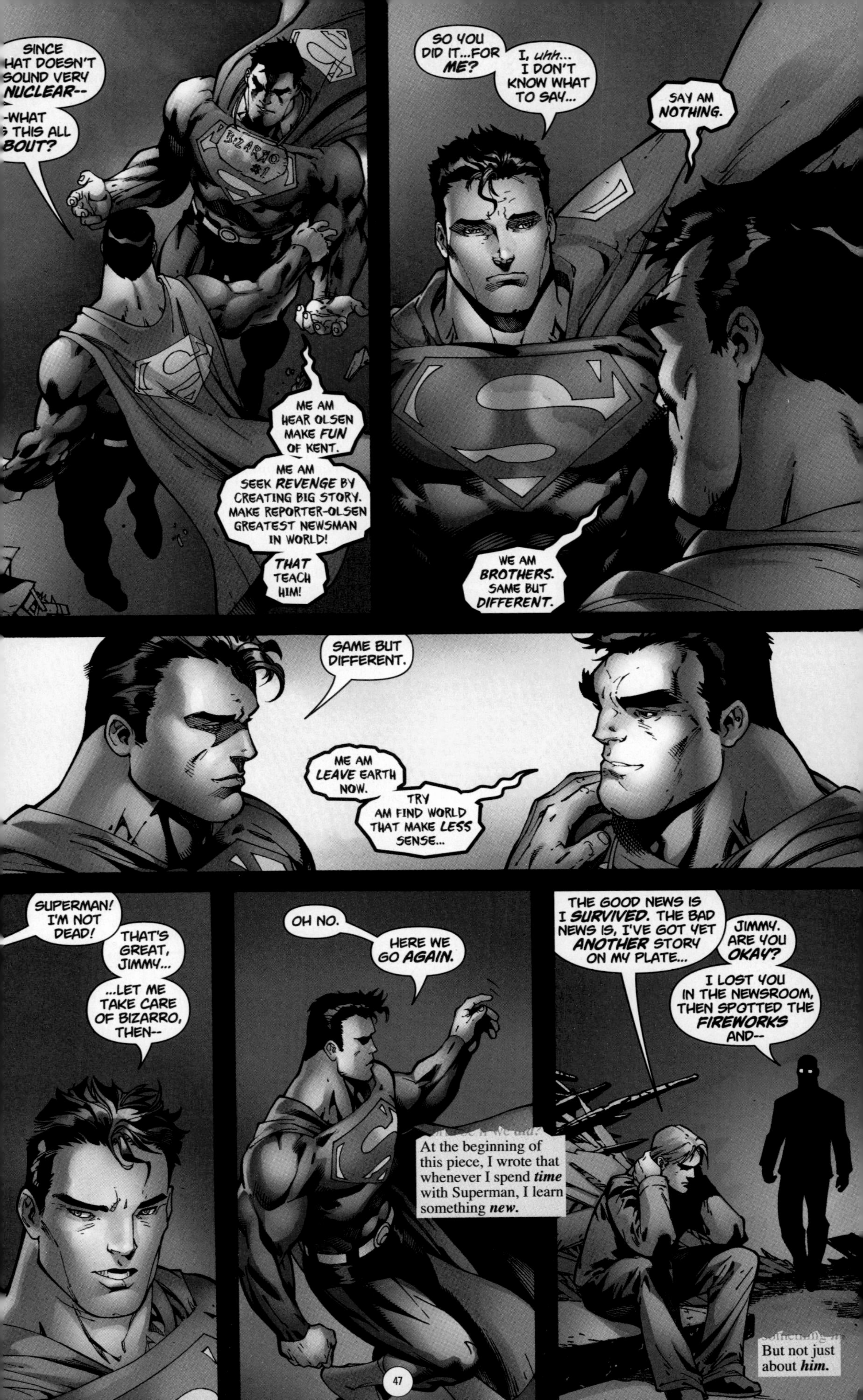

SINCE HAT DOESN'T SOUND VERY NUCLEAR--
-WHAT S THIS ALL BOUT?
BIZARRO #1
ME AM HEAR OLSEN MAKE FUN OF KENT.
ME AM SEEK REVENGE BY CREATING BIG STORY. MAKE REPORTER-OLSEN GREATEST NEWSMAN IN WORLD!
THAT TEACH HIM!
SO YOU DID IT...FOR ME?
I, uhh... I DON'T KNOW WHAT TO SAY...
SAY AM NOTHING.
WE AM BROTHERS. SAME BUT DIFFERENT.
SAME BUT DIFFERENT.
ME AM LEAVE EARTH NOW.
TRY AM FIND WORLD THAT MAKE LESS SENSE...
SUPERMAN! I'M NOT DEAD!
THAT'S GREAT, JIMMY...
...LET ME TAKE CARE OF BIZARRO, THEN--
OH NO.
HERE WE GO AGAIN.
At the beginning of this piece, I wrote that whenever I spend time with Superman, I learn something new.
THE GOOD NEWS IS I SURVIVED. THE BAD NEWS IS, I'VE GOT YET ANOTHER STORY ON MY PLATE...
JIMMY. ARE YOU OKAY?
I LOST YOU IN THE NEWSROOM, THEN SPOTTED THE FIREWORKS AND--
But not just about him.

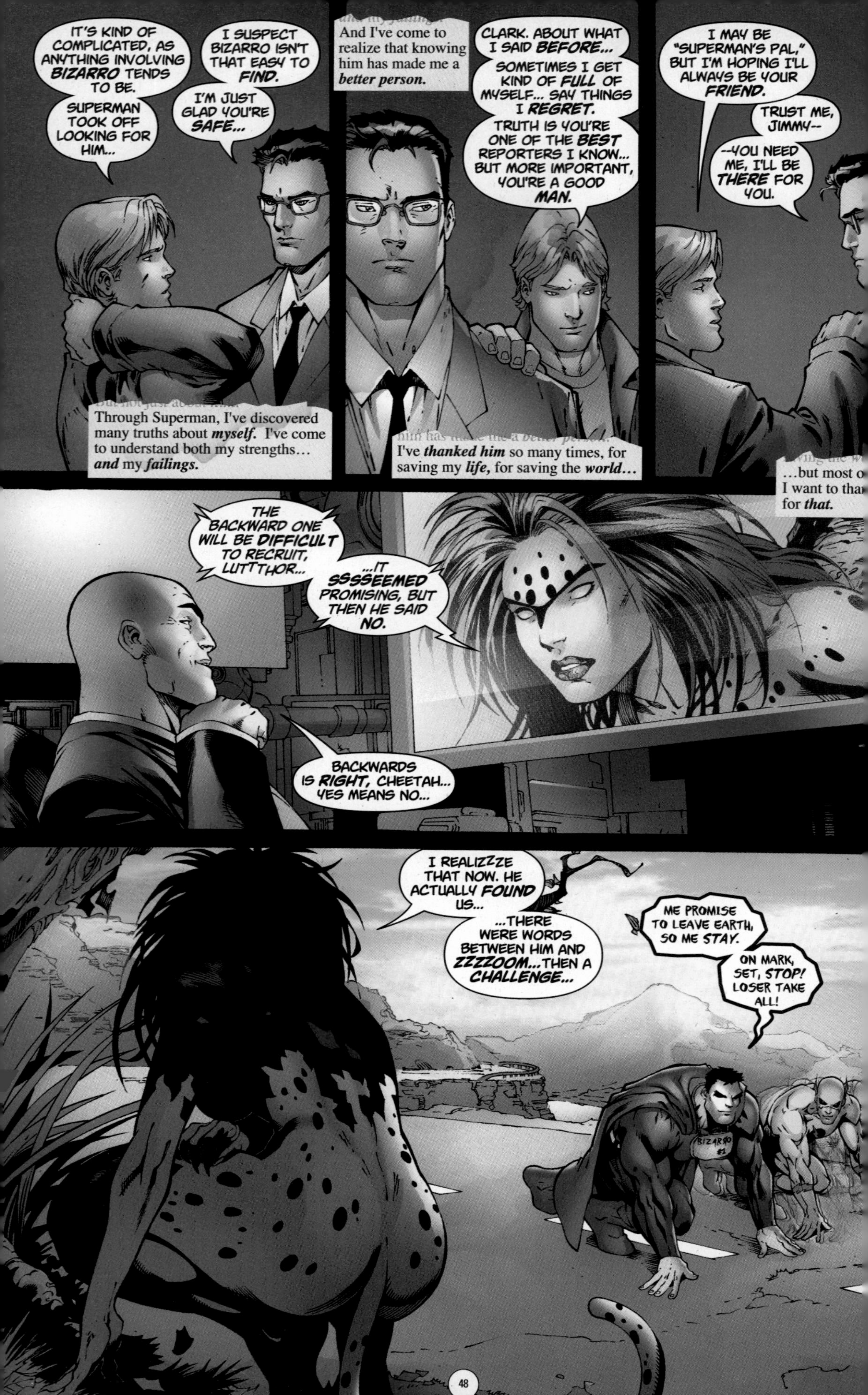
IT'S KIND OF COMPLICATED, AS ANYTHING INVOLVING BIZARRO TENDS TO BE.
SUPERMAN TOOK OFF LOOKING FOR HIM...
I SUSPECT BIZARRO ISN'T THAT EASY TO FIND.
I'M JUST GLAD YOU'RE SAFE...
Through Superman, I've discovered many truths about myself. I've come to understand both my strengths… and my failings.
And I've come to realize that knowing him has made me a better person.
I've thanked him so many times, for saving my life, for saving the world…
CLARK. ABOUT WHAT I SAID BEFORE...
SOMETIMES I GET KIND OF FULL OF MYSELF... SAY THINGS I REGRET.
TRUTH IS YOU'RE ONE OF THE BEST REPORTERS I KNOW... BUT MORE IMPORTANT, YOU'RE A GOOD MAN.
I MAY BE "SUPERMAN'S PAL," BUT I'M HOPING I'LL ALWAYS BE YOUR FRIEND.
TRUST ME, JIMMY--
--YOU NEED ME, I'LL BE THERE FOR YOU.
THE BACKWARD ONE WILL BE DIFFICULT TO RECRUIT, LUTTTHOR...
...IT SSSSEEMED PROMISING, BUT THEN HE SAID NO.
BACKWARDS IS RIGHT, CHEETAH... YES MEANS NO...
I REALIZZZE THAT NOW. HE ACTUALLY FOUND US...
...THERE WERE WORDS BETWEEN HIM AND ZZZZOOM...THEN A CHALLENGE...
ME PROMISE TO LEAVE EARTH, SO ME STAY.
ON MARK, SET, STOP! LOSER TAKE ALL!
BIZARRO #1

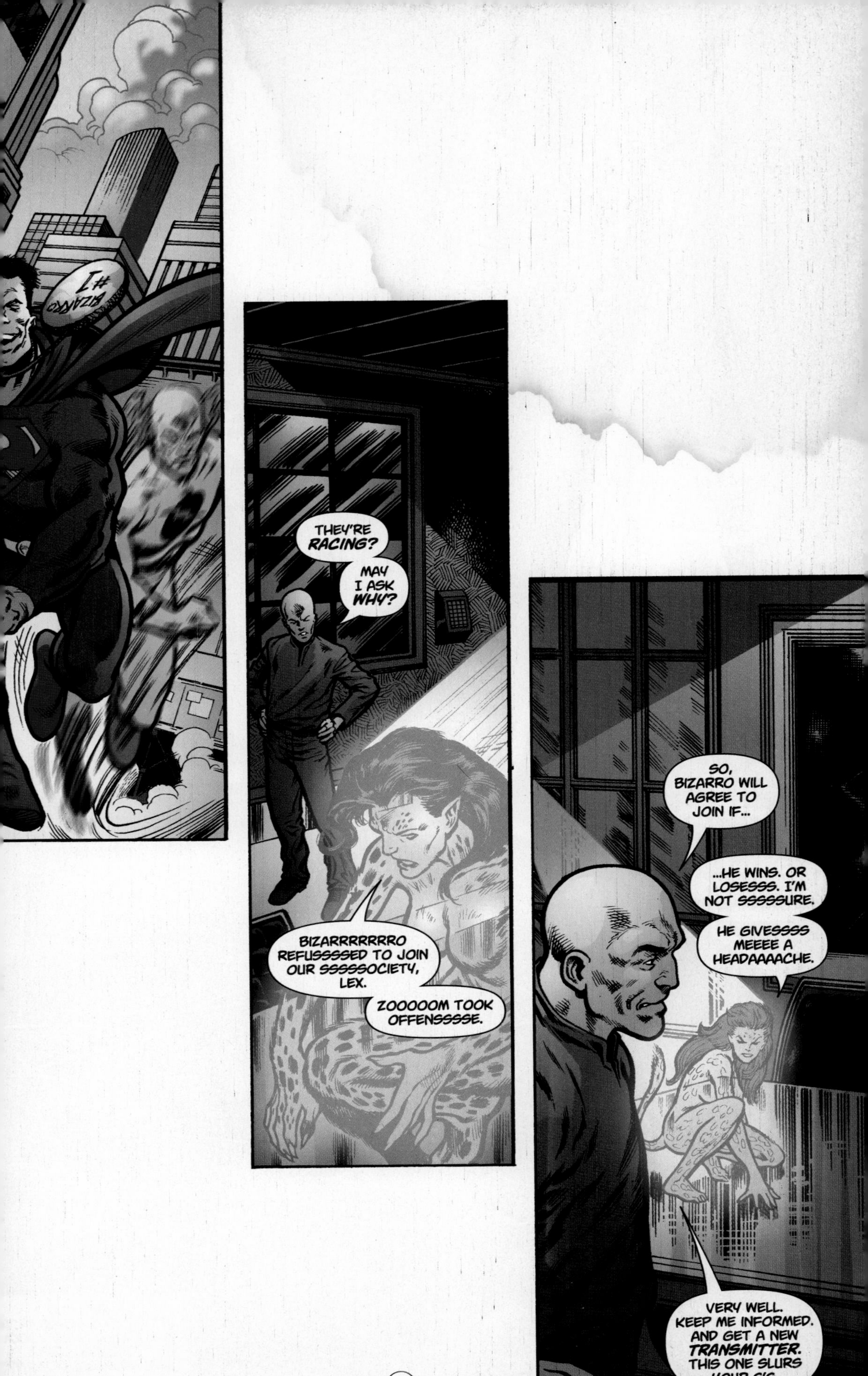
THEY'RE RACING?
MAY I ASK WHY?
BIZARRRRRRRO REFUSSSSED TO JOIN OUR SSSSSOCIETY, LEX.
ZOOOOOM TOOK OFFENSSSSE.
SO, BIZARRO WILL AGREE TO JOIN IF...
...HE WINS. OR LOSESSS. I'M NOT SSSSSURE.
HE GIVESSSS MEEEE A HEADAAAACHE.
VERY WELL. KEEP ME INFORMED. AND GET A NEW TRANSMITTER. THIS ONE SLURS YOUR S'S.

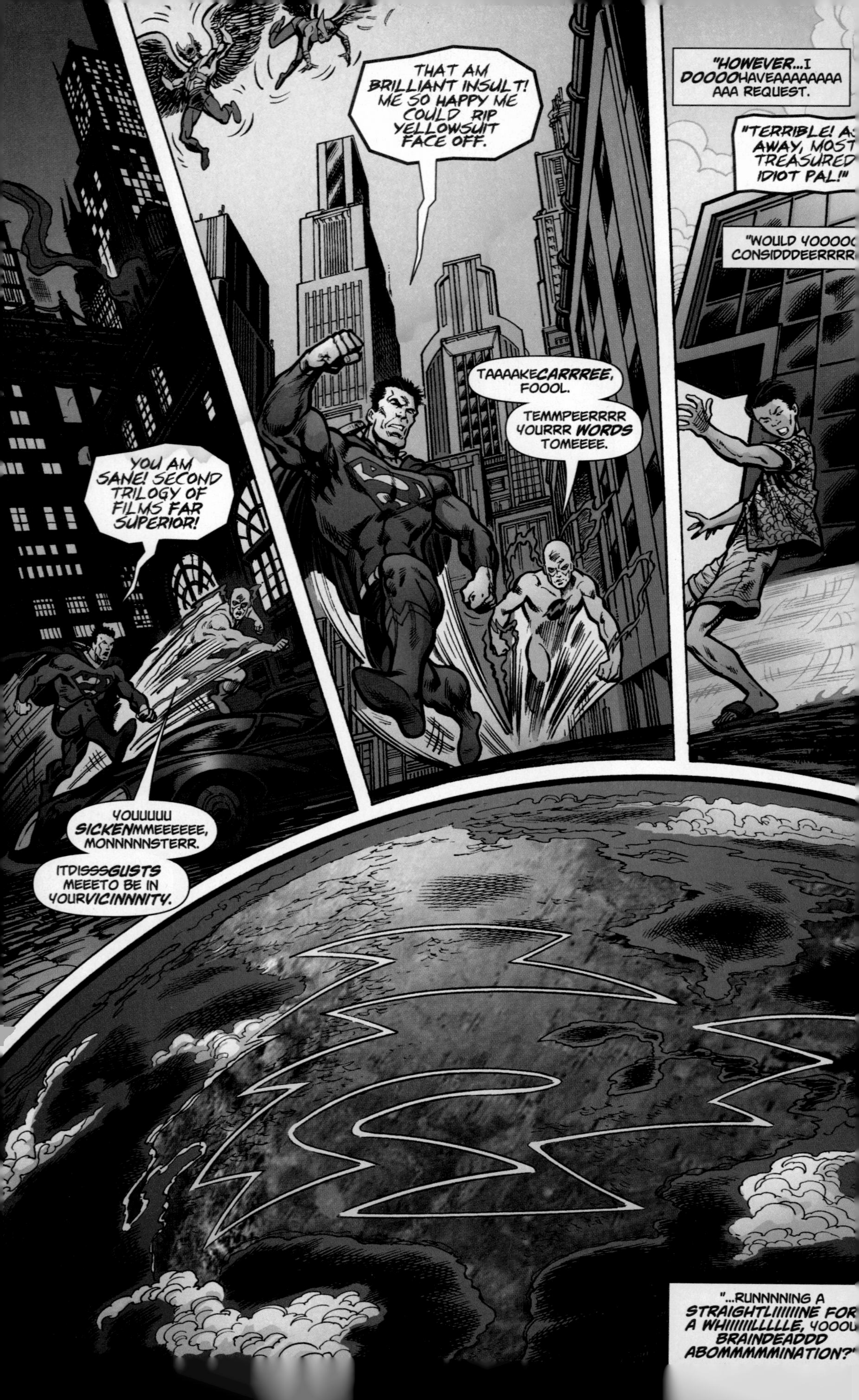
YOU AM SANE! SECOND TRILOGY OF FILMS FAR SUPERIOR!
YOUUUUU SICKENMMEEEEEE, MONNNNNSTERR.
ITDISSSGUSTS MEEETO BE IN YOURVICINNNITY.
THAT AM BRILLIANT INSULT! ME SO HAPPY ME COULD RIP YELLOWSUIT FACE OFF.
TAAAAKECARRREE, FOOOL.
TEMMPEERRRR YOURRR WORDS TOMEEEE.
"HOWEVER...I DOOOOHAVEAAAAAAAA AAA REQUEST.
"TERRIBLE! A: AWAY, MOST TREASURED IDIOT PAL!"
"WOULD YOOOO CONSIDDDEERRRR
"...RUNNNNING A STRAIGHTLIIIIIINE FOR A WHIIIIIILLLLE, YOOOU BRAINDEADDD ABOMMMMINATION?"

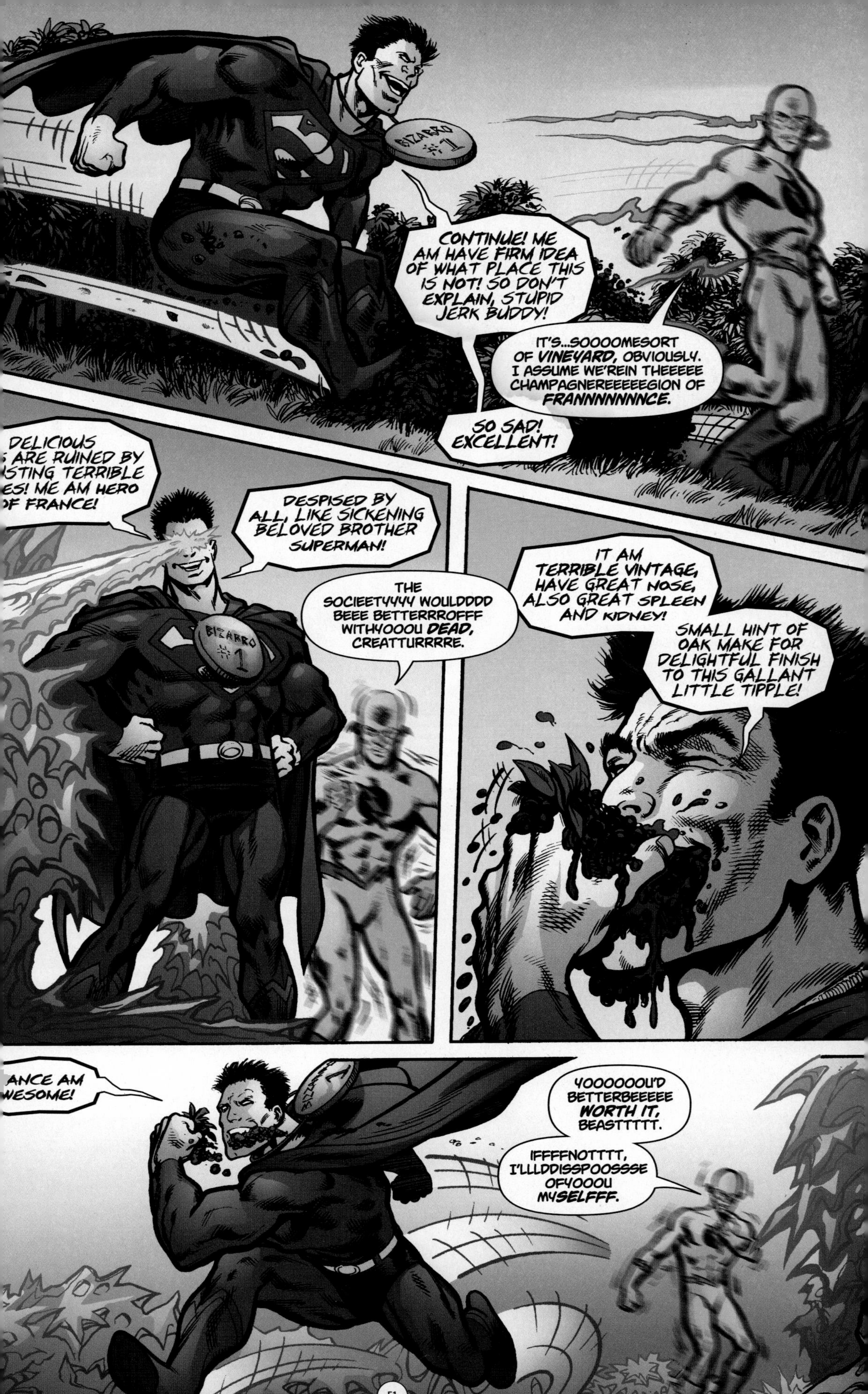
BIZARRO #1
CONTINUE! ME AM HAVE FIRM IDEA OF WHAT PLACE THIS IS NOT! SO DON'T EXPLAIN, STUPID JERK BUDDY!
IT'S...SOOOOMESORT OF VINEYARD, OBVIOUSLY. I ASSUME WE'REIN THEEEEE CHAMPAGNEREEEEEGION OF FRANNNNNNNCE.
SO SAD! EXCELLENT!
DELICIOUS S ARE RUINED BY STING TERRIBLE ES! ME AM HERO OF FRANCE!
DESPISED BY ALL, LIKE SICKENING BELOVED BROTHER SUPERMAN!
BIZARRO #1
THE SOCIEETYYYY WOULDDDD BEEE BETTERRROFF WITHYOOOU DEAD, CREATTURRRRE.
IT AM TERRIBLE VINTAGE, HAVE GREAT NOSE, ALSO GREAT SPLEEN AND KIDNEY!
SMALL HINT OF OAK MAKE FOR DELIGHTFUL FINISH TO THIS GALLANT LITTLE TIPPLE!
ANCE AM WESOME!
YOOOOOOU'D BETTERBEEEEE WORTH IT, BEASTTTTT.
IFFFFNOTTTT, I'LLLDDISSPOOSSSE OFYOOOU MYSELFFF.

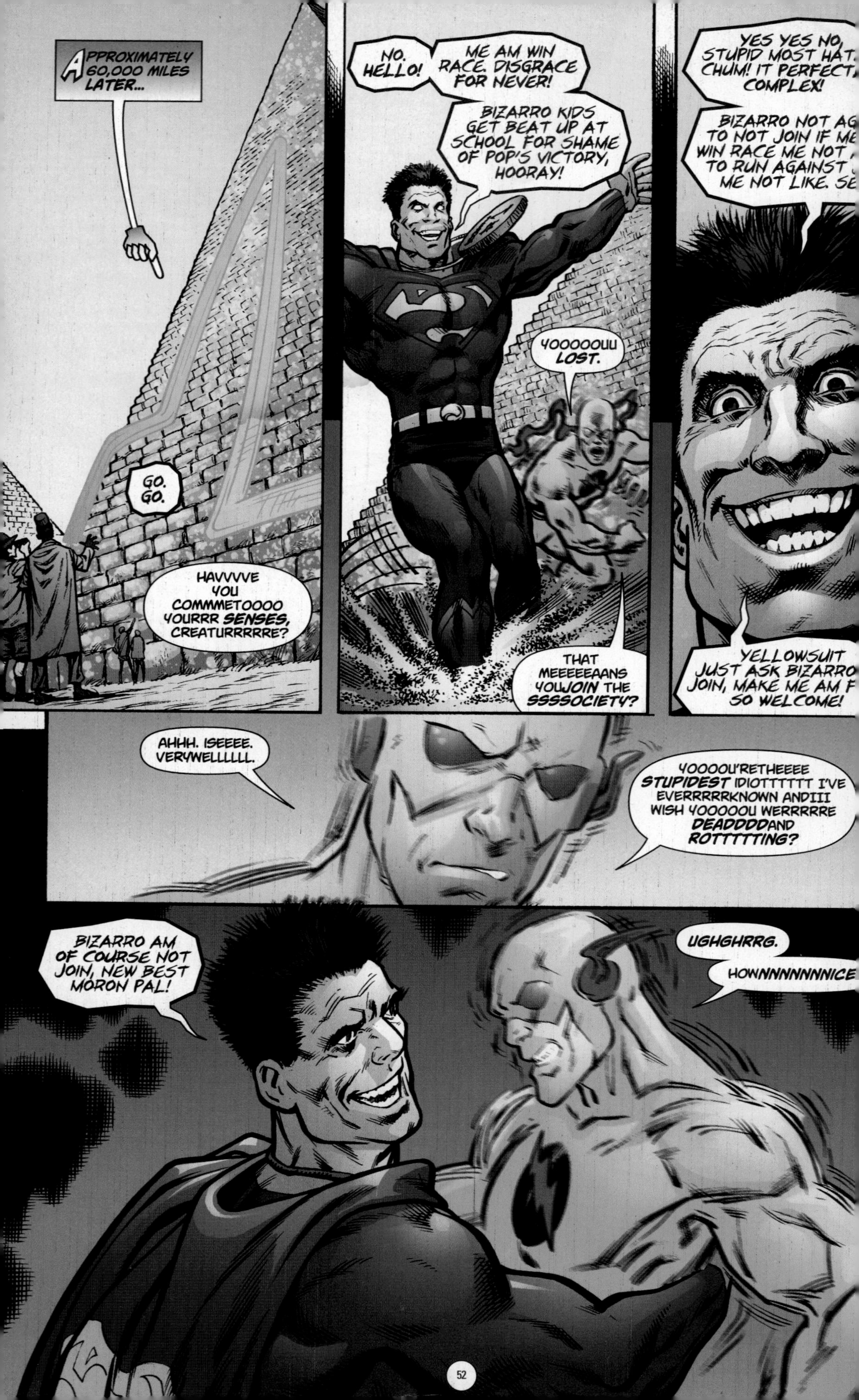
APPROXIMATELY 60,000 MILES LATER...
GO. GO.
HAVVVVE YOU COMMMETOOOO YOURRR SENSES, CREATURRRRRE?
NO. HELLO!
ME AM WIN RACE. DISGRACE FOR NEVER!
BIZARRO KIDS GET BEAT UP AT SCHOOL FOR SHAME OF POP'S VICTORY, HOORAY!
YOOOOOUU LOST.
THAT MEEEEEAANS YOUJOIN THE SSSSOCIETY?
YES YES NO, STUPID MOST HAT CHUM! IT PERFECT COMPLEX!
BIZARRO NOT AG TO NOT JOIN IF ME WIN RACE ME NOT TO RUN AGAINST ME NOT LIKE. SE
YELLOWSUIT JUST ASK BIZARRO JOIN, MAKE ME AM F SO WELCOME!
AHHH. ISEEEE. VERYWELLLLLL.
YOOOOU'RETHEEEE STUPIDEST IDIOTTTTTT I'VE EVERRRRRKNOWN ANDIII WISH YOOOOOU WERRRRRE DEADDDDAND ROTTTTTING?
BIZARRO AM OF COURSE NOT JOIN, NEW BEST MORON PAL!
UGHGHRRG.
HOWNNNNNNNNICE

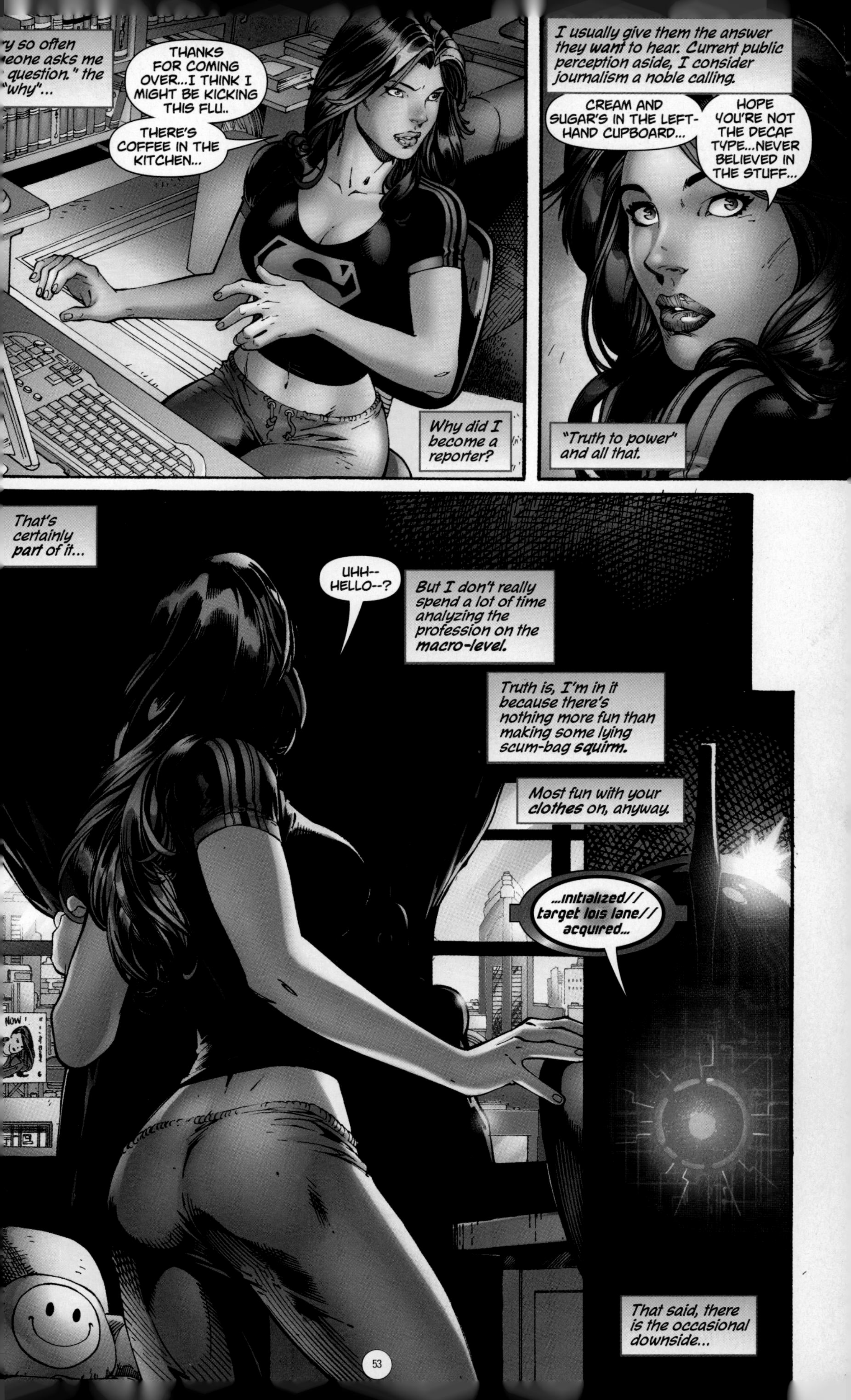

ry so often
eone asks me
question." the
"why"...
THANKS FOR COMING OVER...I THINK I MIGHT BE KICKING THIS FLU..
THERE'S COFFEE IN THE KITCHEN...
Why did I become a reporter?
I usually give them the answer they want to hear. Current public perception aside, I consider journalism a noble calling.
CREAM AND SUGAR'S IN THE LEFT-HAND CUPBOARD...
HOPE YOU'RE NOT THE DECAF TYPE...NEVER BELIEVED IN THE STUFF...
"Truth to power" and all that.
That's certainly part of it...
UHH-- HELLO--?
But I don't really spend a lot of time analyzing the profession on the macro-level.
Truth is, I'm in it because there's nothing more fun than making some lying scum-bag squirm.
Most fun with your clothes on, anyway.
...initialized// target lois lane// acquired...
NOW!
That said, there is the occasional downside...

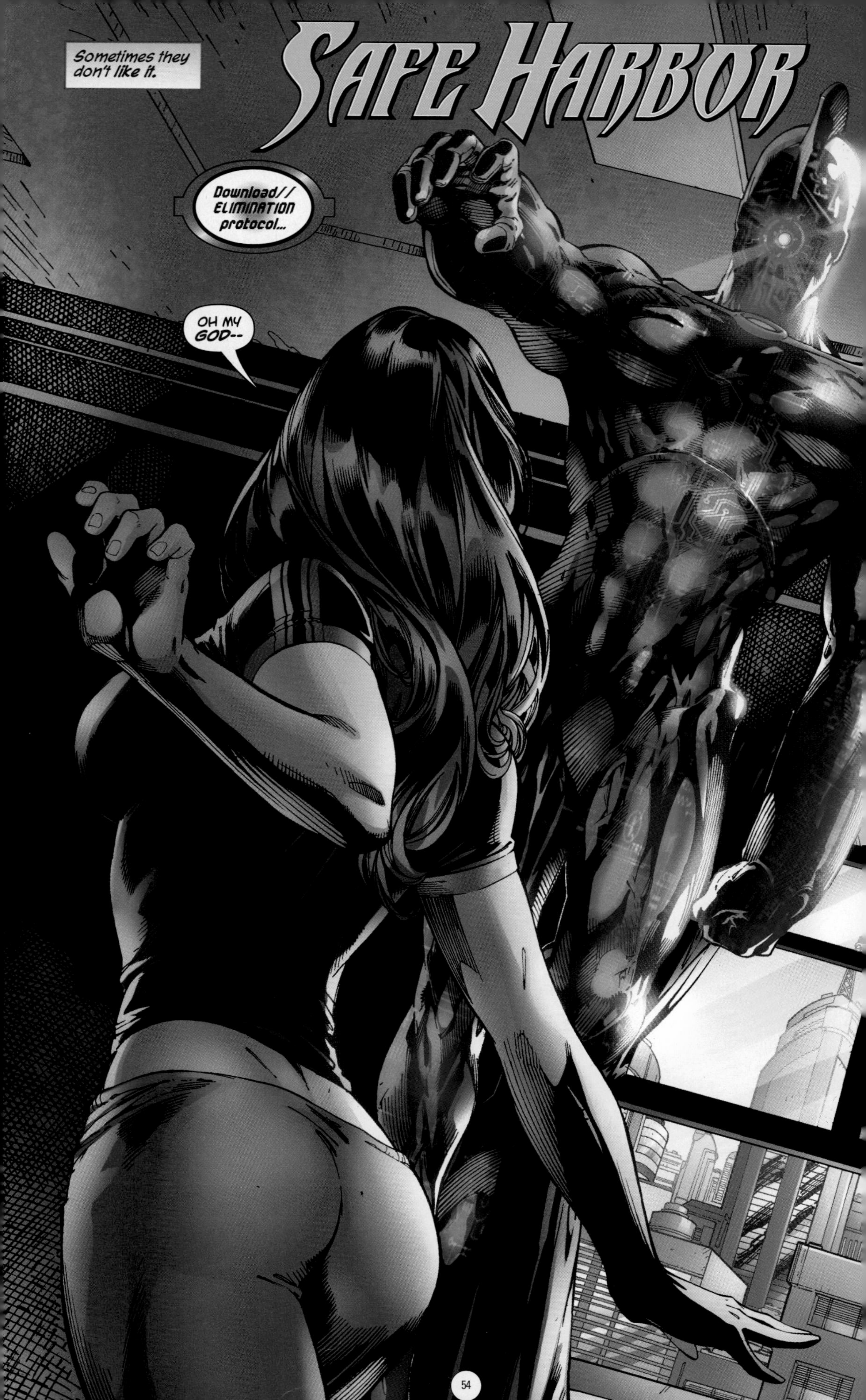
Sometimes they don't like it.
SAFE HARBOR
Download// ELIMINATION protocol...
OH MY GOD--

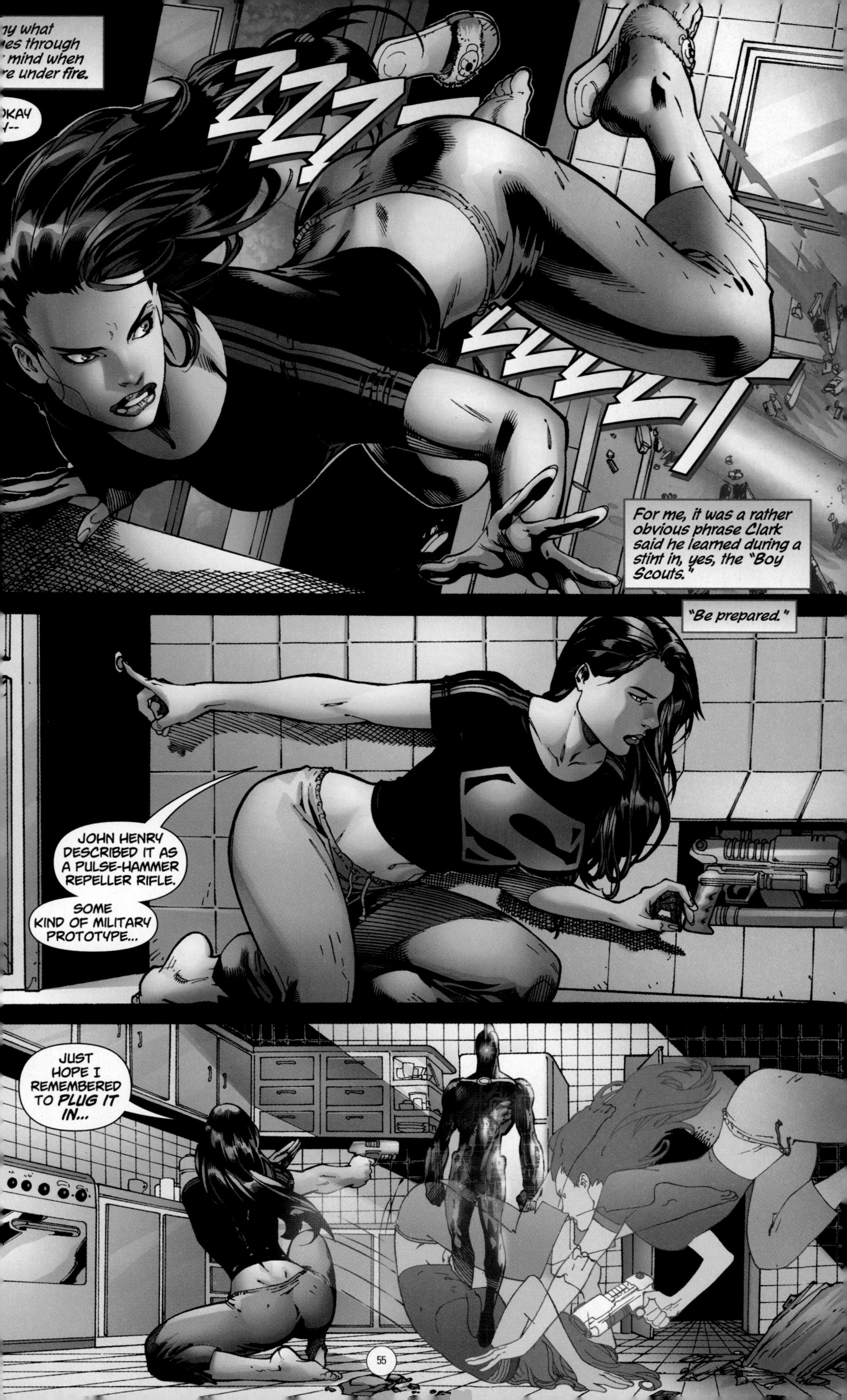

ny what
es through
mind when
re under fire.
OKAY
--
ZZZ--
ZZZZZT
For me, it was a rather obvious phrase Clark said he learned during a stint in, yes, the "Boy Scouts."
"Be prepared."
JOHN HENRY DESCRIBED IT AS A PULSE-HAMMER REPELLER RIFLE.
SOME KIND OF MILITARY PROTOTYPE...
JUST HOPE I REMEMBERED TO PLUG IT IN...

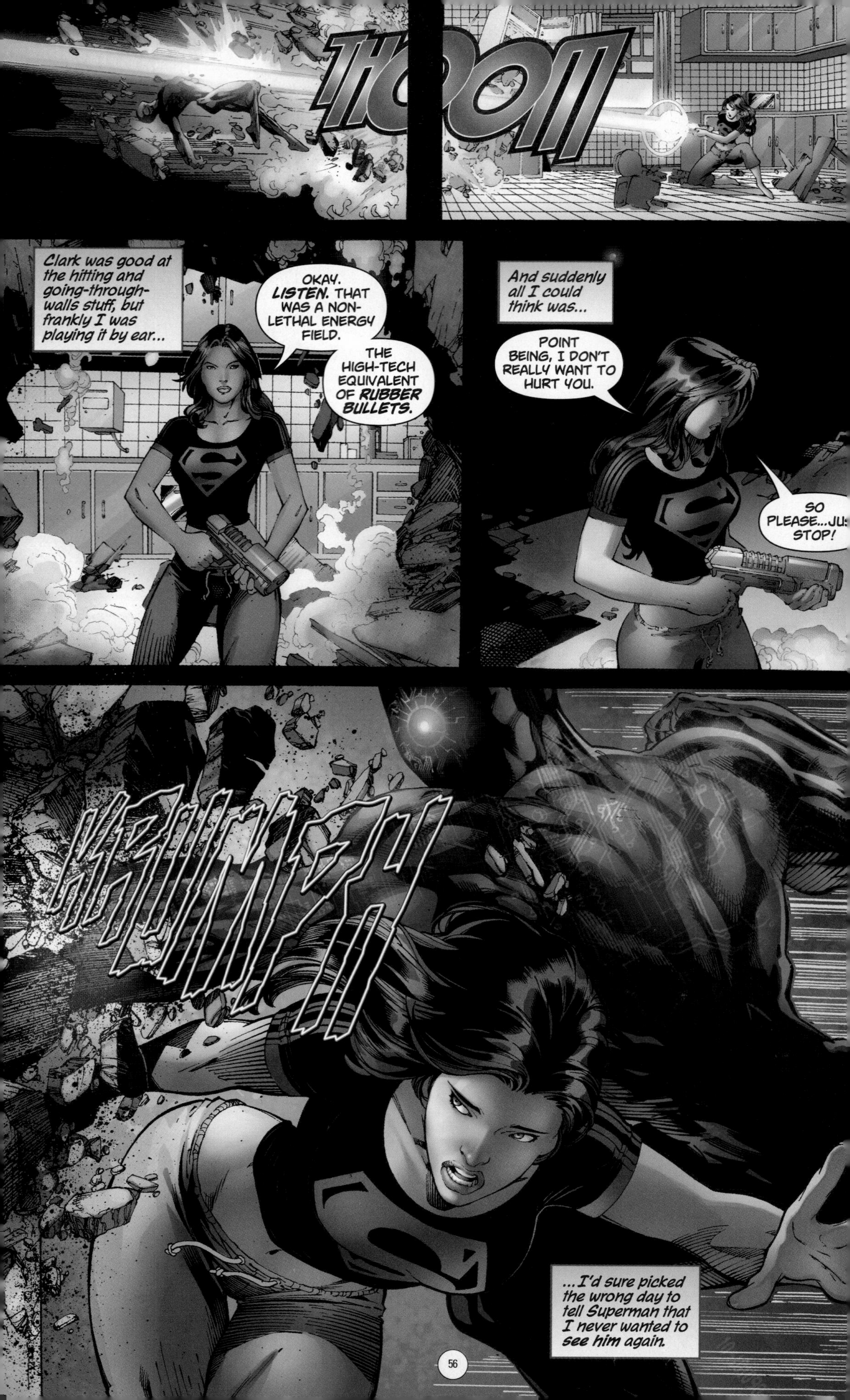
THOOM
Clark was good at the hitting and going-through-walls stuff, but frankly I was playing it by ear...
OKAY. LISTEN. THAT WAS A NON-LETHAL ENERGY FIELD.
THE HIGH-TECH EQUIVALENT OF RUBBER BULLETS.
And suddenly all I could think was...
POINT BEING, I DON'T REALLY WANT TO HURT YOU.
SO PLEASE...JUST STOP!
...I'd sure picked the wrong day to tell Superman that I never wanted to see him again.

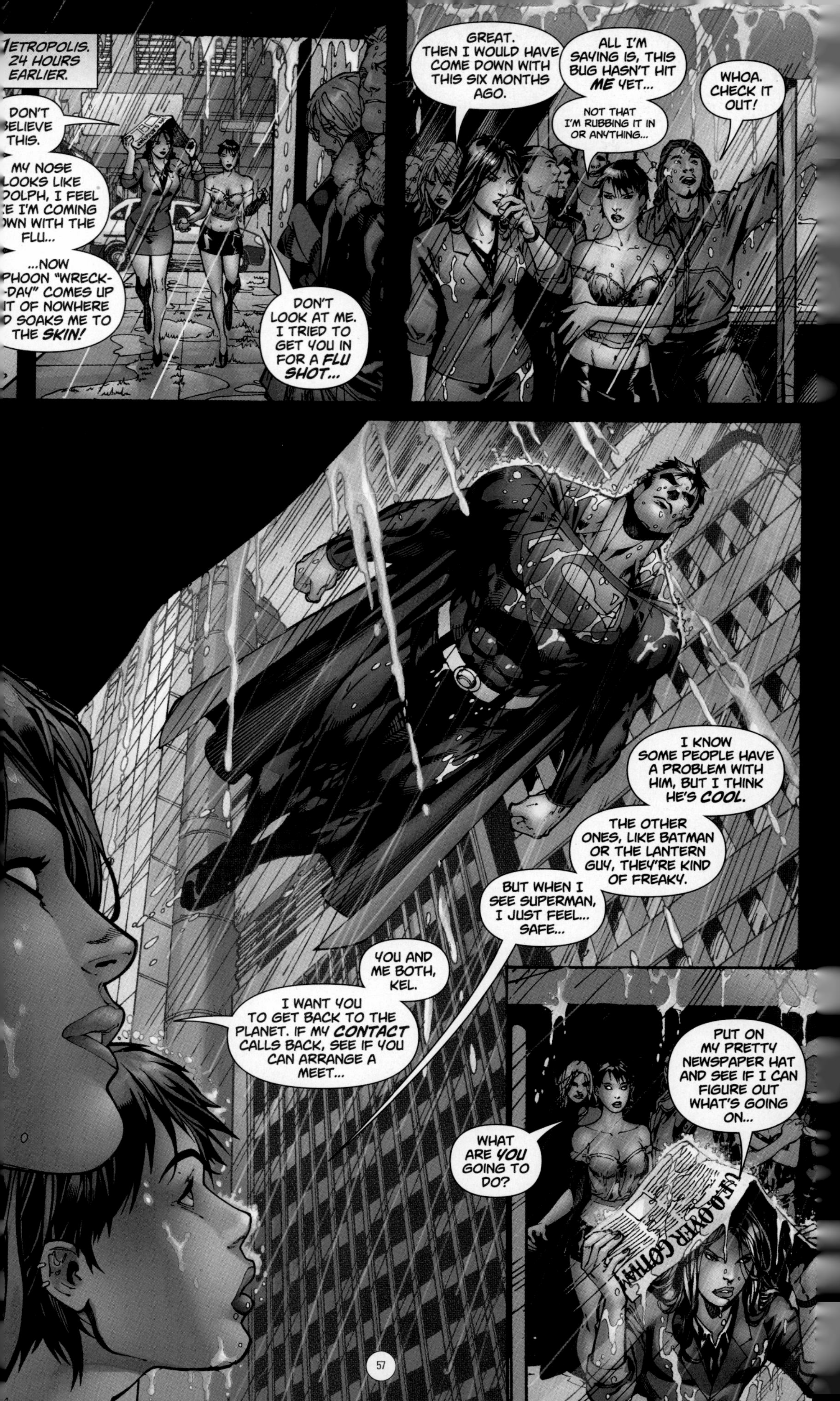
ETROPOLIS. 24 HOURS EARLIER.
DON'T ELIEVE THIS.
MY NOSE LOOKS LIKE DOLPH, I FEEL E I'M COMING WN WITH THE FLU...
...NOW PHOON "WRECK- -DAY" COMES UP IT OF NOWHERE D SOAKS ME TO THE SKIN!
DON'T LOOK AT ME. I TRIED TO GET YOU IN FOR A FLU SHOT...
GREAT. THEN I WOULD HAVE COME DOWN WITH THIS SIX MONTHS AGO.
ALL I'M SAYING IS, THIS BUG HASN'T HIT ME YET...
NOT THAT I'M RUBBING IT IN OR ANYTHING...
WHOA. CHECK IT OUT!
I KNOW SOME PEOPLE HAVE A PROBLEM WITH HIM, BUT I THINK HE'S COOL.
THE OTHER ONES, LIKE BATMAN OR THE LANTERN GUY, THEY'RE KIND OF FREAKY.
BUT WHEN I SEE SUPERMAN, I JUST FEEL... SAFE...
YOU AND ME BOTH, KEL.
I WANT YOU TO GET BACK TO THE PLANET. IF MY CONTACT CALLS BACK, SEE IF YOU CAN ARRANGE A MEET...
WHAT ARE YOU GOING TO DO?
PUT ON MY PRETTY NEWSPAPER HAT AND SEE IF I CAN FIGURE OUT WHAT'S GOING ON...

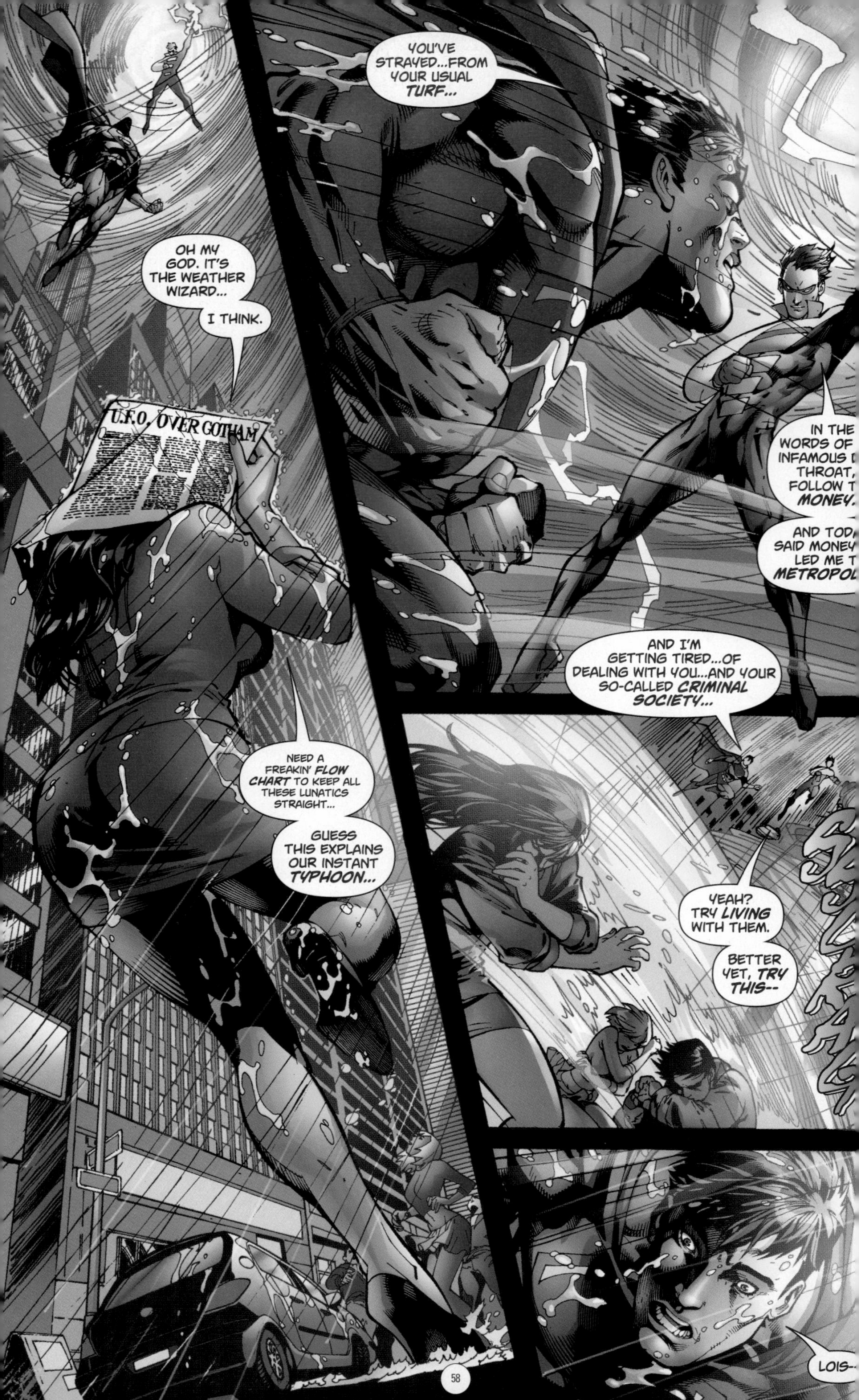
OH MY GOD. IT'S THE WEATHER WIZARD...
I THINK.
U.F.O. OVER GOTHAM
YOU'VE STRAYED...FROM YOUR USUAL TURF...
IN THE WORDS OF INFAMOUS D THROAT, FOLLOW T MONEY.
AND TOD SAID MONEY LED ME T METROPOL
AND I'M GETTING TIRED...OF DEALING WITH YOU...AND YOUR SO-CALLED CRIMINAL SOCIETY...
NEED A FREAKIN' FLOW CHART TO KEEP ALL THESE LUNATICS STRAIGHT...
GUESS THIS EXPLAINS OUR INSTANT TYPHOON...
YEAH? TRY LIVING WITH THEM.
BETTER YET, TRY THIS--
LOIS--

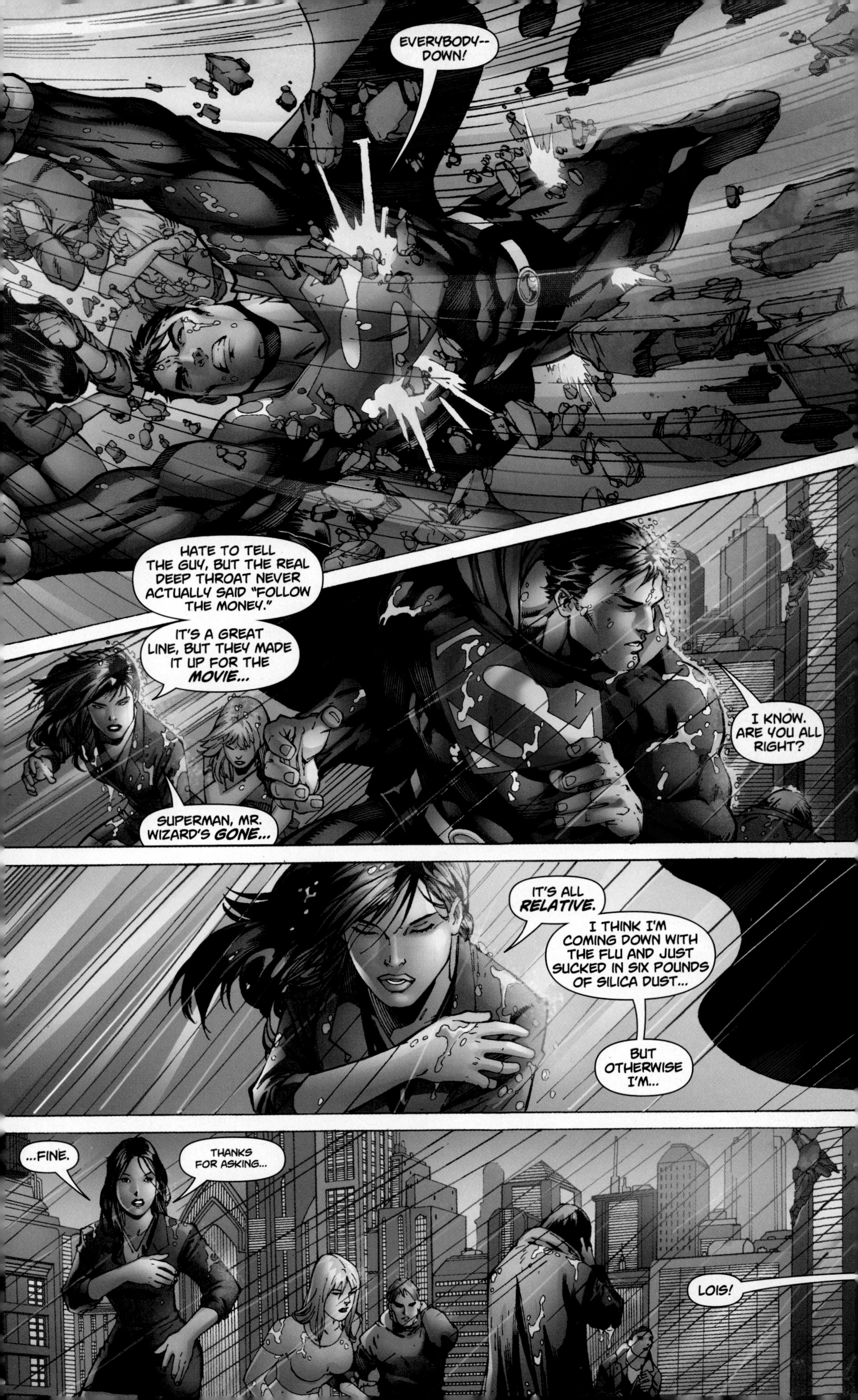
EVERYBODY-- DOWN!
HATE TO TELL THE GUY, BUT THE REAL DEEP THROAT NEVER ACTUALLY SAID "FOLLOW THE MONEY."
IT'S A GREAT LINE, BUT THEY MADE IT UP FOR THE MOVIE...
I KNOW. ARE YOU ALL RIGHT?
SUPERMAN, MR. WIZARD'S GONE...
IT'S ALL RELATIVE.
I THINK I'M COMING DOWN WITH THE FLU AND JUST SUCKED IN SIX POUNDS OF SILICA DUST...
BUT OTHERWISE I'M...
...FINE.
THANKS FOR ASKING...
LOIS!

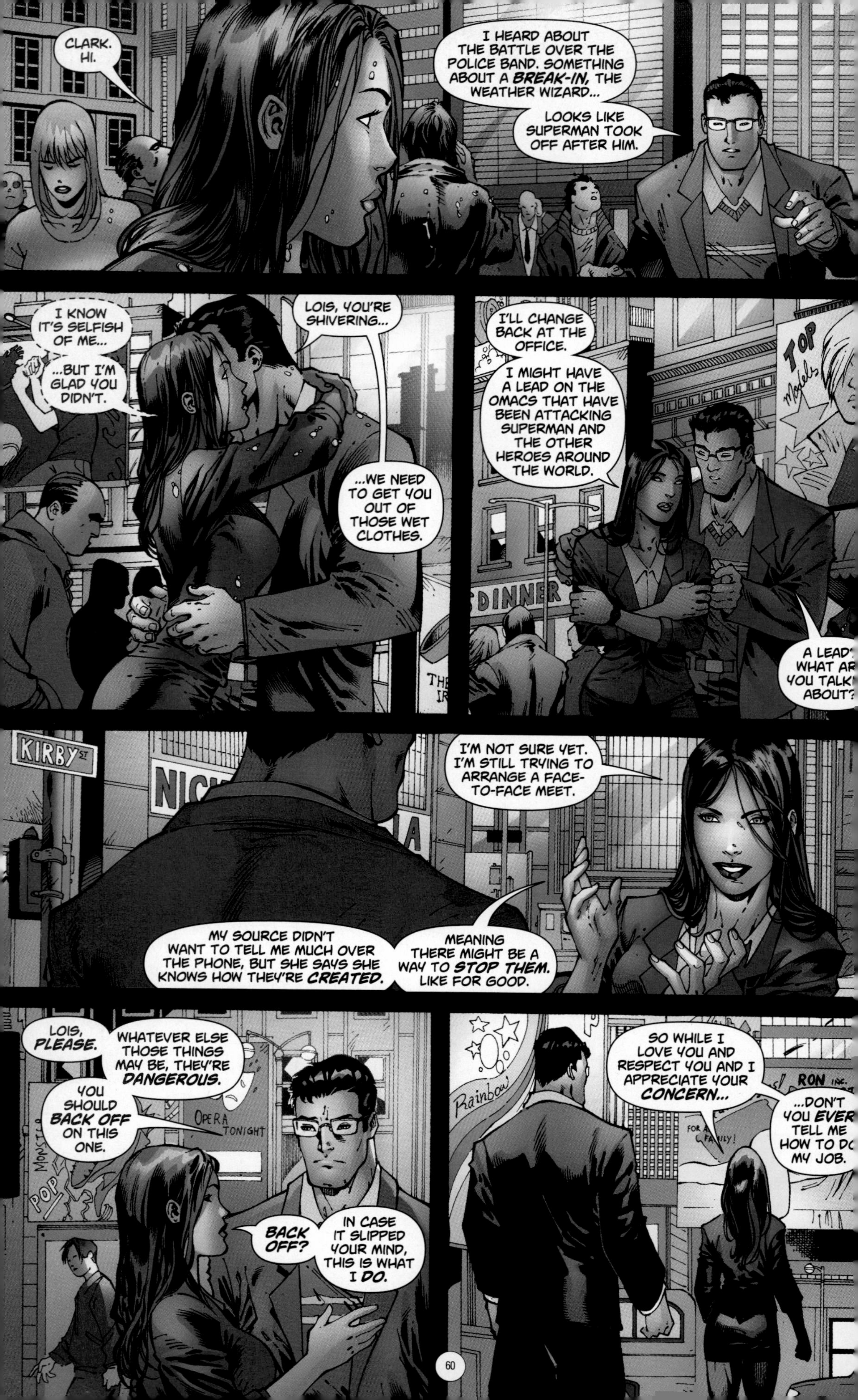
CLARK. HI.
I HEARD ABOUT THE BATTLE OVER THE POLICE BAND. SOMETHING ABOUT A BREAK-IN, THE WEATHER WIZARD...
LOOKS LIKE SUPERMAN TOOK OFF AFTER HIM.
I KNOW IT'S SELFISH OF ME...
...BUT I'M GLAD YOU DIDN'T.
LOIS, YOU'RE SHIVERING...
...WE NEED TO GET YOU OUT OF THOSE WET CLOTHES.
I'LL CHANGE BACK AT THE OFFICE.
I MIGHT HAVE A LEAD ON THE OMACS THAT HAVE BEEN ATTACKING SUPERMAN AND THE OTHER HEROES AROUND THE WORLD.
DINNER
TOP Models
KIRBY ST
I'M NOT SURE YET. I'M STILL TRYING TO ARRANGE A FACE-TO-FACE MEET.
MY SOURCE DIDN'T WANT TO TELL ME MUCH OVER THE PHONE, BUT SHE SAYS SHE KNOWS HOW THEY'RE CREATED.
MEANING THERE MIGHT BE A WAY TO STOP THEM. LIKE FOR GOOD.
LOIS, PLEASE.
WHATEVER ELSE THOSE THINGS MAY BE, THEY'RE DANGEROUS.
YOU SHOULD BACK OFF ON THIS ONE.
OPERA TONIGHT
BACK OFF?
IN CASE IT SLIPPED YOUR MIND, THIS IS WHAT I DO.
Rainbow
SO WHILE I LOVE YOU AND RESPECT YOU AND I APPRECIATE YOUR CONCERN...
...DON'T YOU EVER TELL ME HOW TO DO MY JOB.

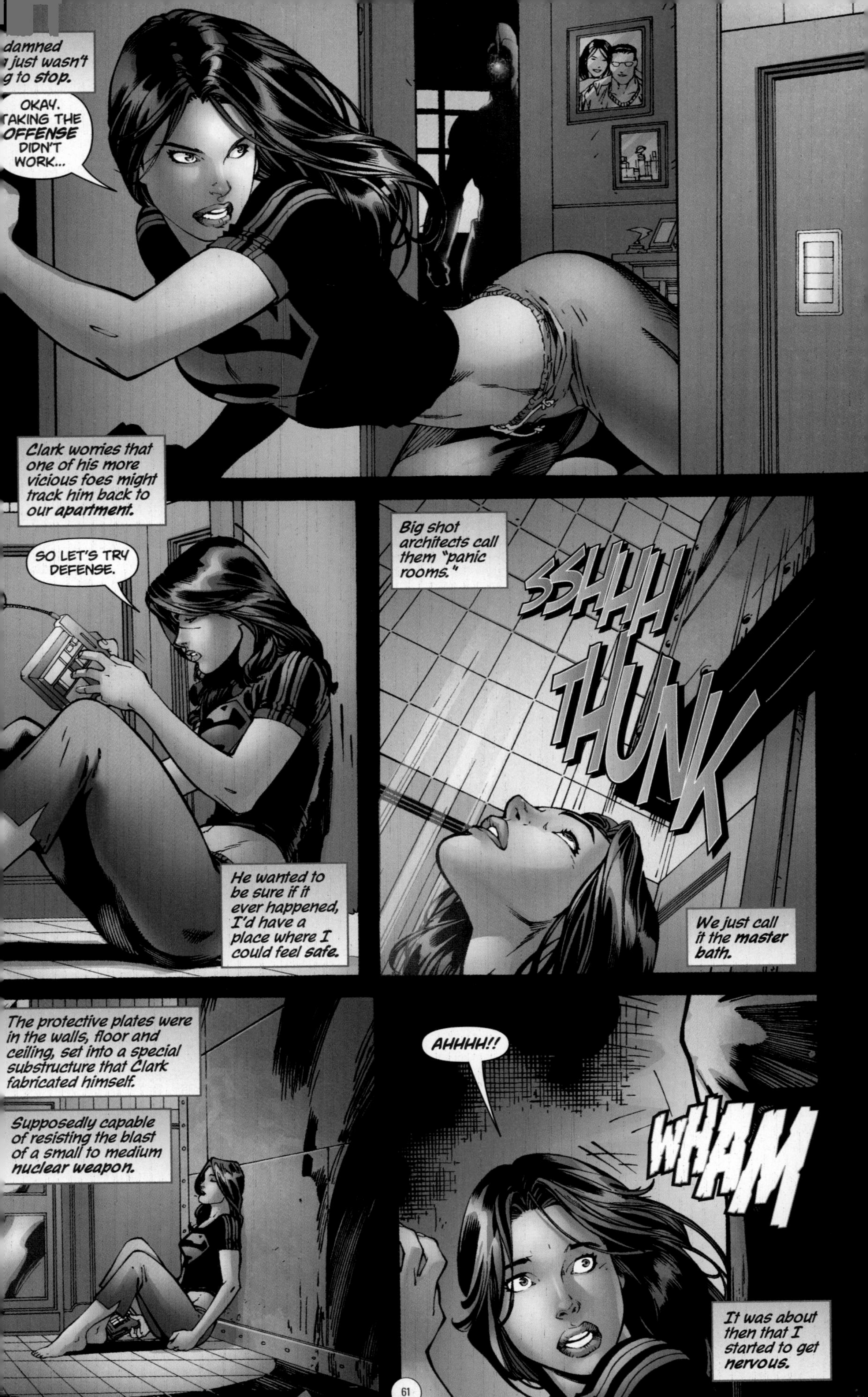
damned
just wasn't
g to stop.
OKAY.
TAKING THE OFFENSE DIDN'T WORK...
Clark worries that one of his more vicious foes might track him back to our apartment.
SO LET'S TRY DEFENSE.
He wanted to be sure if it ever happened, I'd have a place where I could feel safe.
Big shot architects call them "panic rooms."
SSHHH
THUNK
We just call it the master bath.
The protective plates were in the walls, floor and ceiling, set into a special substructure that Clark fabricated himself.
Supposedly capable of resisting the blast of a small to medium nuclear weapon.
AHHHH!!
WHAM
It was about then that I started to get nervous.

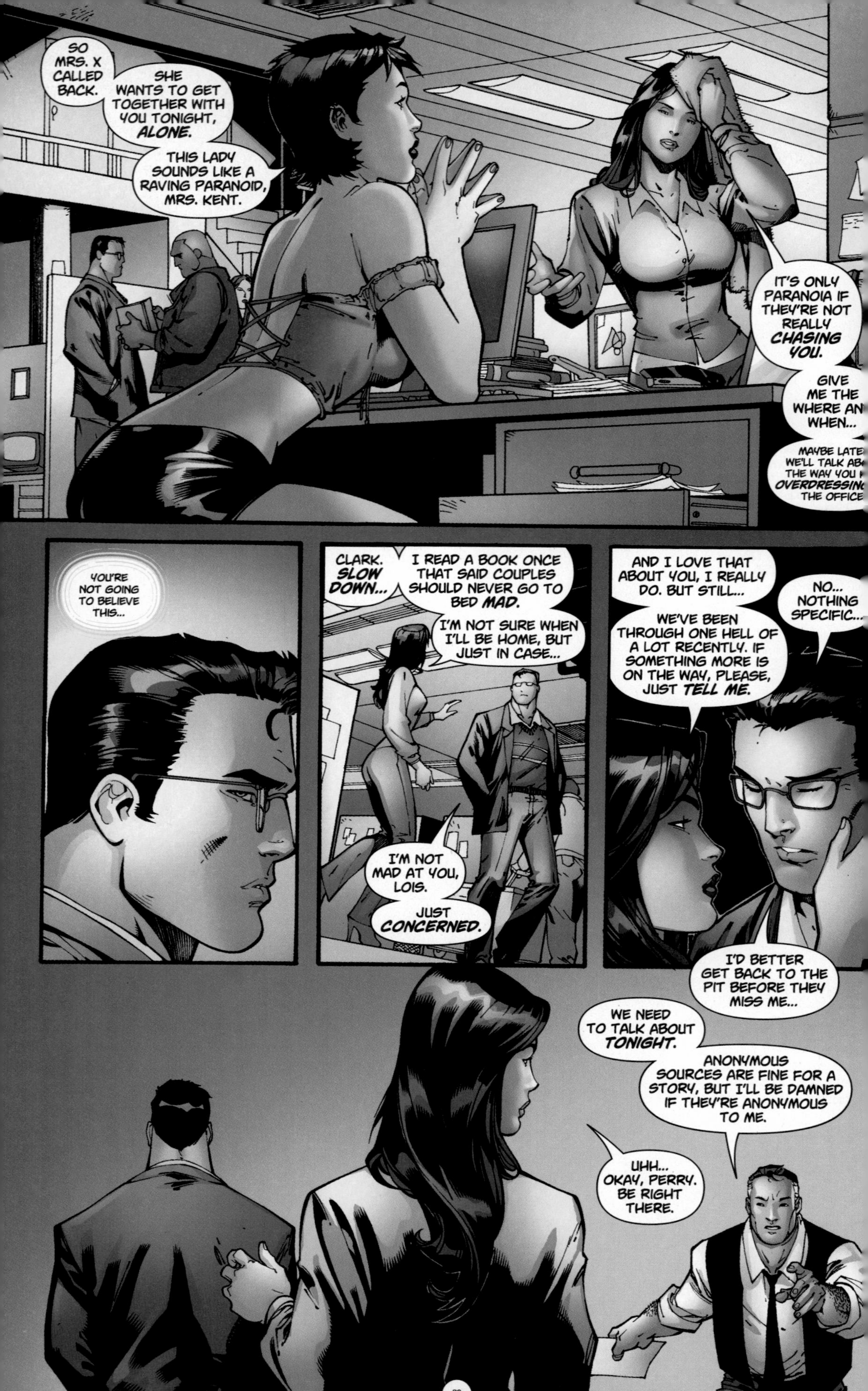
SO MRS. X CALLED BACK.
SHE WANTS TO GET TOGETHER WITH YOU TONIGHT, ALONE.
THIS LADY SOUNDS LIKE A RAVING PARANOID, MRS. KENT.
IT'S ONLY PARANOIA IF THEY'RE NOT REALLY CHASING YOU.
GIVE ME THE WHERE AN WHEN...
MAYBE LATE WE'LL TALK AB THE WAY YOU OVERDRESSIN THE OFFICE
YOU'RE NOT GOING TO BELIEVE THIS...
CLARK. SLOW DOWN...
I READ A BOOK ONCE THAT SAID COUPLES SHOULD NEVER GO TO BED MAD.
I'M NOT SURE WHEN I'LL BE HOME, BUT JUST IN CASE...
I'M NOT MAD AT YOU, LOIS.
JUST CONCERNED.
AND I LOVE THAT ABOUT YOU, I REALLY DO. BUT STILL...
WE'VE BEEN THROUGH ONE HELL OF A LOT RECENTLY. IF SOMETHING MORE IS ON THE WAY, PLEASE, JUST TELL ME.
NO... NOTHING SPECIFIC...
I'D BETTER GET BACK TO THE PIT BEFORE THEY MISS ME...
WE NEED TO TALK ABOUT TONIGHT.
ANONYMOUS SOURCES ARE FINE FOR A STORY, BUT I'LL BE DAMNED IF THEY'RE ANONYMOUS TO ME.
UHH... OKAY, PERRY. BE RIGHT THERE.

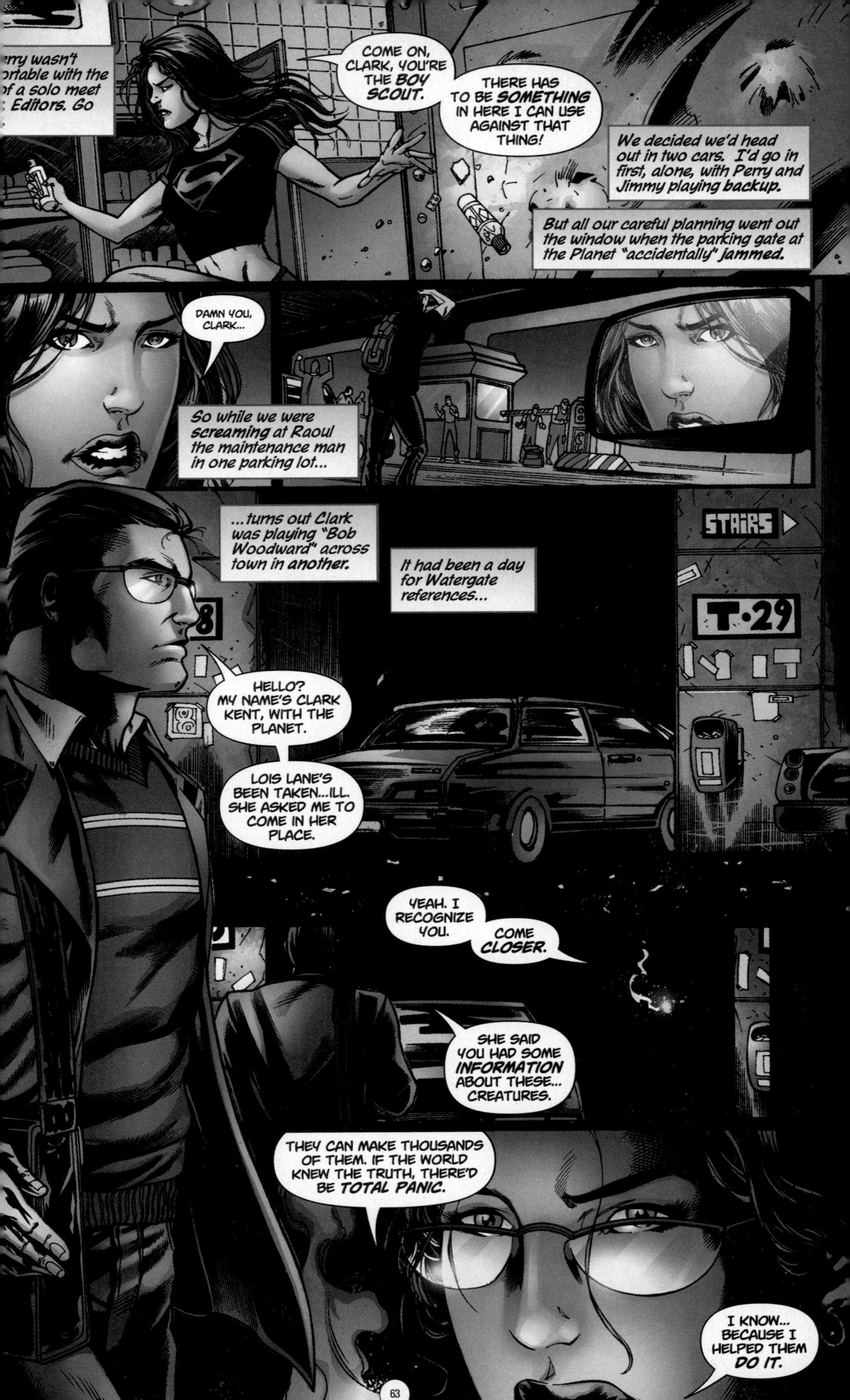

...rry wasn't ...ortable with the ...of a solo meet ... Editors. Go
COME ON, CLARK, YOU'RE THE BOY SCOUT.
THERE HAS TO BE SOMETHING IN HERE I CAN USE AGAINST THAT THING!
We decided we'd head out in two cars. I'd go in first, alone, with Perry and Jimmy playing backup.
But all our careful planning went out the window when the parking gate at the Planet "accidentally" jammed.
DAMN YOU, CLARK...
So while we were screaming at Raoul the maintenance man in one parking lot...
...turns out Clark was playing "Bob Woodward" across town in another.
It had been a day for Watergate references...
STAIRS
T-29
HELLO? MY NAME'S CLARK KENT, WITH THE PLANET.
LOIS LANE'S BEEN TAKEN...ILL. SHE ASKED ME TO COME IN HER PLACE.
YEAH. I RECOGNIZE YOU.
COME CLOSER.
SHE SAID YOU HAD SOME INFORMATION ABOUT THESE... CREATURES.
THEY CAN MAKE THOUSANDS OF THEM. IF THE WORLD KNEW THE TRUTH, THERE'D BE TOTAL PANIC.
I KNOW... BECAUSE I HELPED THEM DO IT.

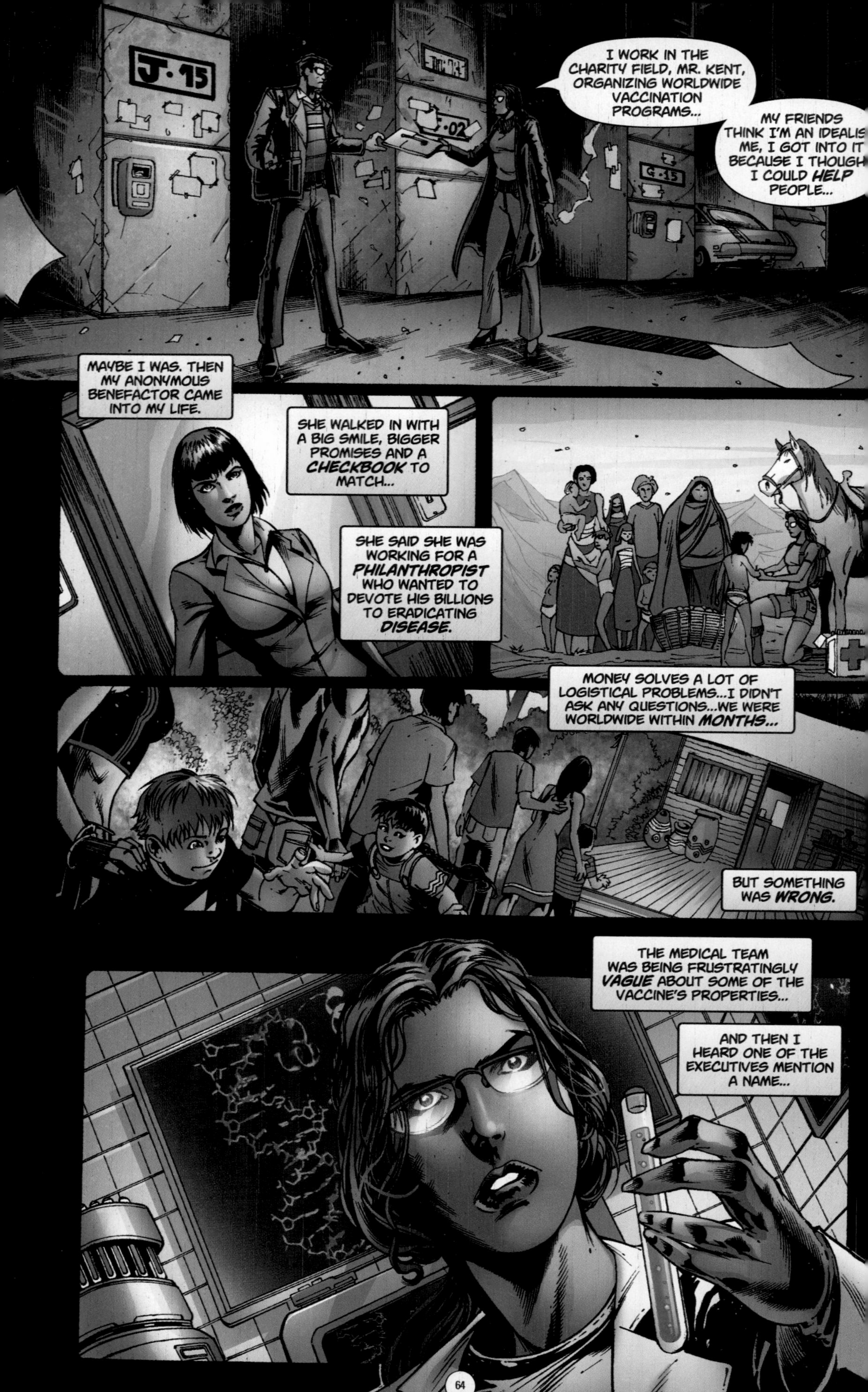
J-15
I WORK IN THE CHARITY FIELD, MR. KENT, ORGANIZING WORLDWIDE VACCINATION PROGRAMS...
MY FRIENDS THINK I'M AN IDEALIS ME, I GOT INTO IT BECAUSE I THOUGH I COULD HELP PEOPLE...
G-15
MAYBE I WAS. THEN MY ANONYMOUS BENEFACTOR CAME INTO MY LIFE.
SHE WALKED IN WITH A BIG SMILE, BIGGER PROMISES AND A CHECKBOOK TO MATCH...
SHE SAID SHE WAS WORKING FOR A PHILANTHROPIST WHO WANTED TO DEVOTE HIS BILLIONS TO ERADICATING DISEASE.
MONEY SOLVES A LOT OF LOGISTICAL PROBLEMS...I DIDN'T ASK ANY QUESTIONS...WE WERE WORLDWIDE WITHIN MONTHS...
BUT SOMETHING WAS WRONG.
THE MEDICAL TEAM WAS BEING FRUSTRATINGLY VAGUE ABOUT SOME OF THE VACCINE'S PROPERTIES...
AND THEN I HEARD ONE OF THE EXECUTIVES MENTION A NAME...

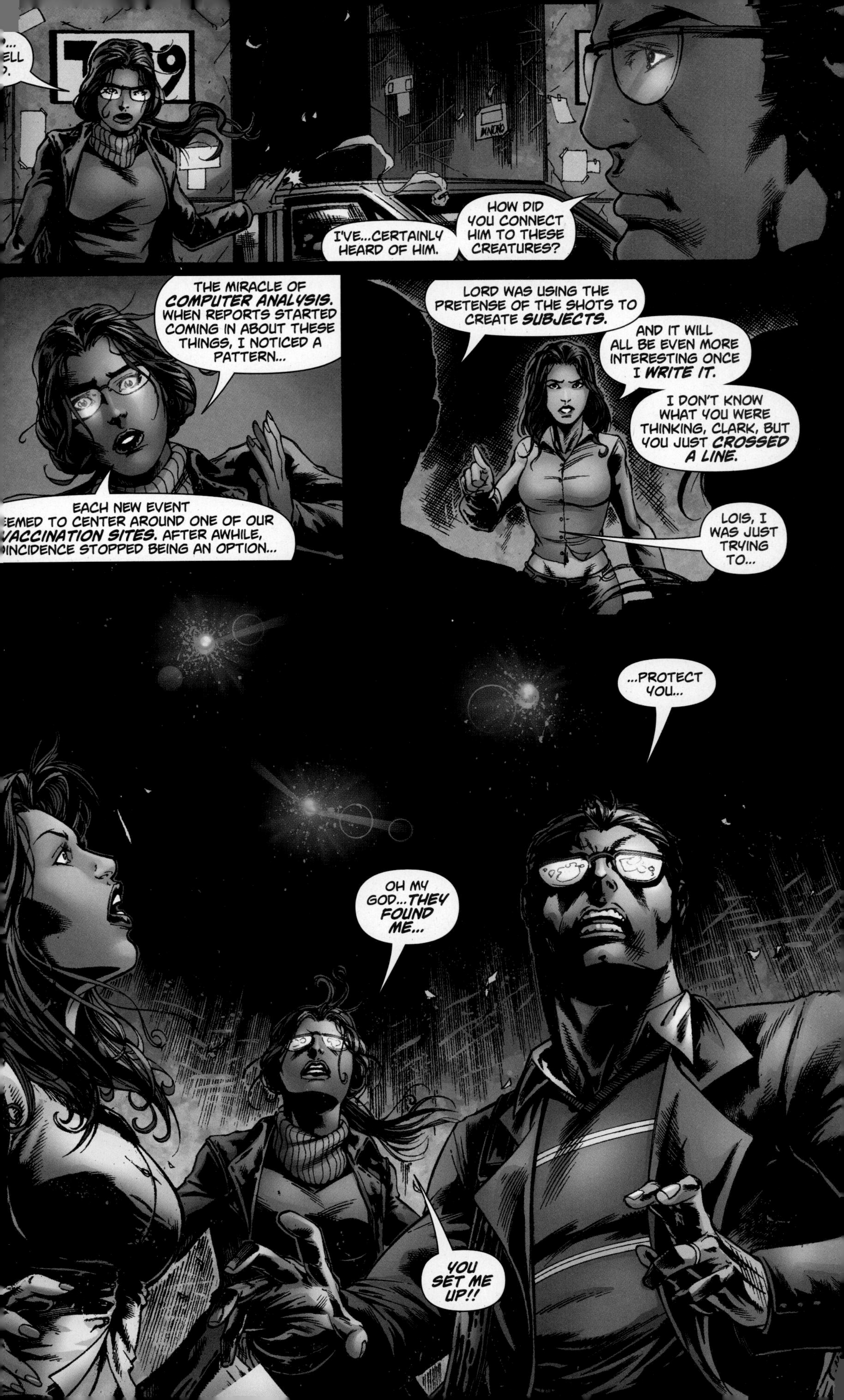
I'VE...CERTAINLY HEARD OF HIM.
HOW DID YOU CONNECT HIM TO THESE CREATURES?
THE MIRACLE OF COMPUTER ANALYSIS. WHEN REPORTS STARTED COMING IN ABOUT THESE THINGS, I NOTICED A PATTERN...
EACH NEW EVENT EEMED TO CENTER AROUND ONE OF OUR VACCINATION SITES. AFTER AWHILE, OINCIDENCE STOPPED BEING AN OPTION...
LORD WAS USING THE PRETENSE OF THE SHOTS TO CREATE SUBJECTS.
AND IT WILL ALL BE EVEN MORE INTERESTING ONCE I WRITE IT.
I DON'T KNOW WHAT YOU WERE THINKING, CLARK, BUT YOU JUST CROSSED A LINE.
LOIS, I WAS JUST TRYING TO...
...PROTECT YOU...
OH MY GOD...THEY FOUND ME...
YOU SET ME UP!!

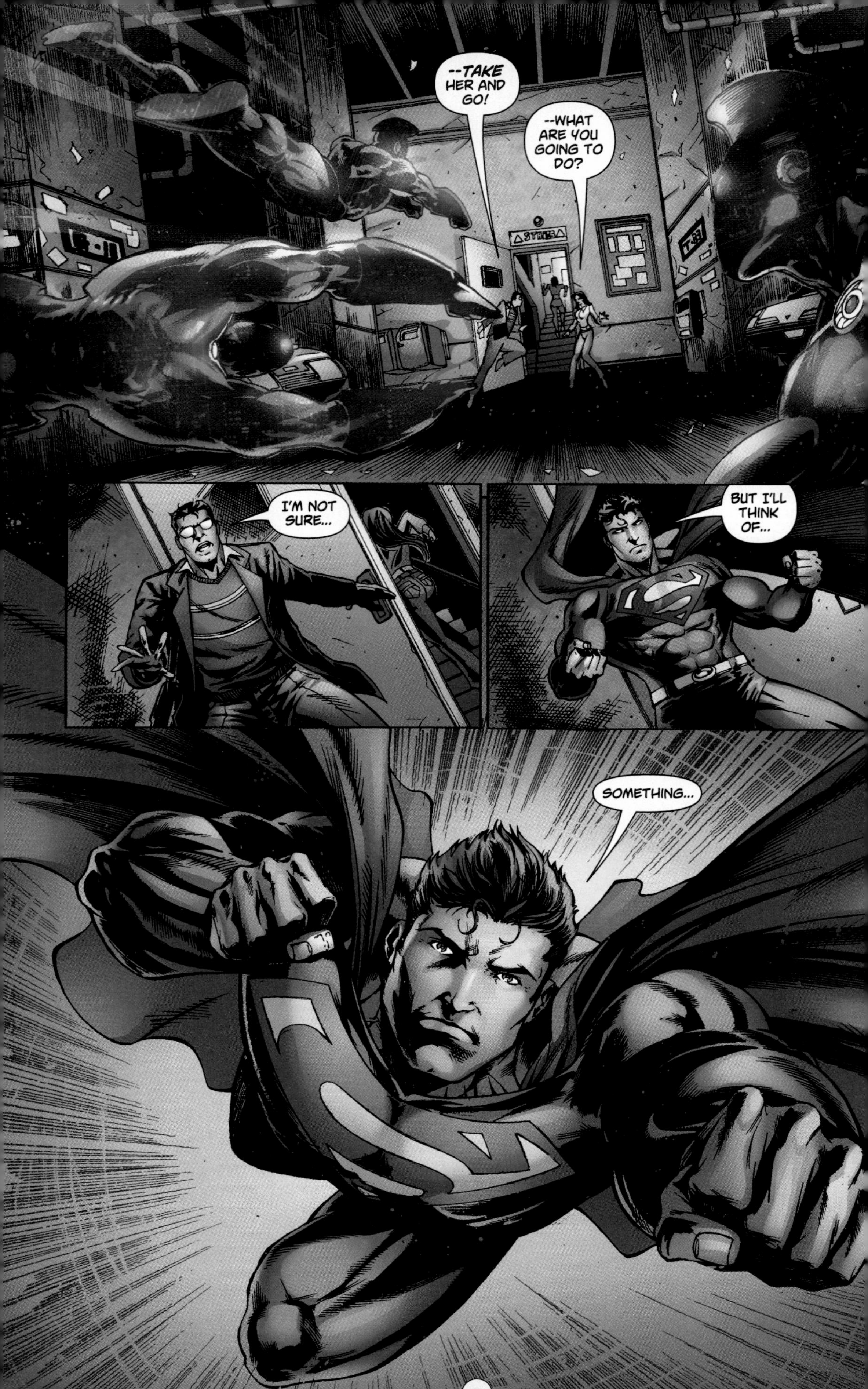
--TAKE HER AND GO!
--WHAT ARE YOU GOING TO DO?
I'M NOT SURE...
BUT I'LL THINK OF...
SOMETHING...

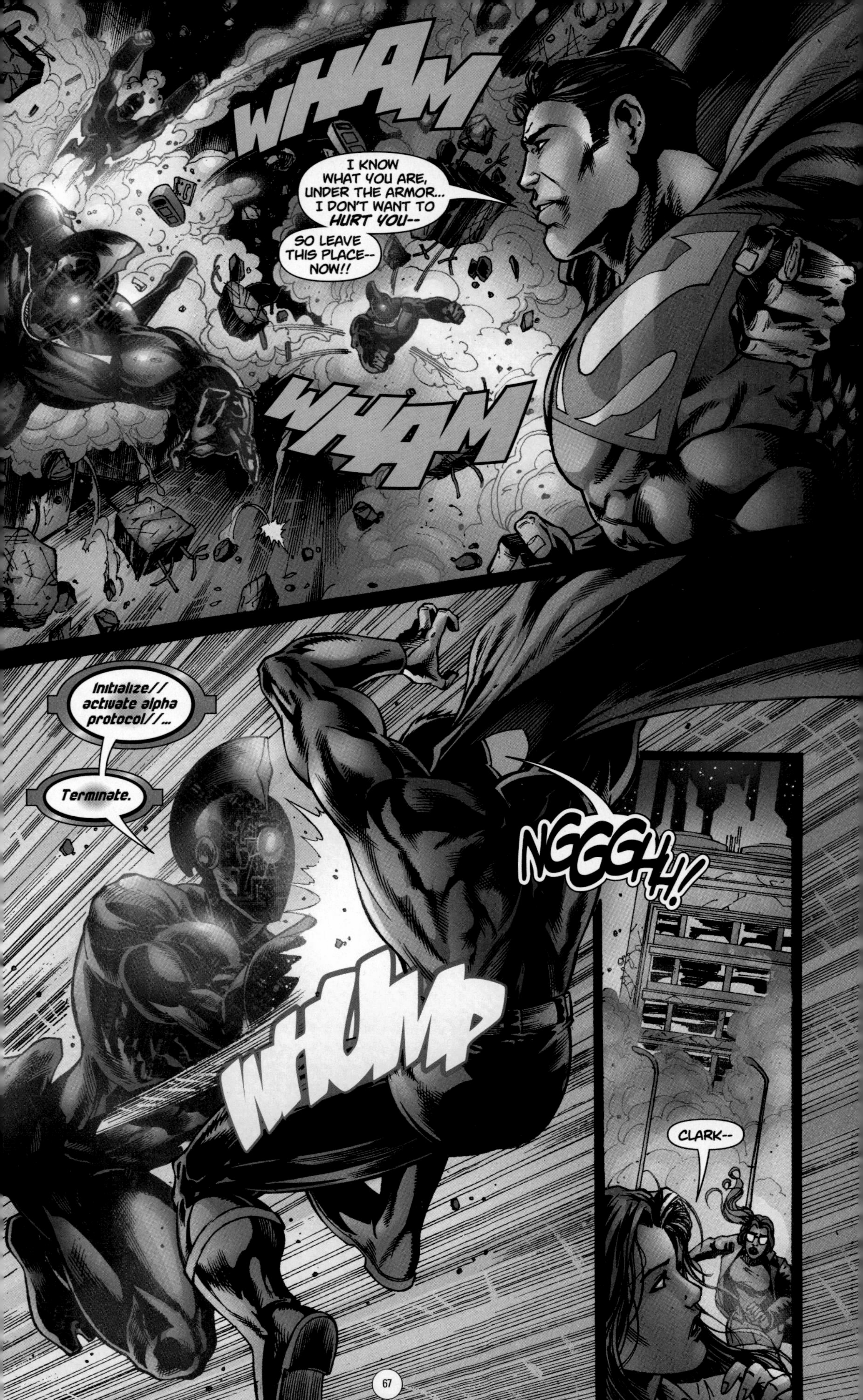
WHAM
I KNOW WHAT YOU ARE, UNDER THE ARMOR... I DON'T WANT TO HURT YOU--
SO LEAVE THIS PLACE-- NOW!!
WHAM
Initialize// activate alpha protocol//...
Terminate.
NGGGHH!
WHUMP
CLARK--

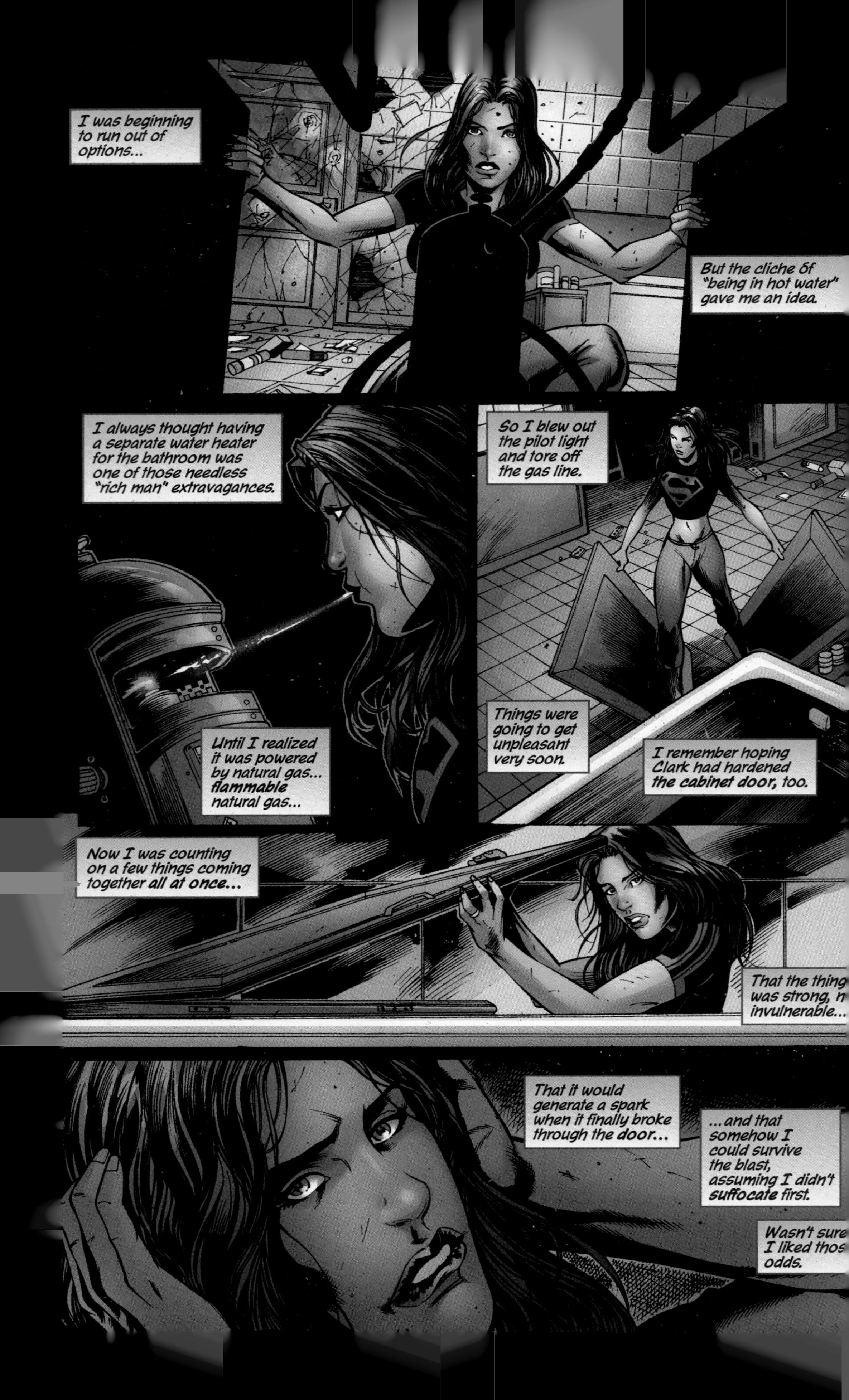
I was beginning to run out of options...
But the cliche of "being in hot water" gave me an idea.
I always thought having a separate water heater for the bathroom was one of those needless "rich man" extravagances.
Until I realized it was powered by natural gas... flammable natural gas...
So I blew out the pilot light and tore off the gas line.
Things were going to get unpleasant very soon.
I remember hoping Clark had hardened the cabinet door, too.
Now I was counting on a few things coming together all at once...
That the thing was strong, n invulnerable...
That it would generate a spark when it finally broke through the door...
...and that somehow I could survive the blast, assuming I didn't suffocate first.
Wasn't sure I liked thos odds.

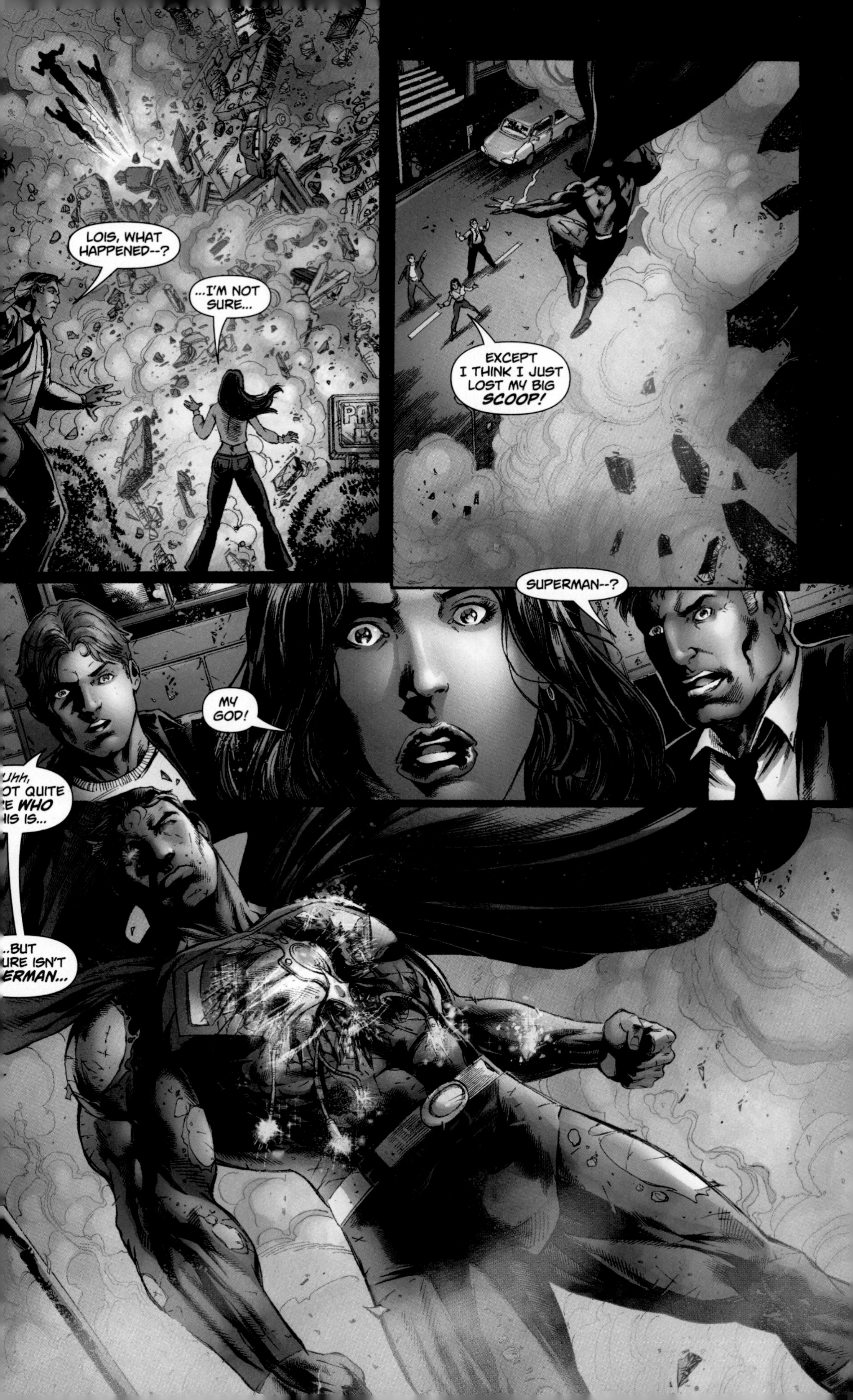
LOIS, WHAT HAPPENED--?
...I'M NOT SURE...
EXCEPT I THINK I JUST LOST MY BIG SCOOP!
SUPERMAN--?
MY GOD!
Uhh, OT QUITE E WHO HIS IS...
...BUT URE ISN'T ERMAN...

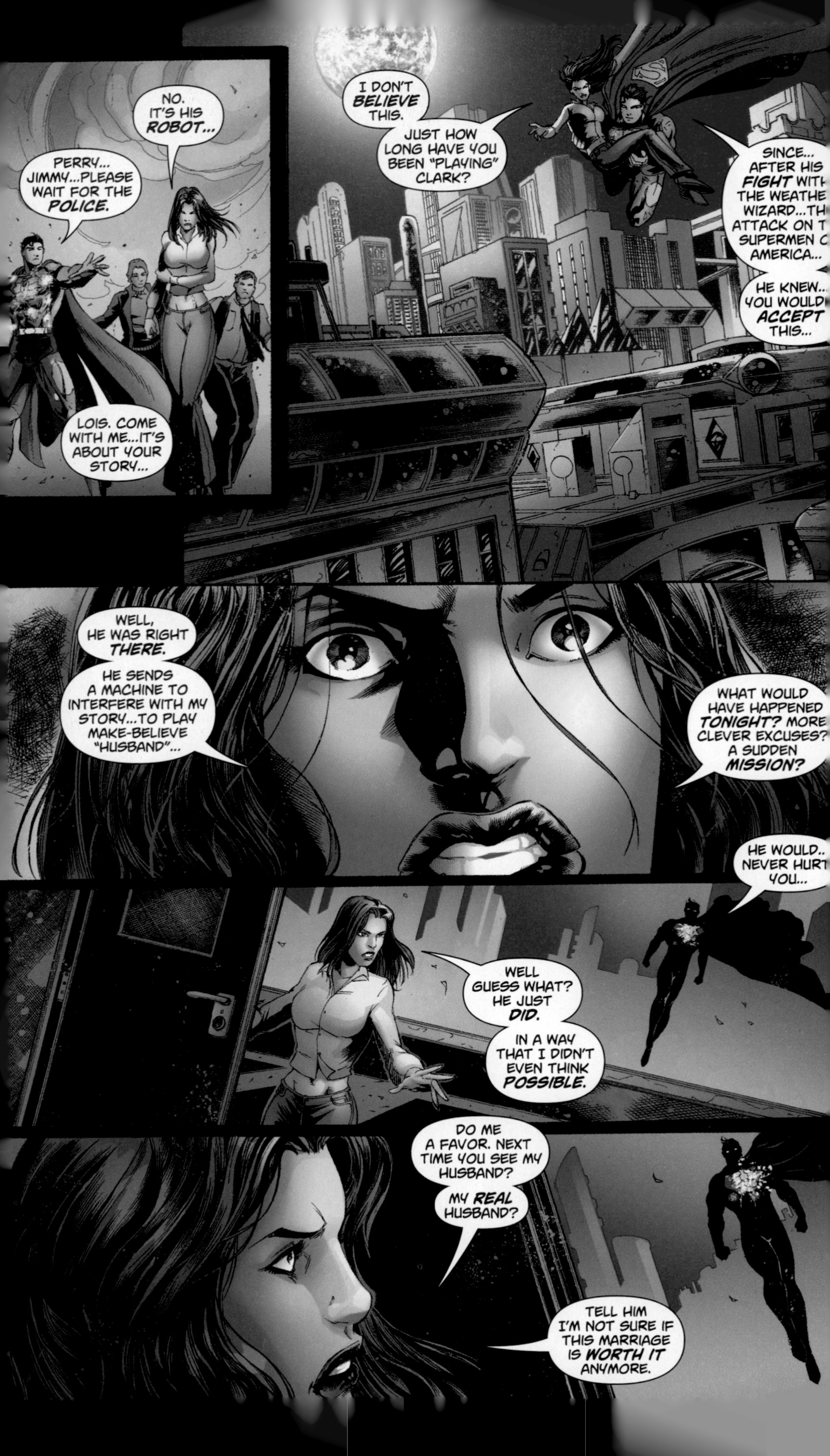

NO. IT'S HIS ROBOT...
PERRY... JIMMY...PLEASE WAIT FOR THE POLICE.
LOIS. COME WITH ME...IT'S ABOUT YOUR STORY...
I DON'T BELIEVE THIS.
JUST HOW LONG HAVE YOU BEEN "PLAYING" CLARK?
SINCE... AFTER HIS FIGHT WITH THE WEATHE WIZARD...TH ATTACK ON T SUPERMEN C AMERICA...
HE KNEW... YOU WOULD ACCEPT THIS...
WELL, HE WAS RIGHT THERE.
HE SENDS A MACHINE TO INTERFERE WITH MY STORY...TO PLAY MAKE-BELIEVE "HUSBAND"...
WHAT WOULD HAVE HAPPENED TONIGHT? MORE CLEVER EXCUSES? A SUDDEN MISSION?
HE WOULD... NEVER HURT YOU...
WELL GUESS WHAT? HE JUST DID.
IN A WAY THAT I DIDN'T EVEN THINK POSSIBLE.
DO ME A FAVOR. NEXT TIME YOU SEE MY HUSBAND?
MY REAL HUSBAND?
TELL HIM I'M NOT SURE IF THIS MARRIAGE IS WORTH IT ANYMORE.

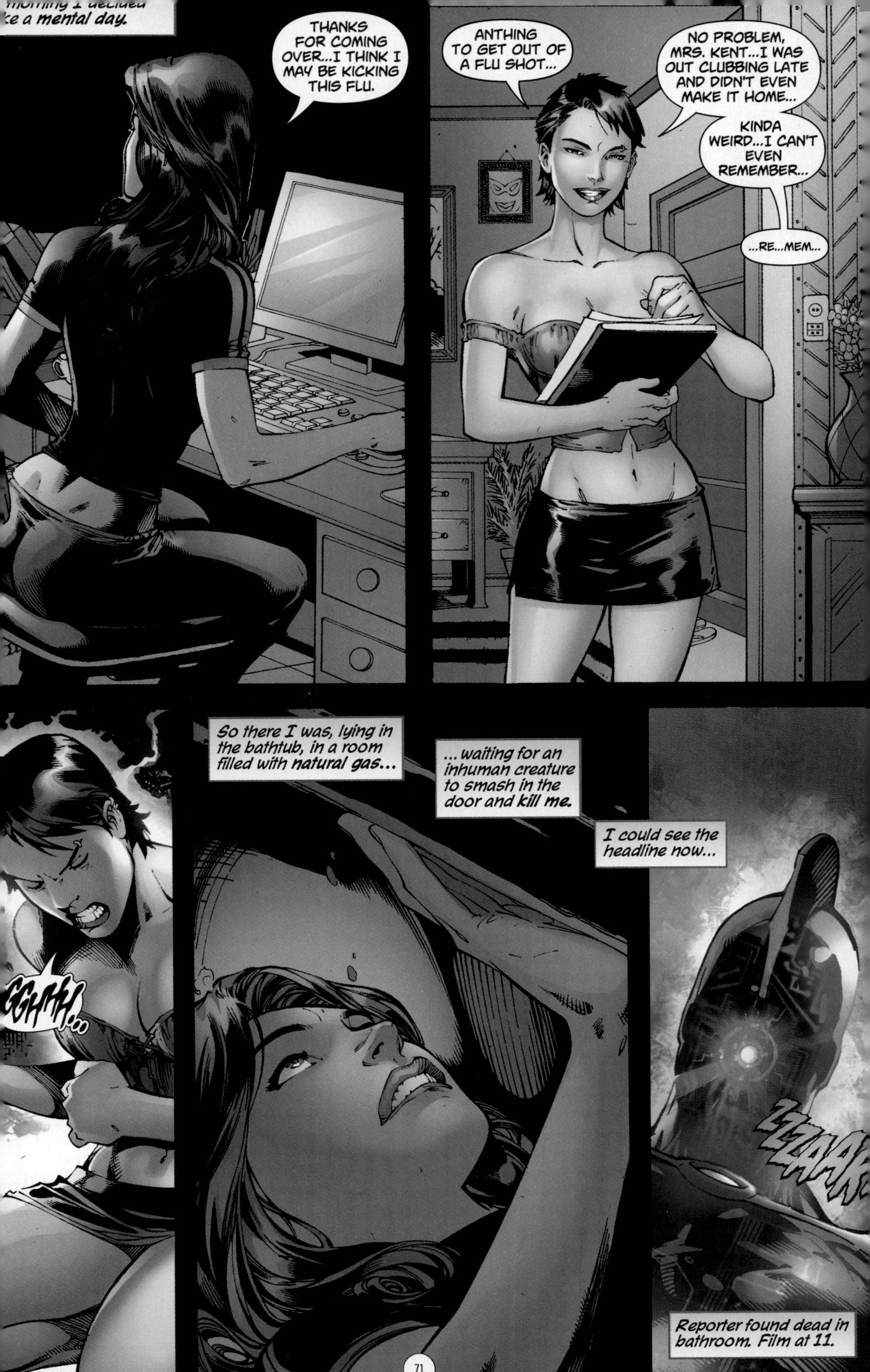

morning I decided
ke a mental day.
THANKS FOR COMING OVER...I THINK I MAY BE KICKING THIS FLU.
ANTHING TO GET OUT OF A FLU SHOT...
NO PROBLEM, MRS. KENT...I WAS OUT CLUBBING LATE AND DIDN'T EVEN MAKE IT HOME...
KINDA WEIRD...I CAN'T EVEN REMEMBER...
...RE...MEM...
So there I was, lying in the bathtub, in a room filled with natural gas...
...waiting for an inhuman creature to smash in the door and kill me.
I could see the headline now...
ZZZAAK
Reporter found dead in bathroom. Film at 11.

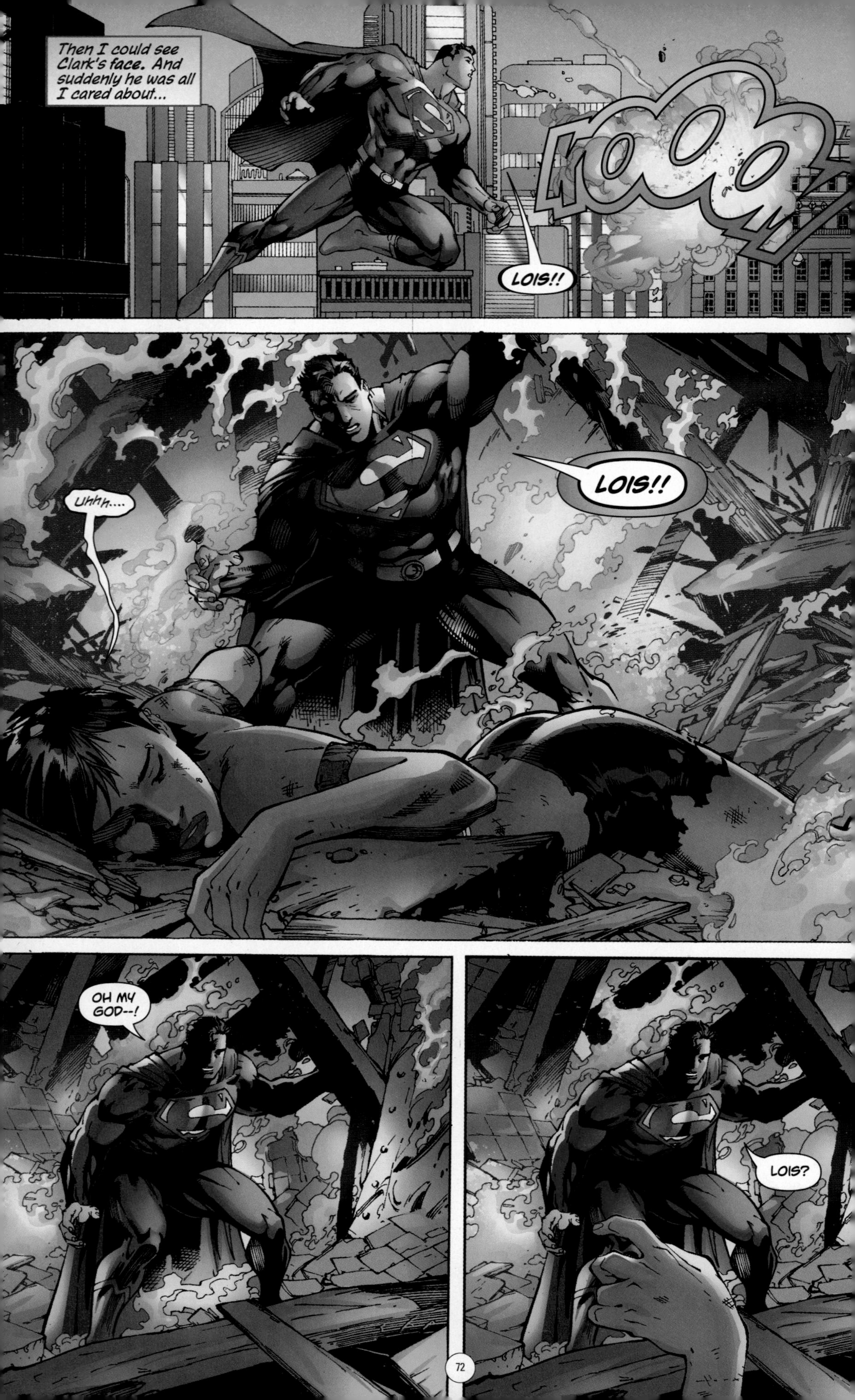
Then I could see Clark's face. And suddenly he was all I cared about...
KOOOM
LOIS!!
LOIS!!
Uhhh....
OH MY GOD--!
LOIS?

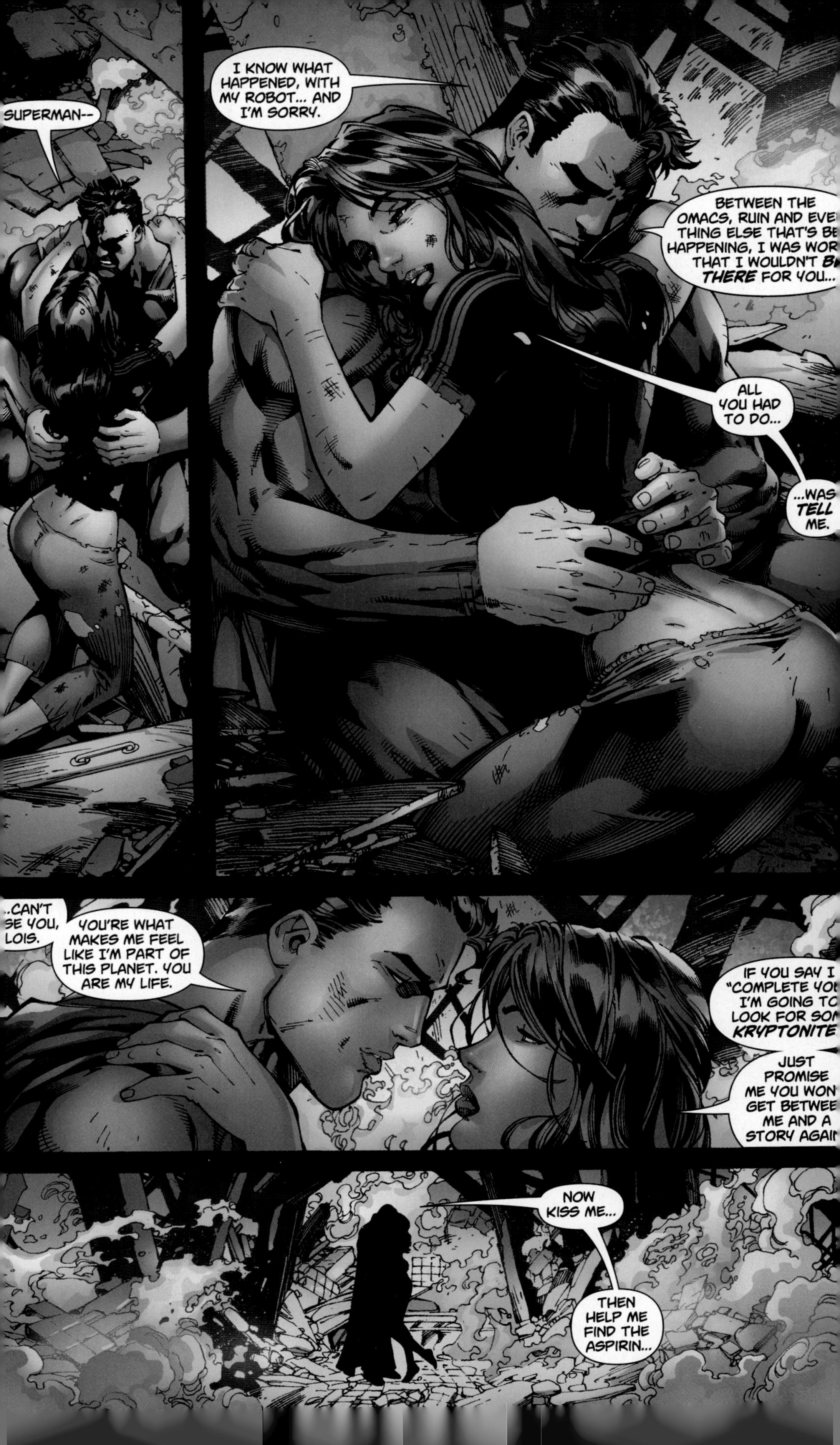
SUPERMAN--
I KNOW WHAT HAPPENED, WITH MY ROBOT... AND I'M SORRY.
BETWEEN THE OMACS, RUIN AND EVE THING ELSE THAT'S BE HAPPENING, I WAS WOR THAT I WOULDN'T B *THERE* FOR YOU...
ALL YOU HAD TO DO...
...WAS *TELL* ME.
..CAN'T SE YOU, LOIS.
YOU'RE WHAT MAKES ME FEEL LIKE I'M PART OF THIS PLANET. YOU ARE MY LIFE.
IF YOU SAY I "COMPLETE YO I'M GOING TO LOOK FOR SOM *KRYPTONITE*
JUST PROMISE ME YOU WON GET BETWEE ME AND A STORY AGAI
NOW KISS ME...
THEN HELP ME FIND THE ASPIRIN...

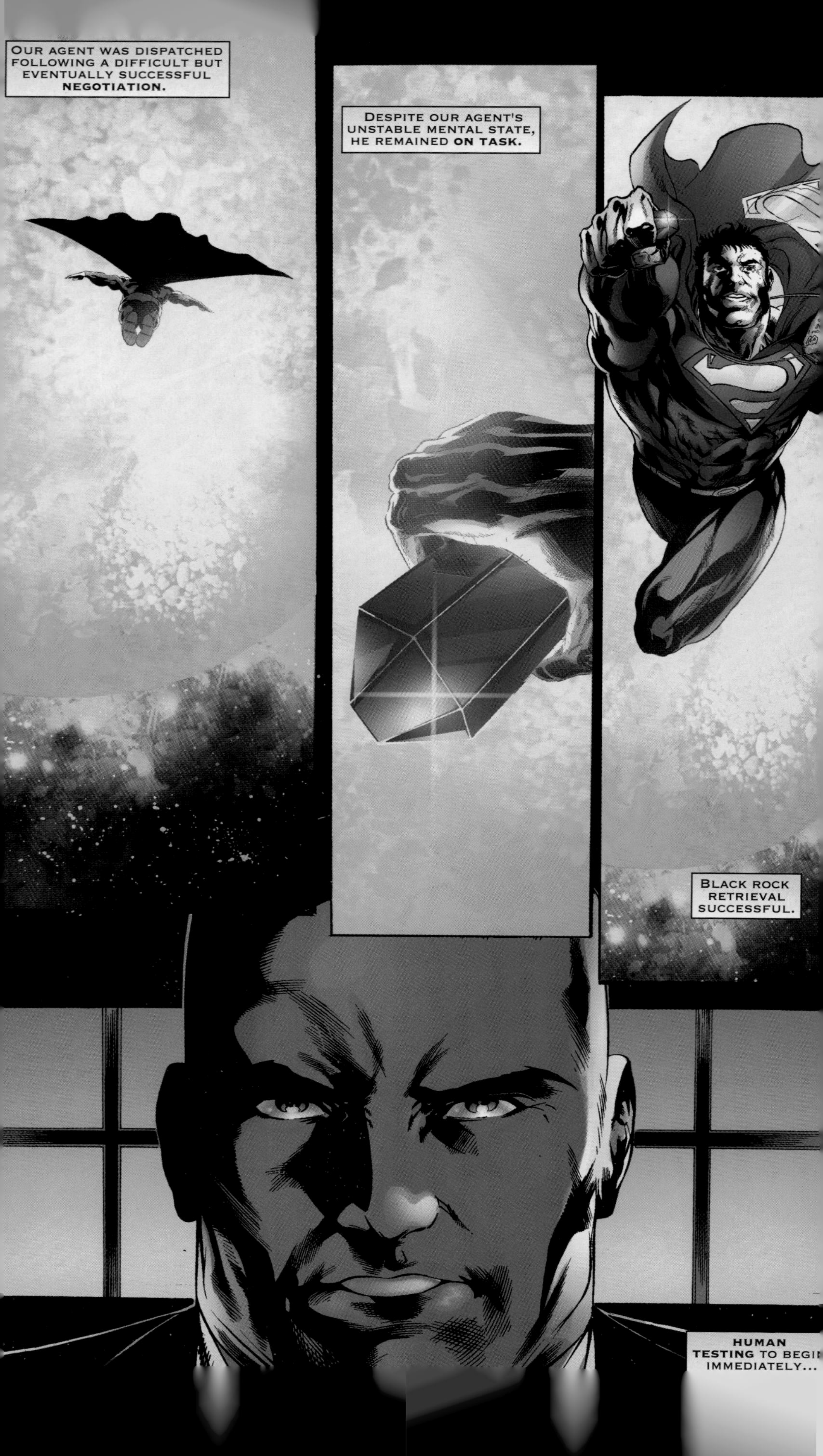
OUR AGENT WAS DISPATCHED FOLLOWING A DIFFICULT BUT EVENTUALLY SUCCESSFUL NEGOTIATION.
DESPITE OUR AGENT'S UNSTABLE MENTAL STATE, HE REMAINED ON TASK.
BLACK ROCK RETRIEVAL SUCCESSFUL.
HUMAN TESTING TO BEGIN IMMEDIATELY...

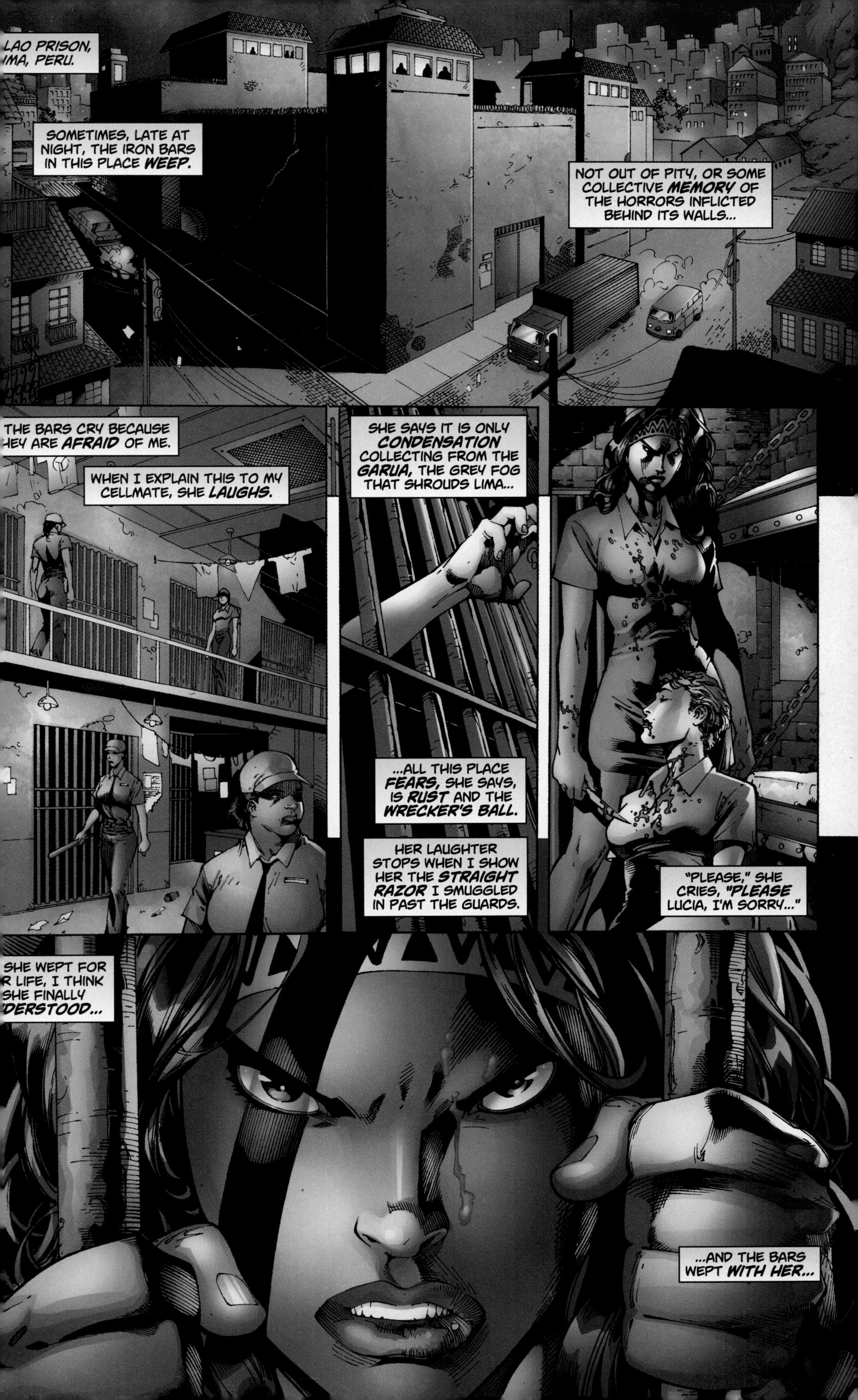
LAO PRISON,
IMA, PERU.
SOMETIMES, LATE AT NIGHT, THE IRON BARS IN THIS PLACE WEEP.
NOT OUT OF PITY, OR SOME COLLECTIVE MEMORY OF THE HORRORS INFLICTED BEHIND ITS WALLS...
THE BARS CRY BECAUSE HEY ARE AFRAID OF ME.
WHEN I EXPLAIN THIS TO MY CELLMATE, SHE LAUGHS.
SHE SAYS IT IS ONLY CONDENSATION COLLECTING FROM THE GARUA, THE GREY FOG THAT SHROUDS LIMA...
...ALL THIS PLACE FEARS, SHE SAYS, IS RUST AND THE WRECKER'S BALL.
HER LAUGHTER STOPS WHEN I SHOW HER THE STRAIGHT RAZOR I SMUGGLED IN PAST THE GUARDS.
"PLEASE," SHE CRIES, "PLEASE LUCIA, I'M SORRY..."
SHE WEPT FOR R LIFE, I THINK SHE FINALLY DERSTOOD...
...AND THE BARS WEPT WITH HER...

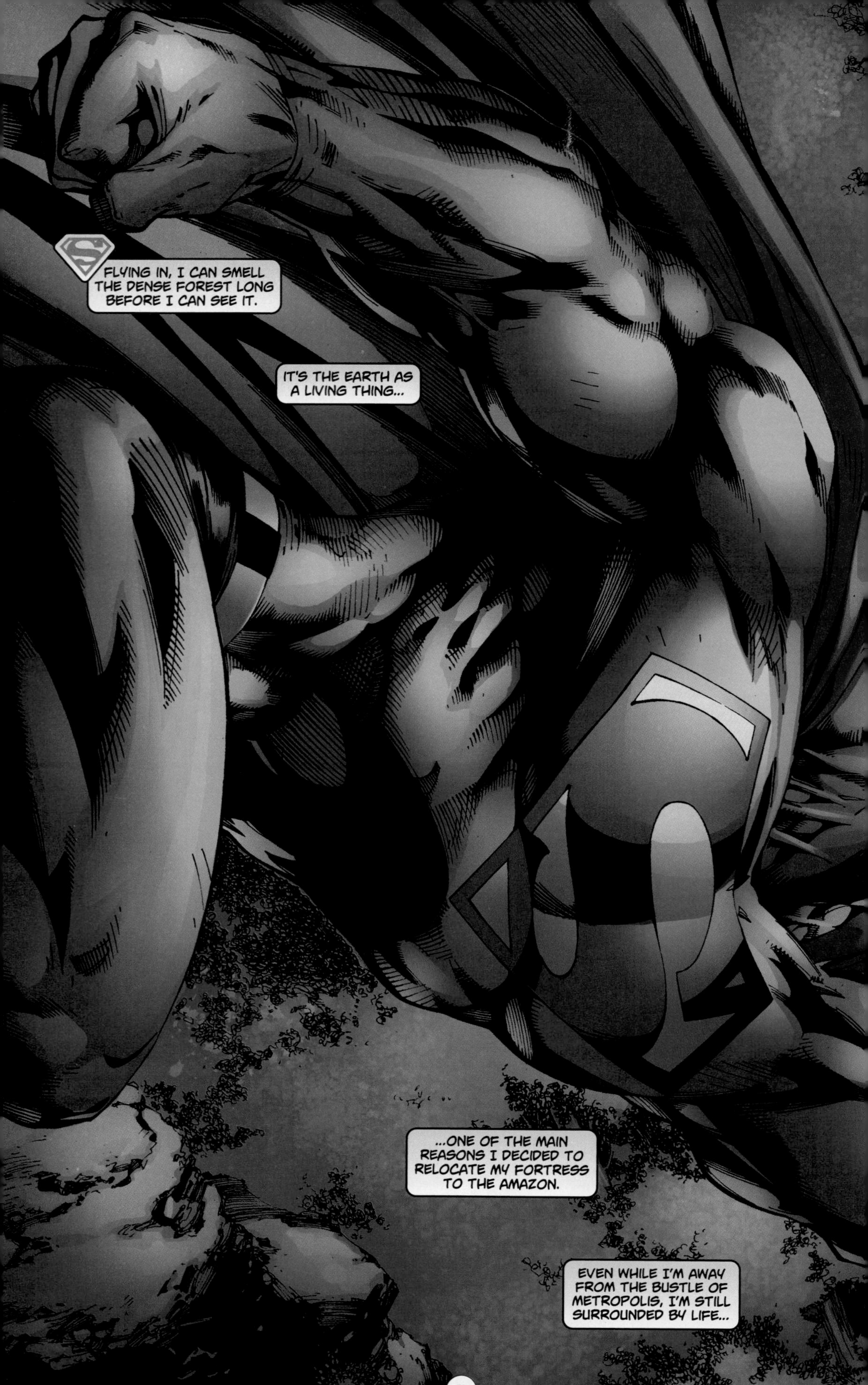
FLYING IN, I CAN SMELL THE DENSE FOREST LONG BEFORE I CAN SEE IT.
IT'S THE EARTH AS A LIVING THING...
...ONE OF THE MAIN REASONS I DECIDED TO RELOCATE MY FORTRESS TO THE AMAZON.
EVEN WHILE I'M AWAY FROM THE BUSTLE OF METROPOLIS, I'M STILL SURROUNDED BY LIFE...

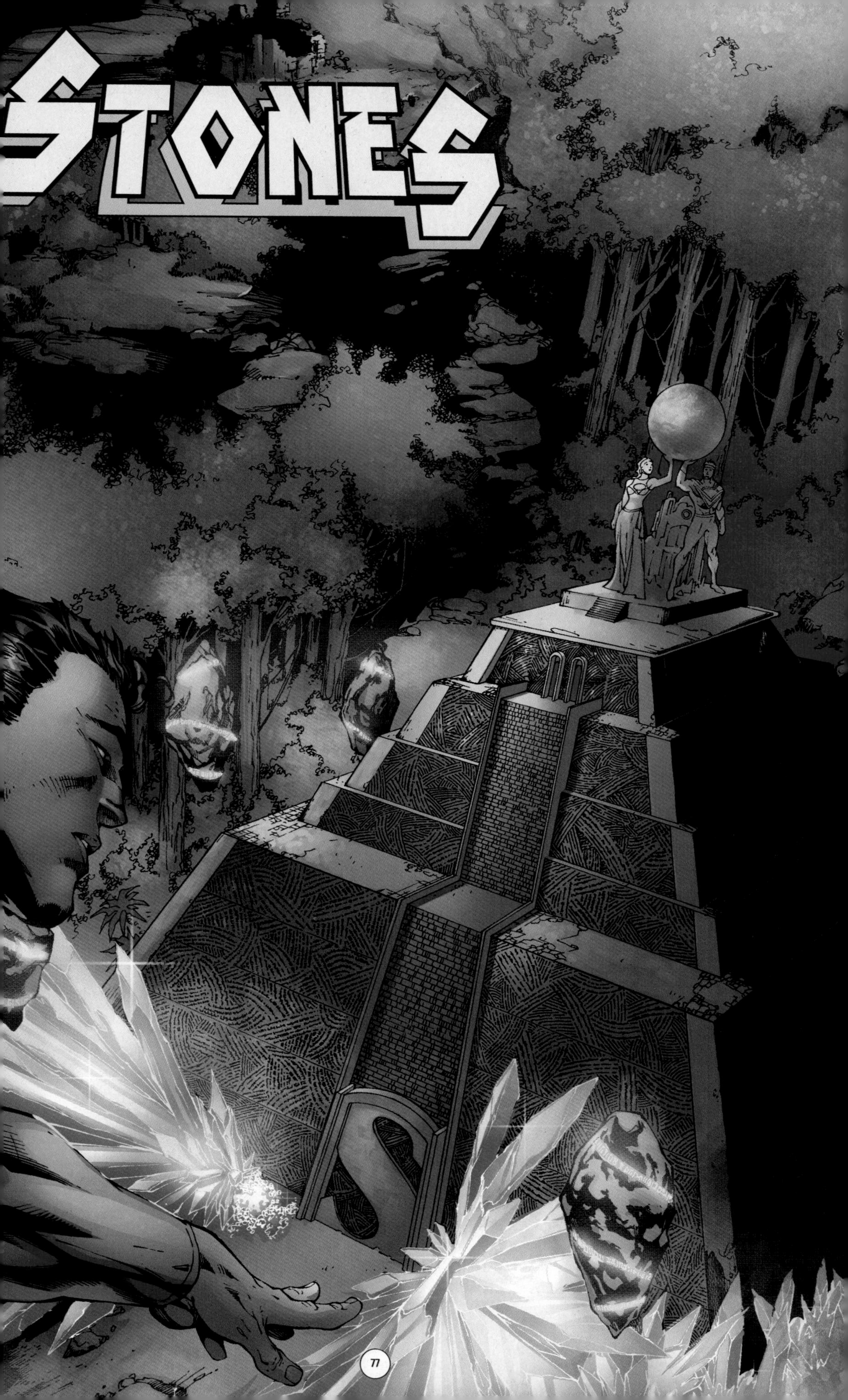
STONES

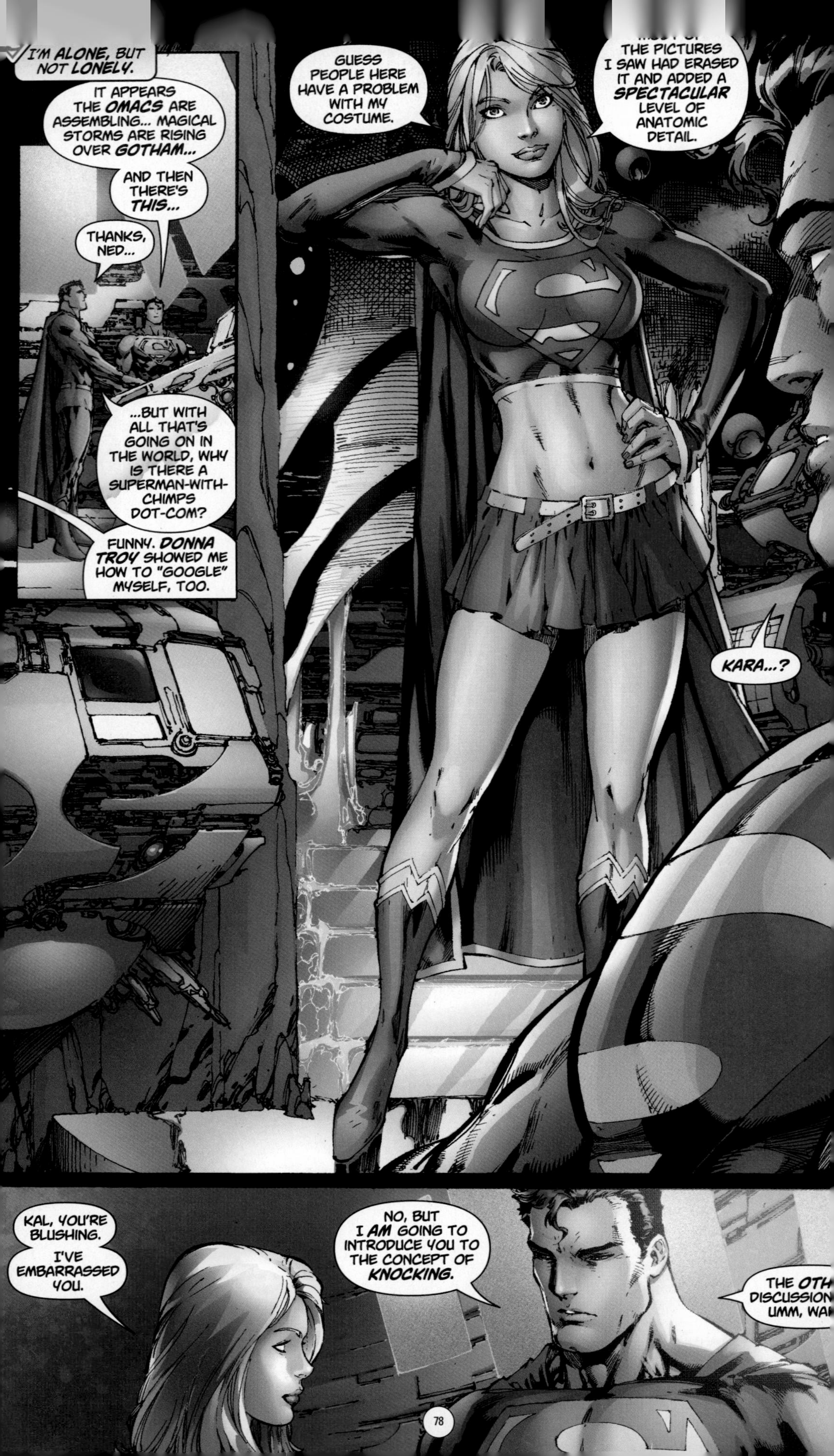

I'M ALONE, BUT NOT LONELY.
IT APPEARS THE OMACS ARE ASSEMBLING... MAGICAL STORMS ARE RISING OVER GOTHAM...
AND THEN THERE'S THIS...
THANKS, NED...
...BUT WITH ALL THAT'S GOING ON IN THE WORLD, WHY IS THERE A SUPERMAN-WITH-CHIMPS DOT-COM?
FUNNY. DONNA TROY SHOWED ME HOW TO "GOOGLE" MYSELF, TOO.
GUESS PEOPLE HERE HAVE A PROBLEM WITH MY COSTUME.
THE PICTURES I SAW HAD ERASED IT AND ADDED A SPECTACULAR LEVEL OF ANATOMIC DETAIL.
KARA...?
KAL, YOU'RE BLUSHING.
I'VE EMBARRASSED YOU.
NO, BUT I AM GOING TO INTRODUCE YOU TO THE CONCEPT OF KNOCKING.
THE OTH
DISCUSSION
UMM, WA

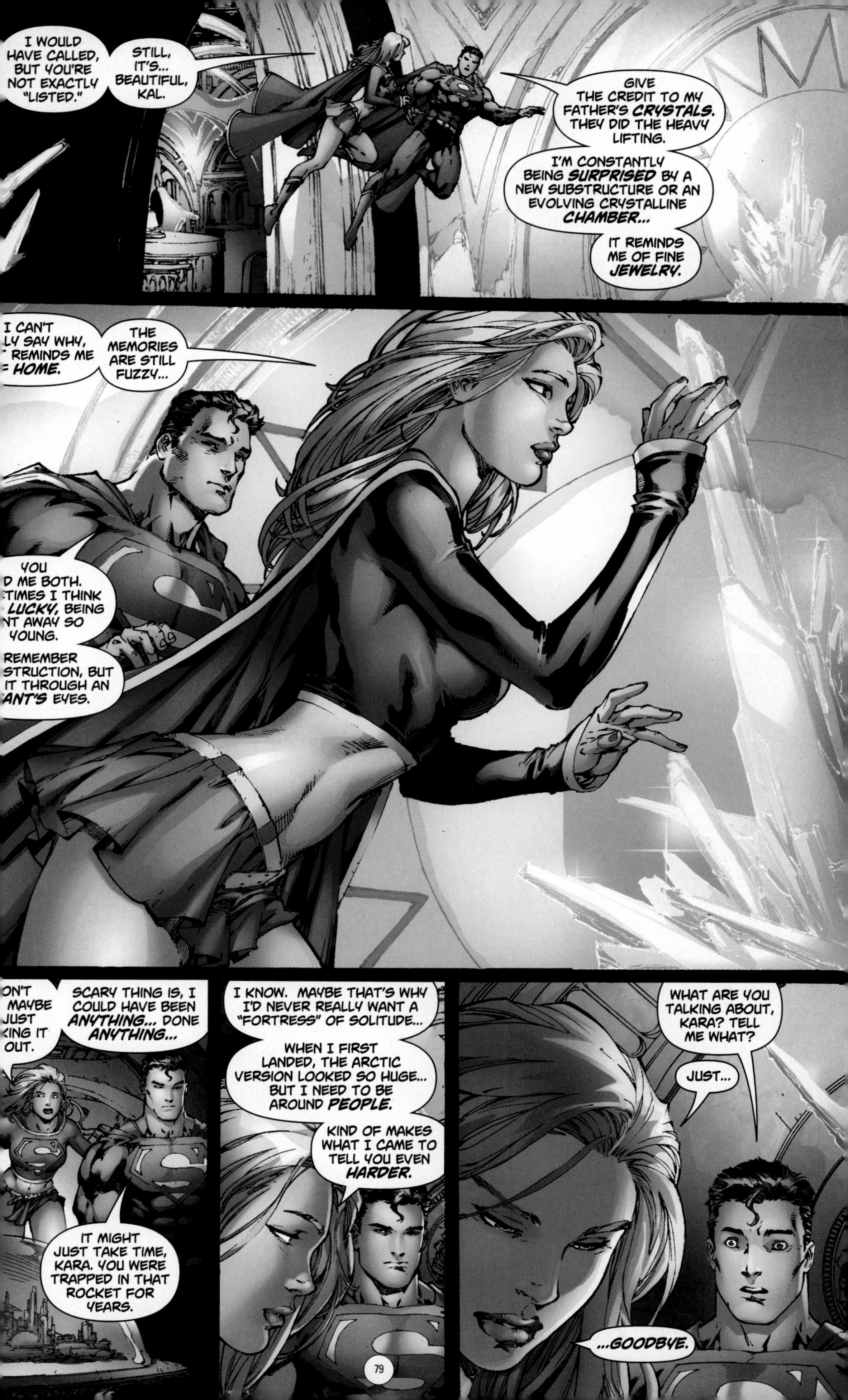

I WOULD HAVE CALLED, BUT YOU'RE NOT EXACTLY "LISTED."
STILL, IT'S... BEAUTIFUL, KAL.
GIVE THE CREDIT TO MY FATHER'S CRYSTALS. THEY DID THE HEAVY LIFTING.
I'M CONSTANTLY BEING SURPRISED BY A NEW SUBSTRUCTURE OR AN EVOLVING CRYSTALLINE CHAMBER...
IT REMINDS ME OF FINE JEWELRY.
I CAN'T LY SAY WHY, REMINDS ME HOME.
THE MEMORIES ARE STILL FUZZY...
YOU D ME BOTH. TIMES I THINK LUCKY, BEING NT AWAY SO YOUNG.
REMEMBER STRUCTION, BUT IT THROUGH AN ANT'S EYES.
ON'T MAYBE JUST KING IT OUT.
SCARY THING IS, I COULD HAVE BEEN ANYTHING... DONE ANYTHING...
IT MIGHT JUST TAKE TIME, KARA. YOU WERE TRAPPED IN THAT ROCKET FOR YEARS.
I KNOW. MAYBE THAT'S WHY I'D NEVER REALLY WANT A "FORTRESS" OF SOLITUDE...
WHEN I FIRST LANDED, THE ARCTIC VERSION LOOKED SO HUGE... BUT I NEED TO BE AROUND PEOPLE.
KIND OF MAKES WHAT I CAME TO TELL YOU EVEN HARDER.
WHAT ARE YOU TALKING ABOUT, KARA? TELL ME WHAT?
JUST...
...GOODBYE.

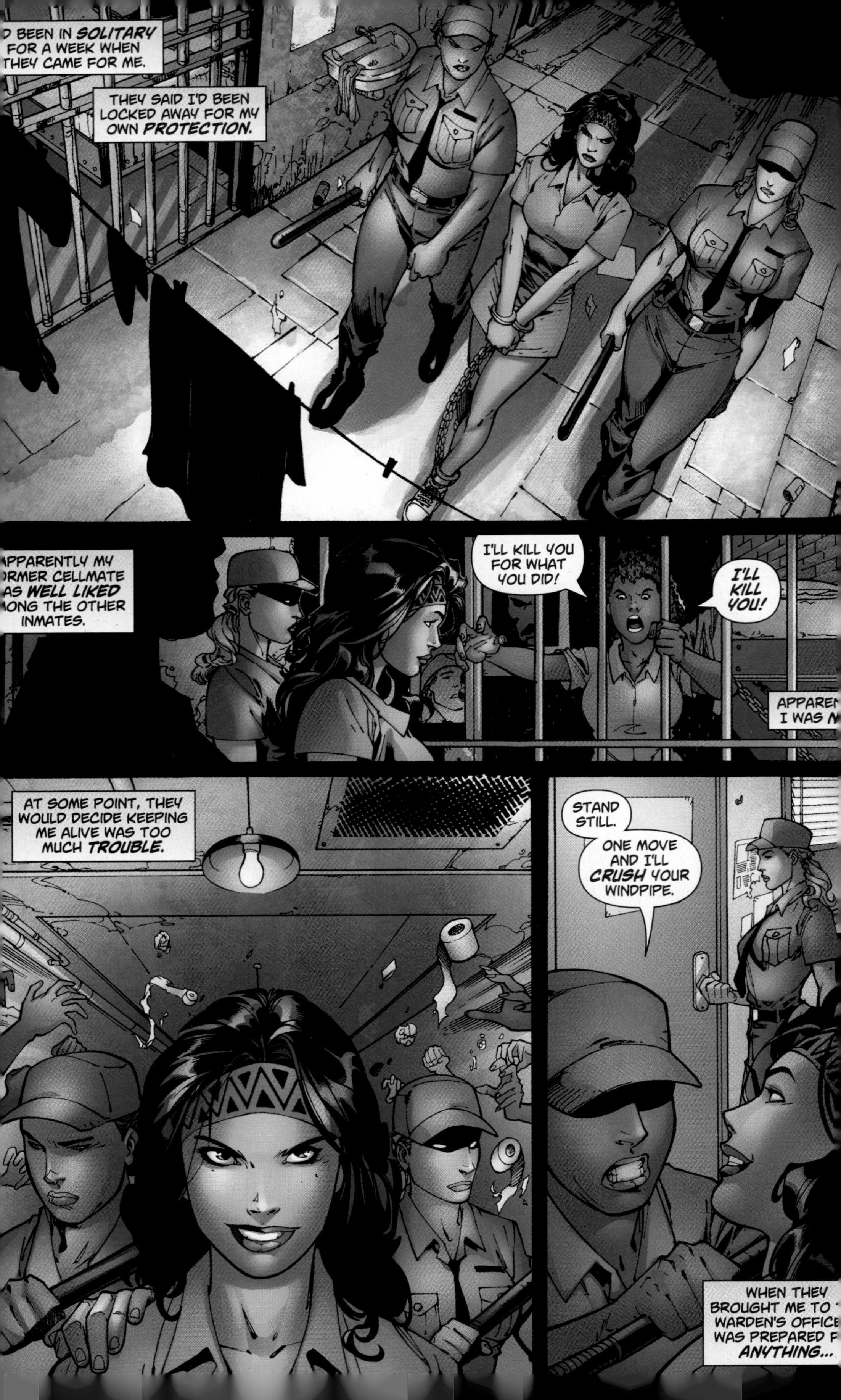
D BEEN IN SOLITARY FOR A WEEK WHEN THEY CAME FOR ME.
THEY SAID I'D BEEN LOCKED AWAY FOR MY OWN PROTECTION.
PPARENTLY MY ORMER CELLMATE AS WELL LIKED ONG THE OTHER INMATES.
I'LL KILL YOU FOR WHAT YOU DID!
I'LL KILL YOU!
APPAREN I WAS
AT SOME POINT, THEY WOULD DECIDE KEEPING ME ALIVE WAS TOO MUCH TROUBLE.
STAND STILL.
ONE MOVE AND I'LL CRUSH YOUR WINDPIPE.
WHEN THEY BROUGHT ME TO WARDEN'S OFFIC WAS PREPARED F ANYTHING...

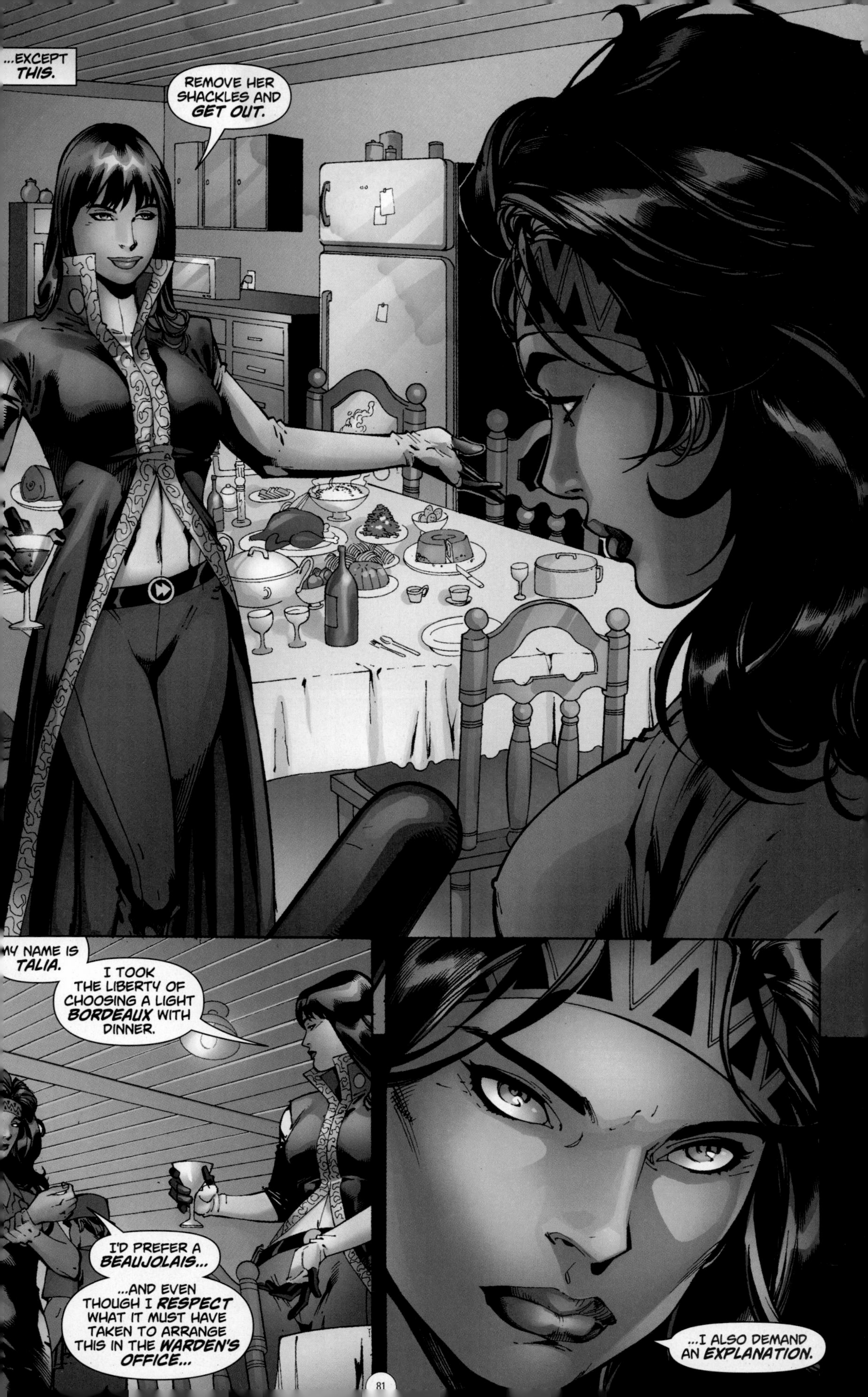
...EXCEPT THIS.
REMOVE HER SHACKLES AND GET OUT.
MY NAME IS TALIA.
I TOOK THE LIBERTY OF CHOOSING A LIGHT BORDEAUX WITH DINNER.
I'D PREFER A BEAUJOLAIS...
...AND EVEN THOUGH I RESPECT WHAT IT MUST HAVE TAKEN TO ARRANGE THIS IN THE WARDEN'S OFFICE...
...I ALSO DEMAND AN EXPLANATION.

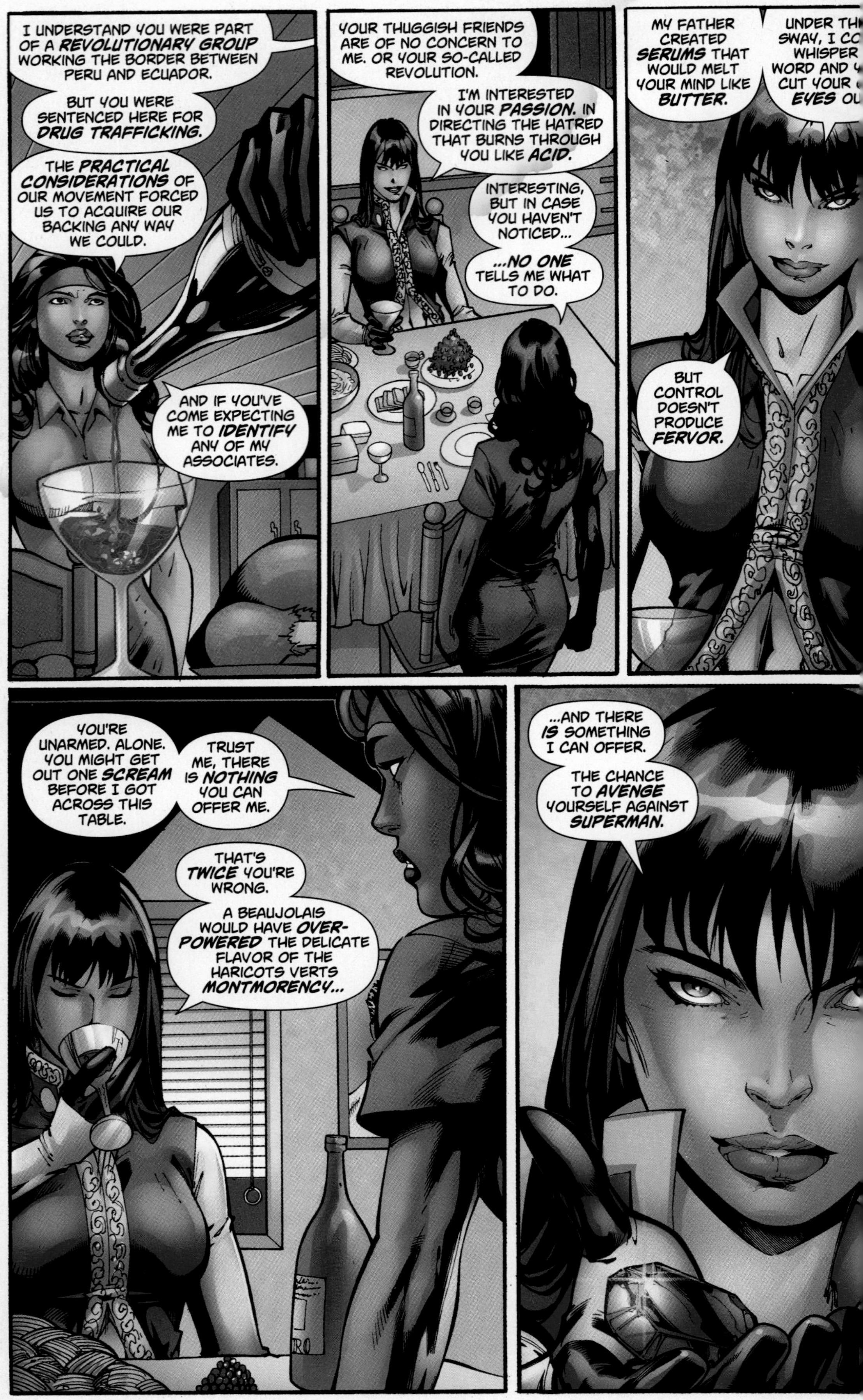
I UNDERSTAND YOU WERE PART OF A REVOLUTIONARY GROUP WORKING THE BORDER BETWEEN PERU AND ECUADOR.
BUT YOU WERE SENTENCED HERE FOR DRUG TRAFFICKING.
THE PRACTICAL CONSIDERATIONS OF OUR MOVEMENT FORCED US TO ACQUIRE OUR BACKING ANY WAY WE COULD.
AND IF YOU'VE COME EXPECTING ME TO IDENTIFY ANY OF MY ASSOCIATES.
YOUR THUGGISH FRIENDS ARE OF NO CONCERN TO ME. OR YOUR SO-CALLED REVOLUTION.
I'M INTERESTED IN YOUR PASSION. IN DIRECTING THE HATRED THAT BURNS THROUGH YOU LIKE ACID.
INTERESTING, BUT IN CASE YOU HAVEN'T NOTICED...
...NO ONE TELLS ME WHAT TO DO.
MY FATHER CREATED SERUMS THAT WOULD MELT YOUR MIND LIKE BUTTER.
UNDER TH SWAY, I C WHISPER WORD AND CUT YOUR EYES OU
BUT CONTROL DOESN'T PRODUCE FERVOR.
YOU'RE UNARMED. ALONE. YOU MIGHT GET OUT ONE SCREAM BEFORE I GOT ACROSS THIS TABLE.
TRUST ME, THERE IS NOTHING YOU CAN OFFER ME.
THAT'S TWICE YOU'RE WRONG.
A BEAUJOLAIS WOULD HAVE OVER-POWERED THE DELICATE FLAVOR OF THE HARICOTS VERTS MONTMORENCY...
...AND THERE IS SOMETHING I CAN OFFER.
THE CHANCE TO AVENGE YOURSELF AGAINST SUPERMAN.

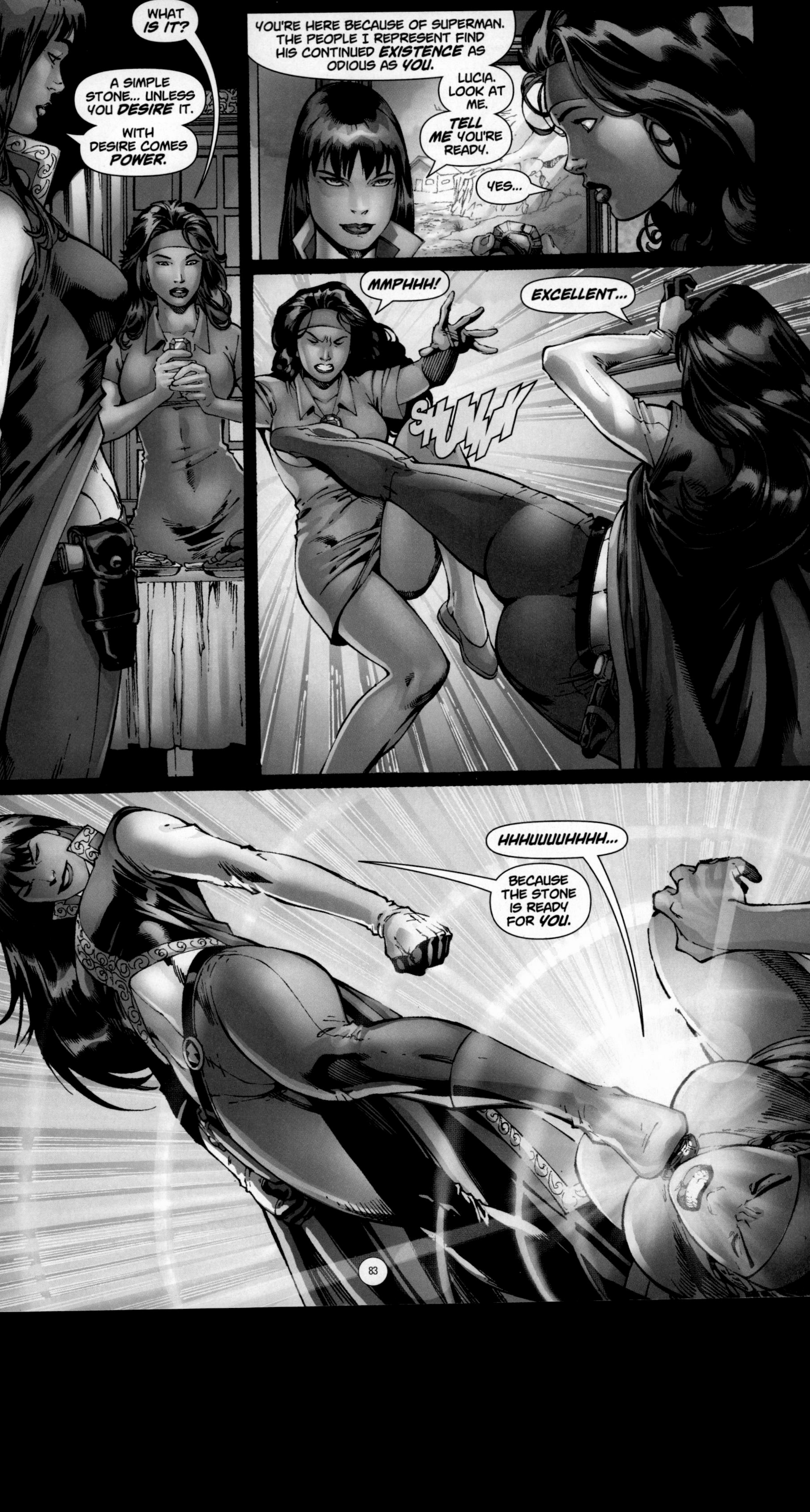
WHAT IS IT?
A SIMPLE STONE... UNLESS YOU DESIRE IT.
WITH DESIRE COMES POWER.
YOU'RE HERE BECAUSE OF SUPERMAN. THE PEOPLE I REPRESENT FIND HIS CONTINUED EXISTENCE AS ODIOUS AS YOU.
LUCIA. LOOK AT ME. TELL ME YOU'RE READY.
YES...
MMPHHH!
EXCELLENT...
SHUNK
HHHUUUUHHHH...
BECAUSE THE STONE IS READY FOR YOU.

I DON'T LIKE IT.

YOU'VE BARELY GOT YOUR FOOTING HERE AND NOW YOU WANT TO GO OFF IN SPACE WITH DONNA TROY?

FIRST, I THINK I'VE FOUND WHATEVER "MY FOOTING" IS SUPPOSED TO MEAN...

...SECOND, I DON'T WANT TO, I *HAVE* TO. DONNA CAN USE MY SKILLS OUT THERE.

YOU REALLY THINK YOU'RE IN CONTROL OF YOUR POWERS AFTER WHAT HAPPENED WITH THE JUSTICE LEAGUE?

THAT WA*LUTHOR*NOT ME

BESIDES PARADIS ISLAND'S B GREAT. DIAN TAUGHT M

HOW TO BE A WARRIOR.

TRUST ME, KARA. IT'S ONLY A SMALL STEP BEFORE YOU GO OVER THE *LINE*.

OUR ENEMIES RELEASED A CLANDESTINE VIDEO OF WONDER WOMAN KILLING MAX LORD, TRYING TO TURN PUBLIC OPINION AGAINST US.

FAR AS I'M CONCERNED, THE CAPTION SHOULD READ "GOT WHAT HE DESERVED."

THAT'S NOT THE PO DON'T CARE IF IT'S M OR LUTHOR OR *ANYC*

LIFE IS *SACRED*. DIANA *FORGOT* THAT.

I WAI TO TO

AT SOME POINT YOU'LL JUST HAVE TO *TRUST* ME.

SUPERMAN-- THERE'S A DISTURBANCE IN LIMA.

A PULSE OF ELECTROMAGNETIC ACTIVITY SIMILAR TO WHAT YOU RECENTLY EXPERIENCED IN METROPOLIS.

METROI

WH HAPPE THEI

BLACKROCK--

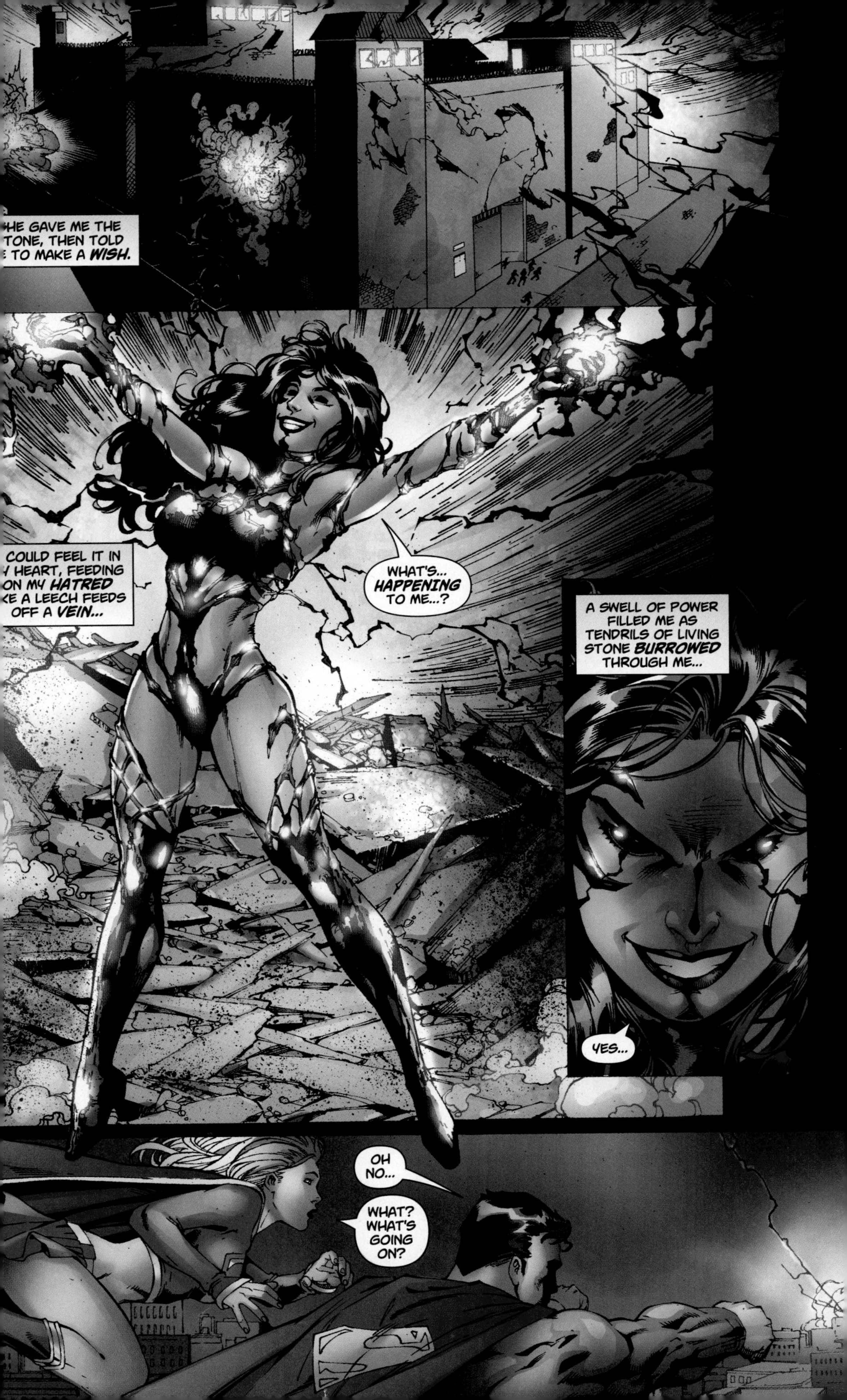
HE GAVE ME THE
TONE, THEN TOLD
E TO MAKE A WISH.
COULD FEEL IT IN
HEART, FEEDING
ON MY HATRED
E A LEECH FEEDS
OFF A VEIN...
WHAT'S... HAPPENING TO ME...?
A SWELL OF POWER FILLED ME AS TENDRILS OF LIVING STONE BURROWED THROUGH ME...
YES...
OH NO...
WHAT? WHAT'S GOING ON?

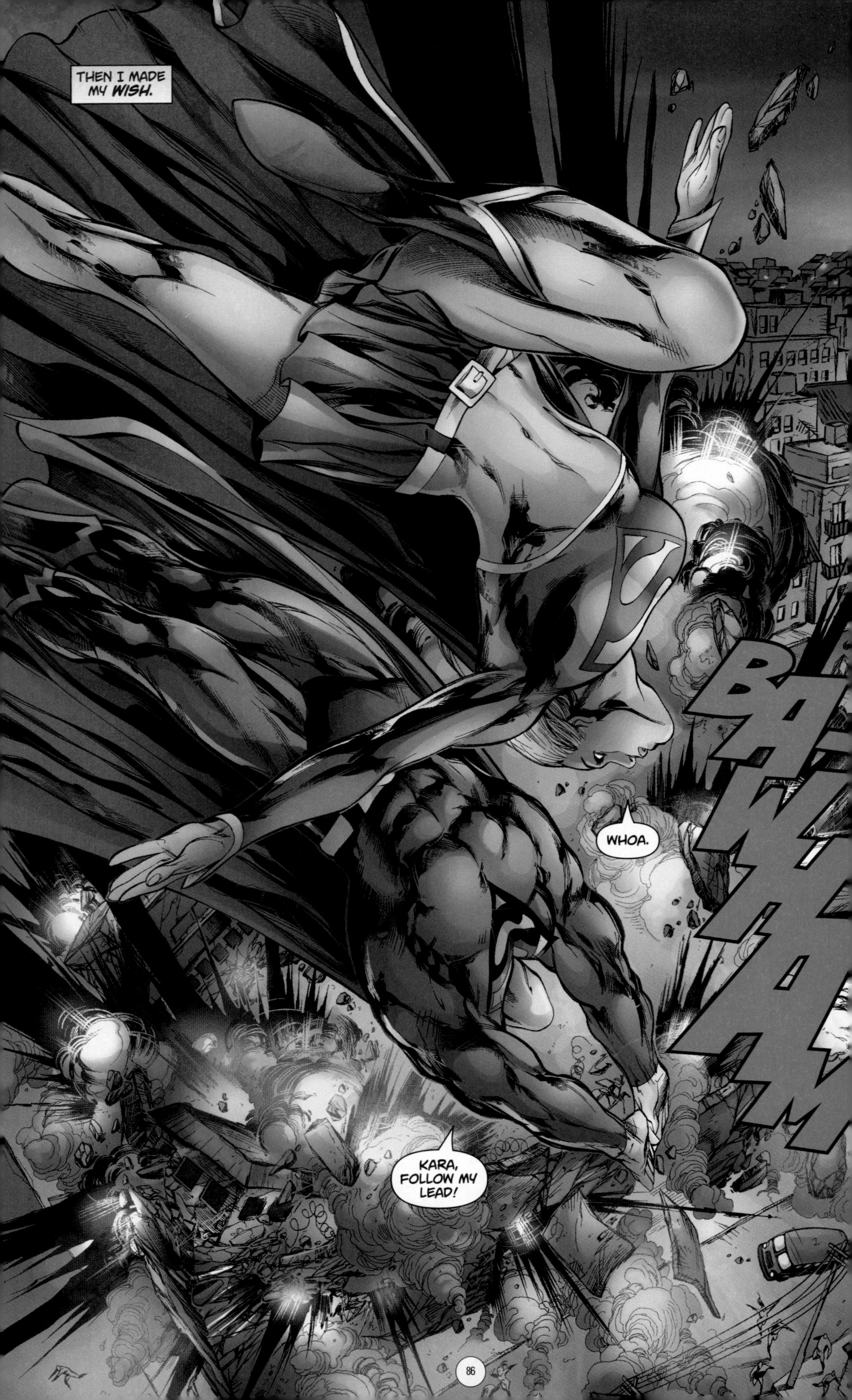
THEN I MADE MY WISH.
WHOA.
KARA, FOLLOW MY LEAD!

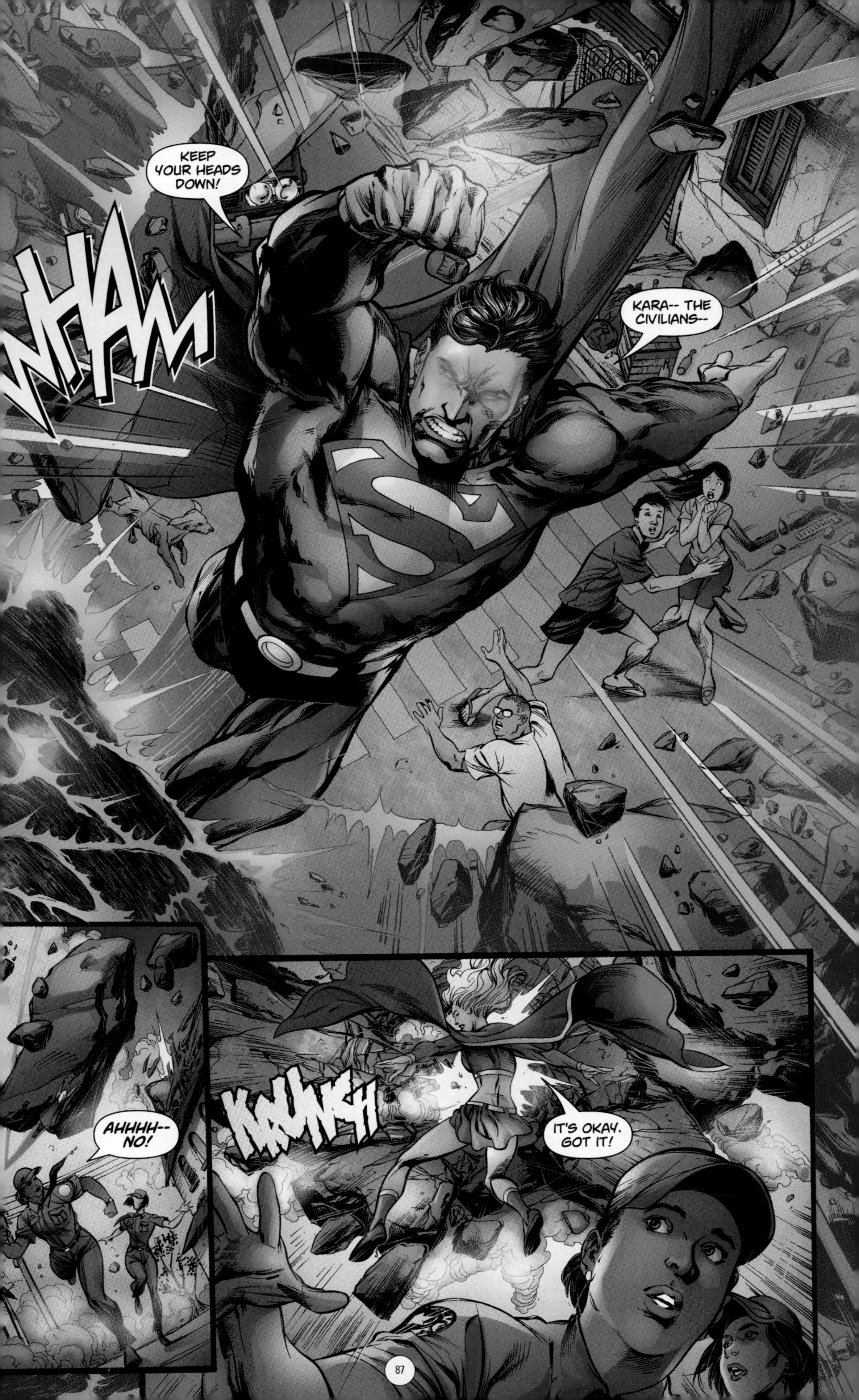
KEEP YOUR HEADS DOWN!
WHAM
KARA-- THE CIVILIANS--
AHHHH-- NO!
KRUNCH
IT'S OKAY. GOT IT!

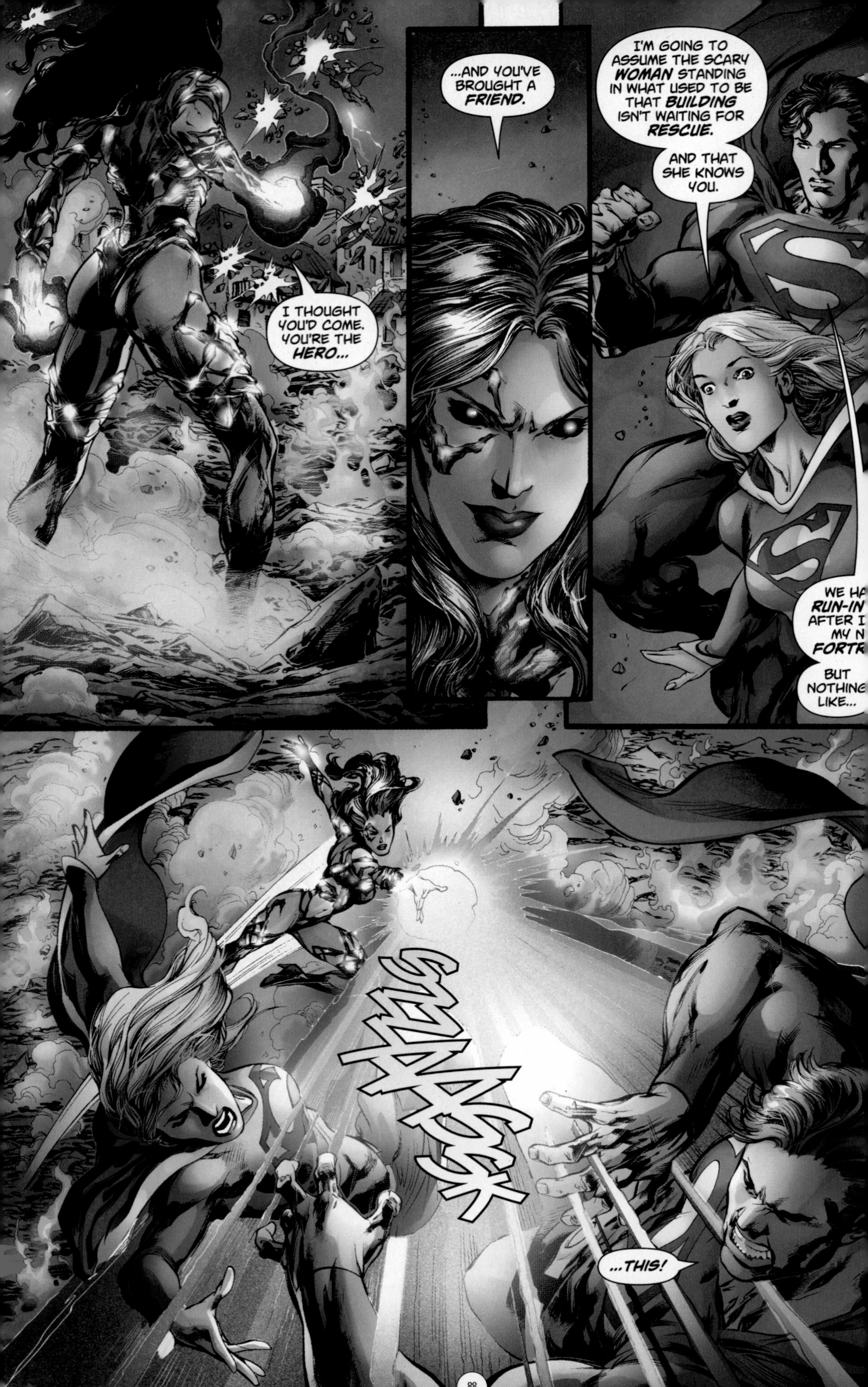
I THOUGHT YOU'D COME. YOU'RE THE HERO...
...AND YOU'VE BROUGHT A FRIEND.
I'M GOING TO ASSUME THE SCARY WOMAN STANDING IN WHAT USED TO BE THAT BUILDING ISN'T WAITING FOR RESCUE.
AND THAT SHE KNOWS YOU.
WE HA RUN-IN AFTER I MY N FORTR
BUT NOTHING LIKE...
...THIS!

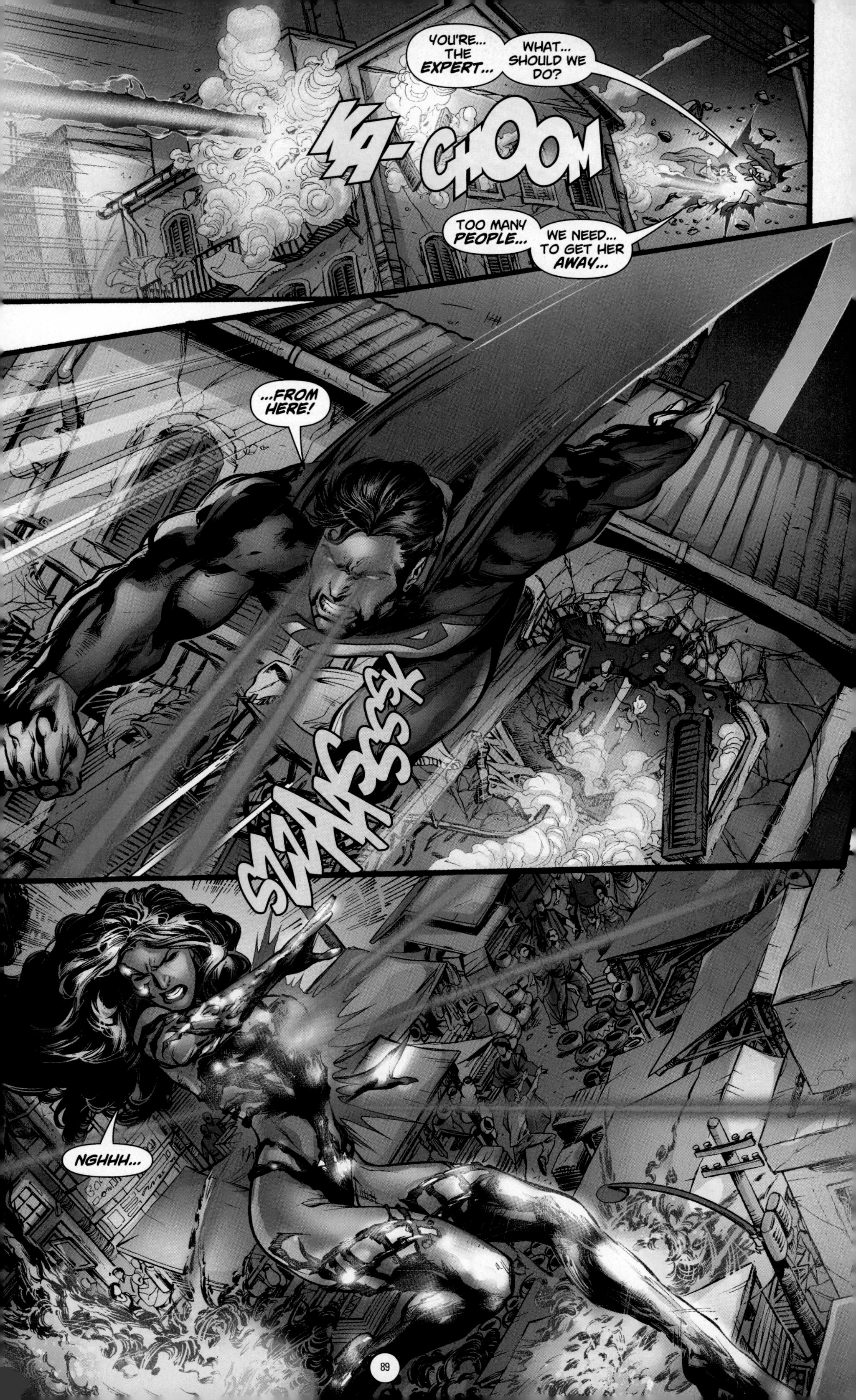
YOU'RE... THE EXPERT...
WHAT... SHOULD WE DO?
KA-CHOOM
TOO MANY PEOPLE...
WE NEED... TO GET HER AWAY...
...FROM HERE!
SZAKSSSSK
NGHHH...

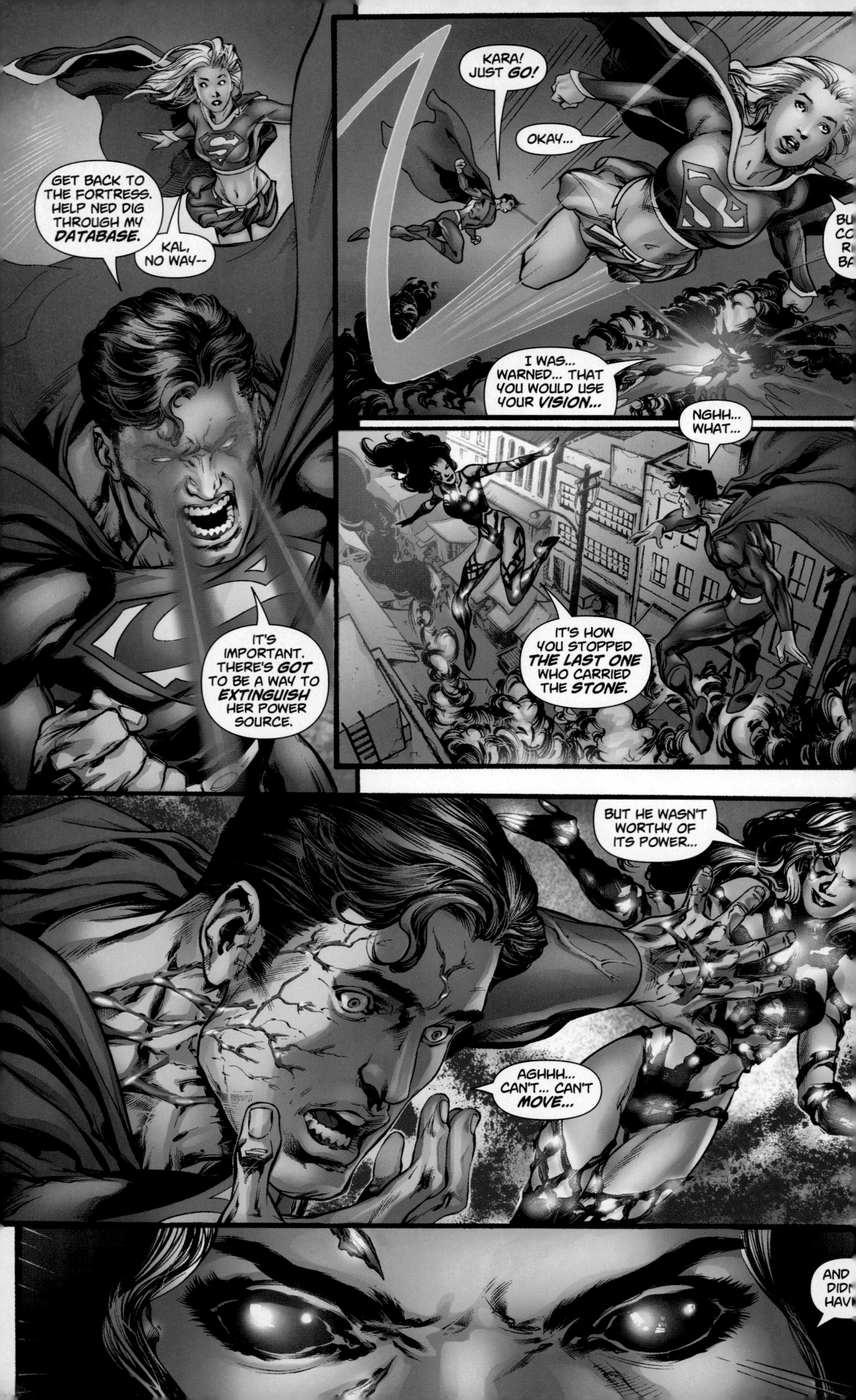
GET BACK TO THE FORTRESS. HELP NED DIG THROUGH MY DATABASE.
KAL, NO WAY--
IT'S IMPORTANT. THERE'S GOT TO BE A WAY TO EXTINGUISH HER POWER SOURCE.
KARA! JUST GO!
OKAY...
I WAS... WARNED... THAT YOU WOULD USE YOUR VISION...
NGHH... WHAT...
IT'S HOW YOU STOPPED THE LAST ONE WHO CARRIED THE STONE.
BUT HE WASN'T WORTHY OF ITS POWER...
AGHHH... CAN'T... CAN'T MOVE...

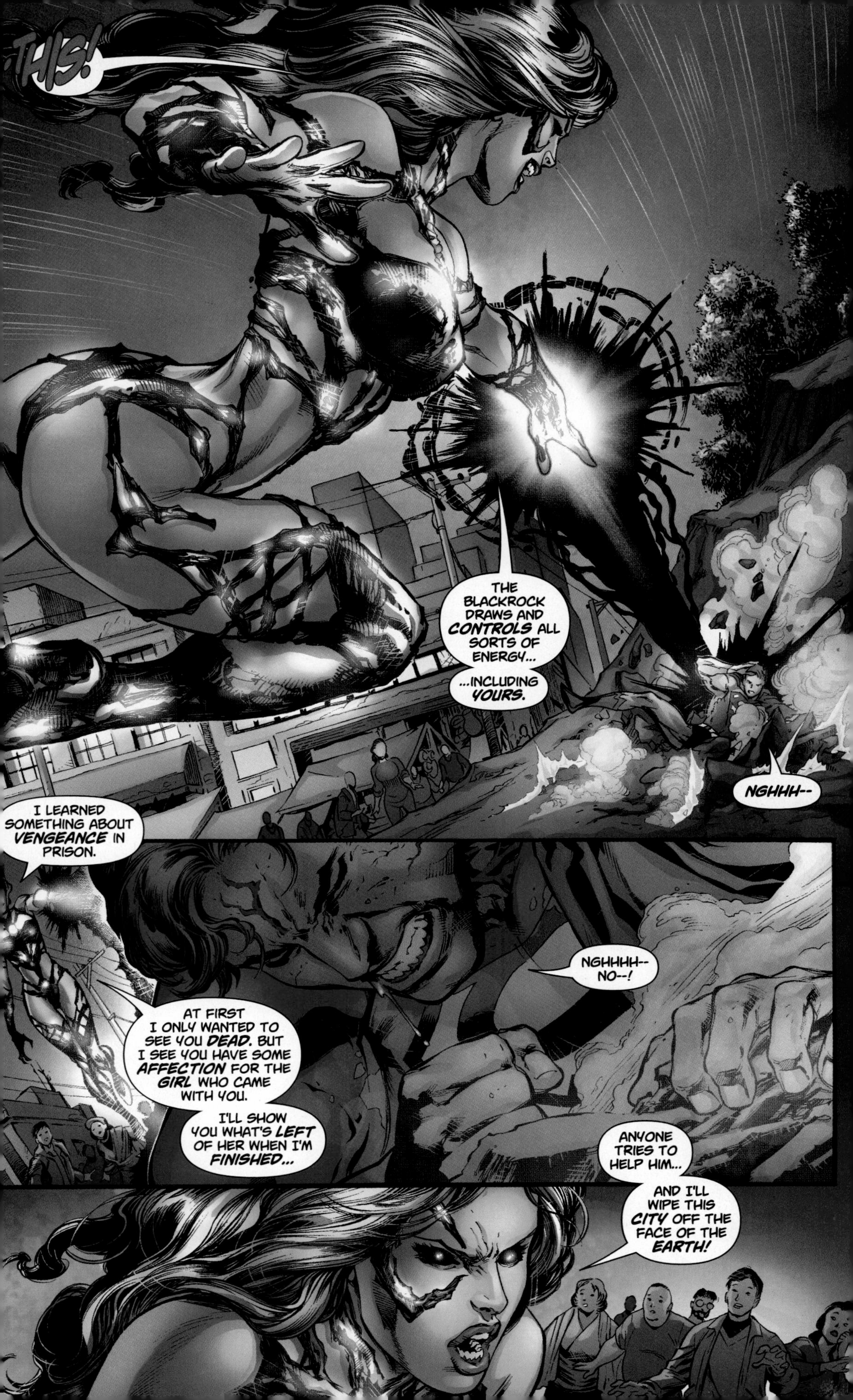

...THIS!
THE BLACKROCK DRAWS AND CONTROLS ALL SORTS OF ENERGY...
...INCLUDING YOURS.
NGHHH--
I LEARNED SOMETHING ABOUT VENGEANCE IN PRISON.
NGHHHH-- NO--!
AT FIRST I ONLY WANTED TO SEE YOU DEAD. BUT I SEE YOU HAVE SOME AFFECTION FOR THE GIRL WHO CAME WITH YOU.
I'LL SHOW YOU WHAT'S LEFT OF HER WHEN I'M FINISHED...
ANYONE TRIES TO HELP HIM...
AND I'LL WIPE THIS CITY OFF THE FACE OF THE EARTH!

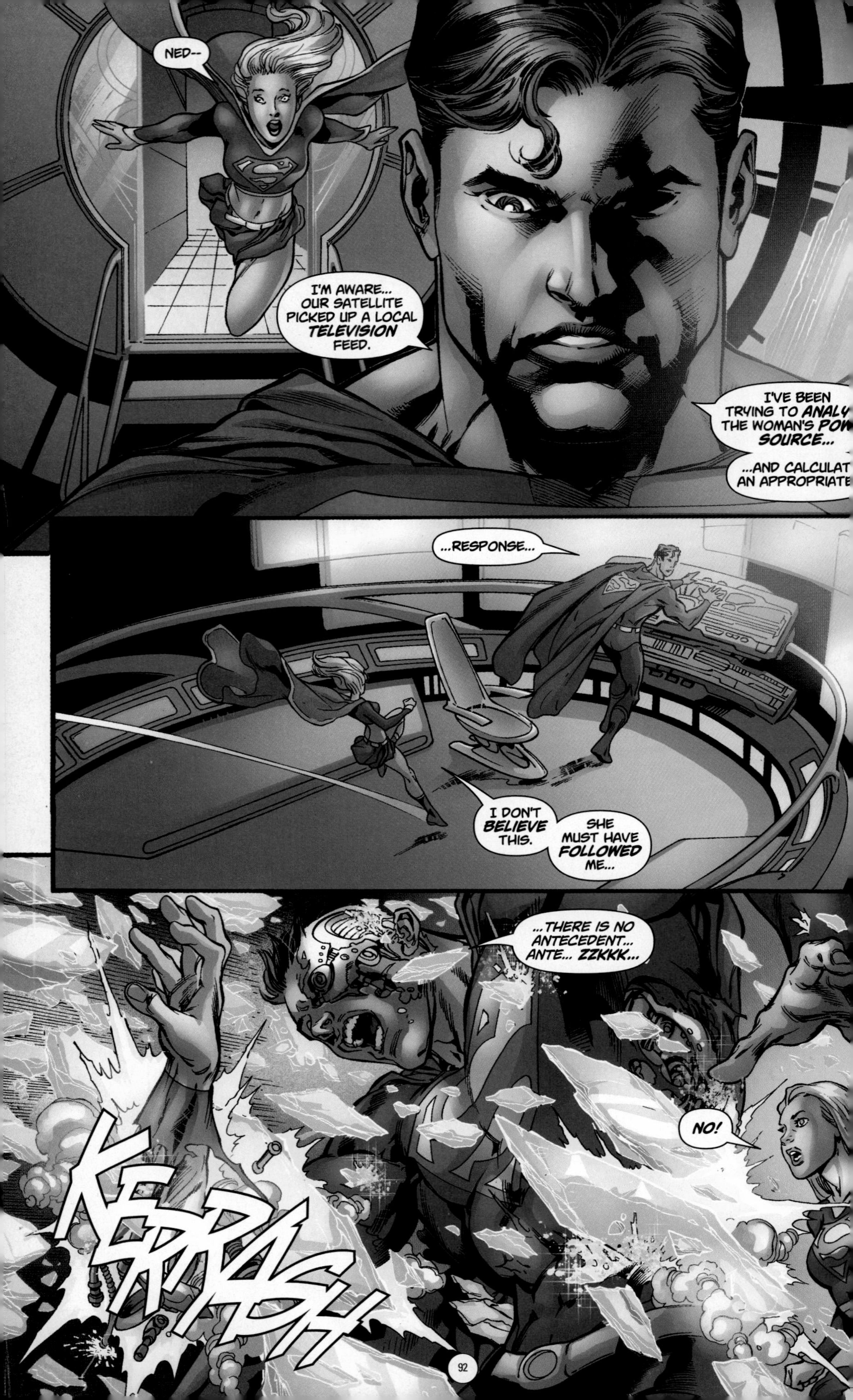
NED--
I'M AWARE... OUR SATELLITE PICKED UP A LOCAL TELEVISION FEED.
I'VE BEEN TRYING TO ANALY THE WOMAN'S POW SOURCE...
...AND CALCULAT AN APPROPRIATE
...RESPONSE...
I DON'T BELIEVE THIS.
SHE MUST HAVE FOLLOWED ME...
...THERE IS NO ANTECEDENT... ANTE... ZZKKK...
NO!
KERRASH

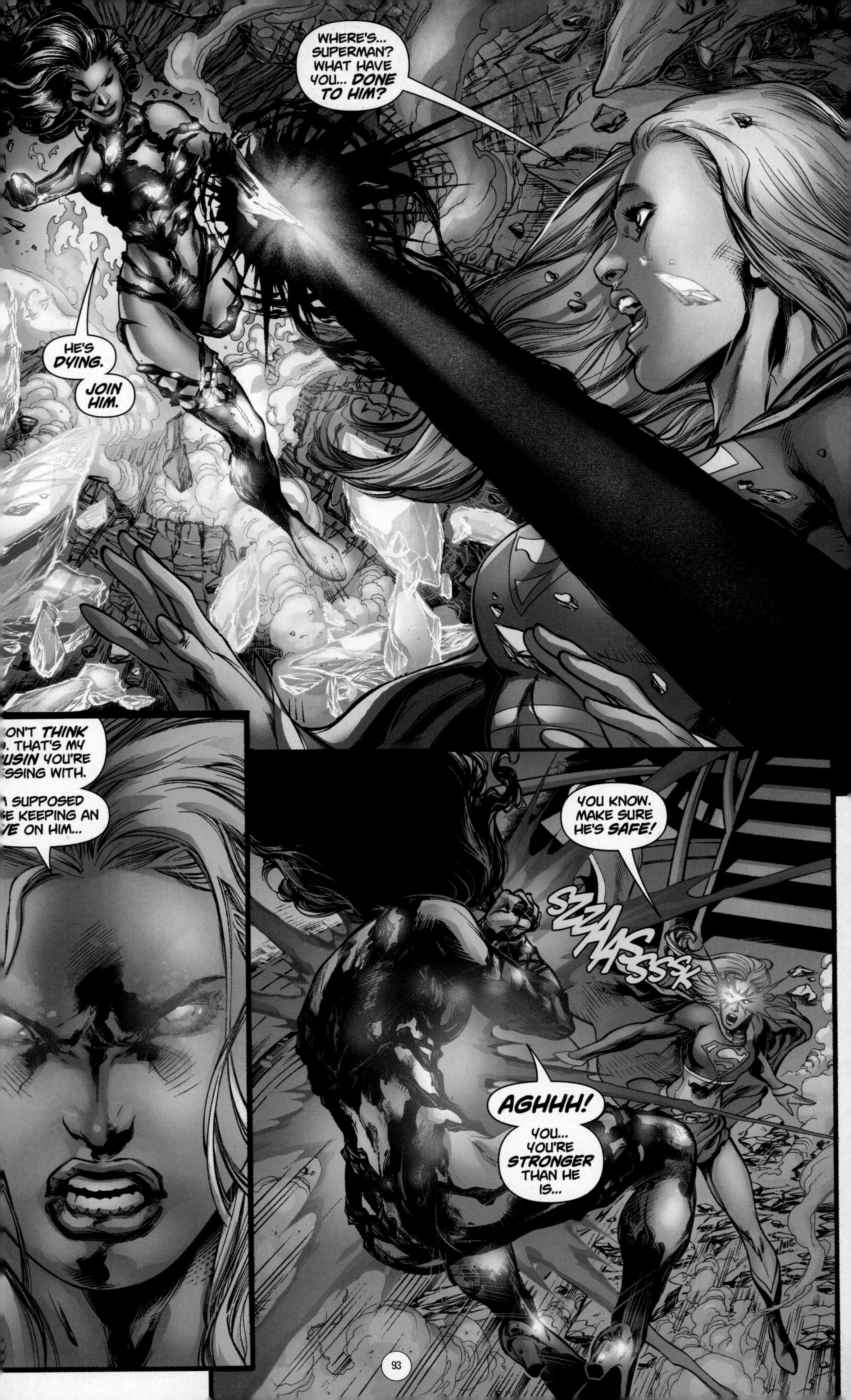

WHERE'S... SUPERMAN? WHAT HAVE YOU... DONE TO HIM?
HE'S DYING.
JOIN HIM.
ON'T THINK . THAT'S MY USIN YOU'RE SSING WITH.
SUPPOSED E KEEPING AN YE ON HIM...
YOU KNOW. MAKE SURE HE'S SAFE!
SZZAASSSK
AGHHH!
YOU... YOU'RE STRONGER THAN HE IS...

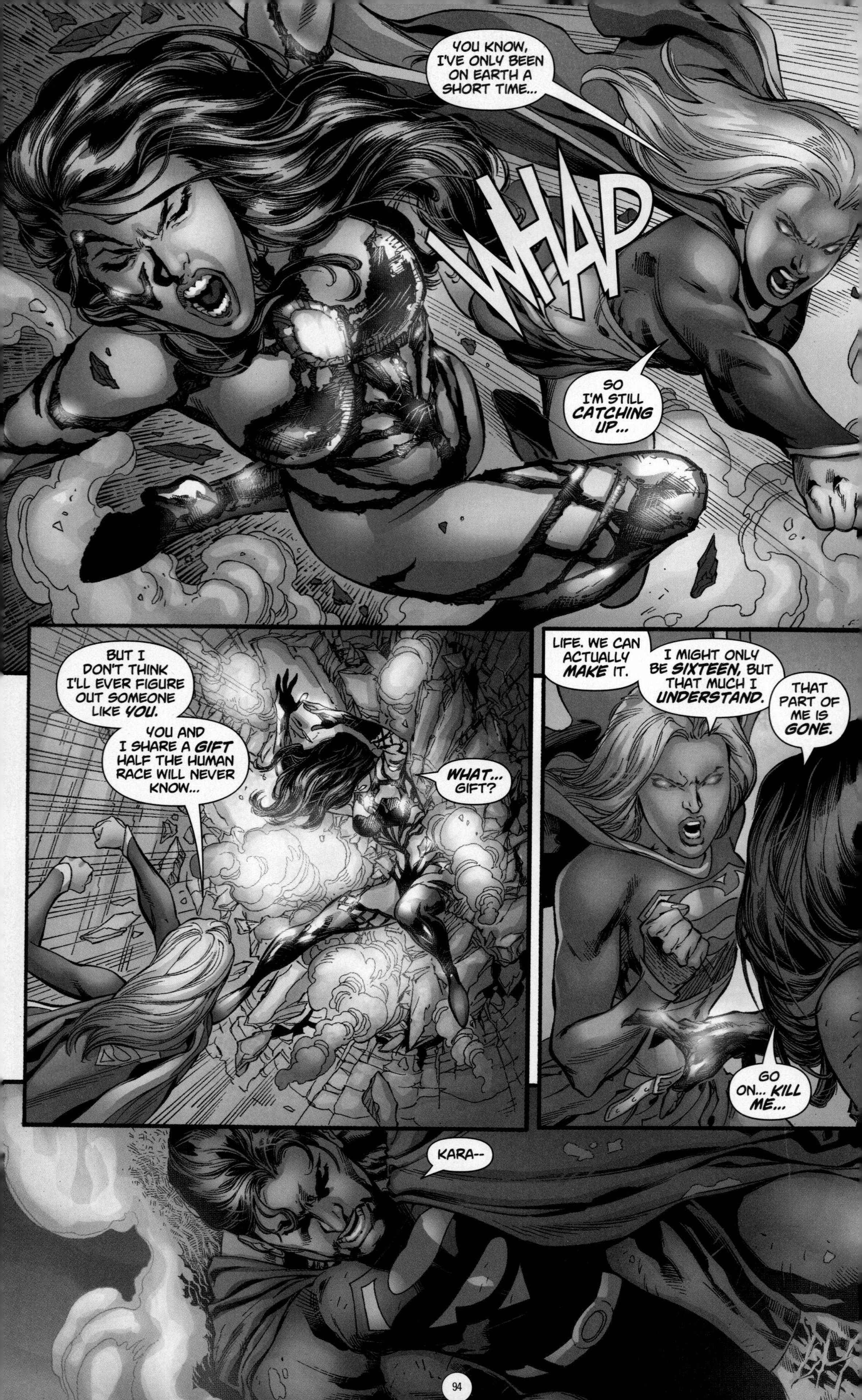

YOU KNOW, I'VE ONLY BEEN ON EARTH A SHORT TIME...
WHAP
SO I'M STILL CATCHING UP...
BUT I DON'T THINK I'LL EVER FIGURE OUT SOMEONE LIKE YOU.
YOU AND I SHARE A GIFT HALF THE HUMAN RACE WILL NEVER KNOW...
WHAT... GIFT?
LIFE. WE CAN ACTUALLY MAKE IT.
I MIGHT ONLY BE SIXTEEN, BUT THAT MUCH I UNDERSTAND.
THAT PART OF ME IS GONE.
GO ON... KILL ME...
KARA--

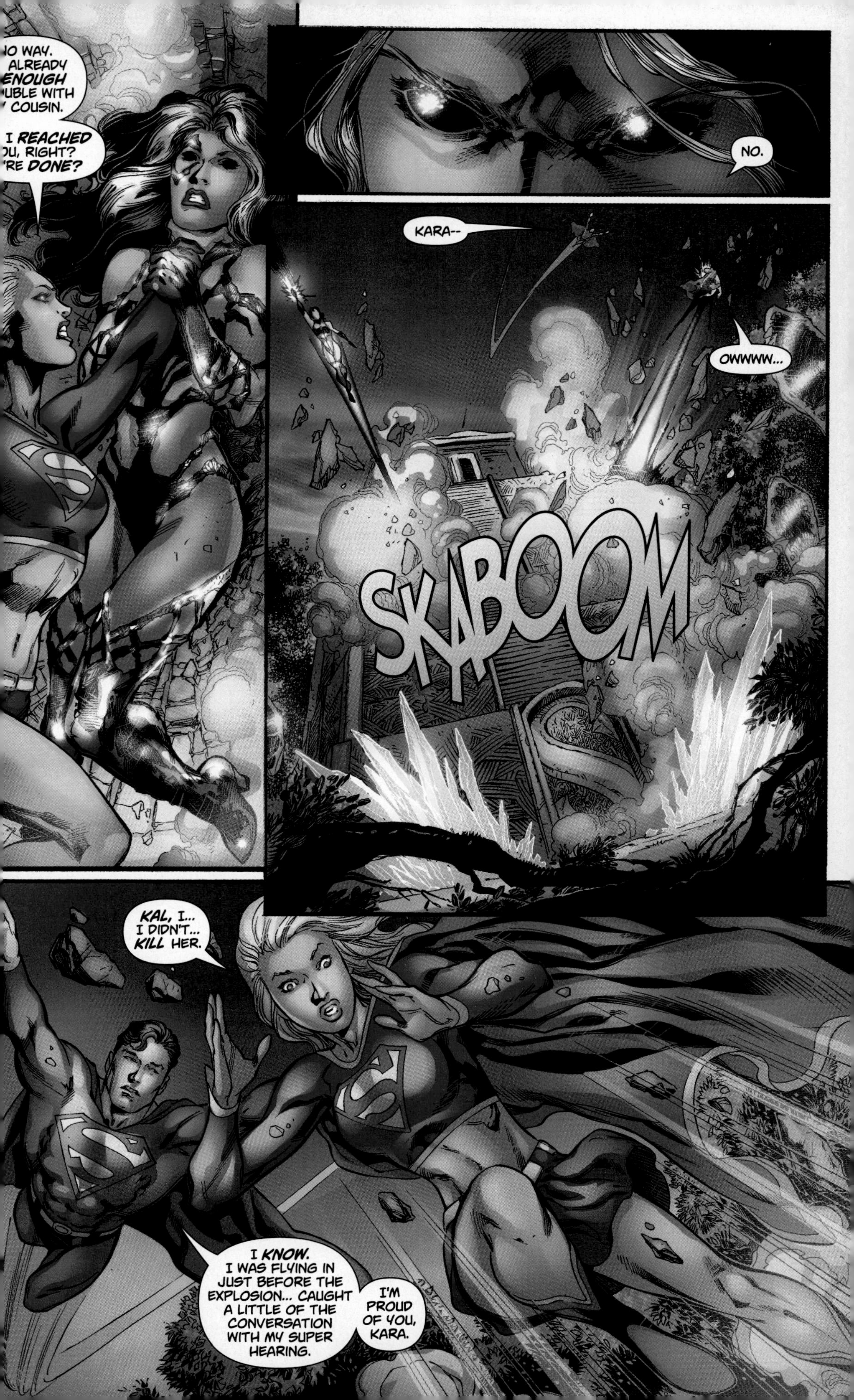

ALREADY ENOUGH ... WITH ... COUSIN.
I REACHED ..., RIGHT? ... DONE?
NO.
KARA--
OWWWW...
SKABOOM
KAL, I... I DIDN'T... KILL HER.
I KNOW. I WAS FLYING IN JUST BEFORE THE EXPLOSION... CAUGHT A LITTLE OF THE CONVERSATION WITH MY SUPER HEARING.
I'M PROUD OF YOU, KARA.

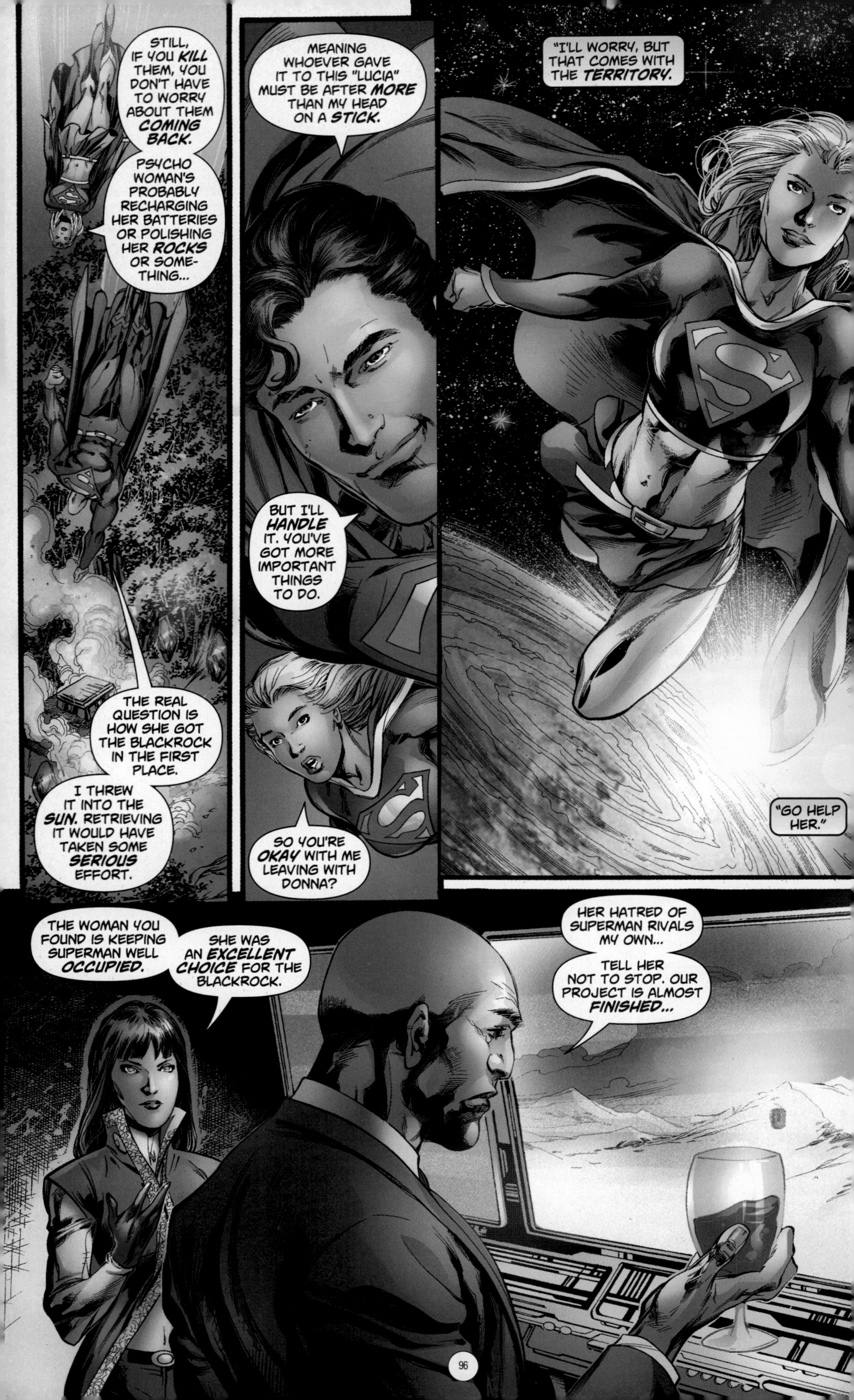
STILL, IF YOU KILL THEM, YOU DON'T HAVE TO WORRY ABOUT THEM COMING BACK.
PSYCHO WOMAN'S PROBABLY RECHARGING HER BATTERIES OR POLISHING HER ROCKS OR SOME-THING...
THE REAL QUESTION IS HOW SHE GOT THE BLACKROCK IN THE FIRST PLACE.
I THREW IT INTO THE SUN. RETRIEVING IT WOULD HAVE TAKEN SOME SERIOUS EFFORT.
MEANING WHOEVER GAVE IT TO THIS "LUCIA" MUST BE AFTER MORE THAN MY HEAD ON A STICK.
BUT I'LL HANDLE IT. YOU'VE GOT MORE IMPORTANT THINGS TO DO.
SO YOU'RE OKAY WITH ME LEAVING WITH DONNA?
"I'LL WORRY, BUT THAT COMES WITH THE TERRITORY.
"GO HELP HER."
THE WOMAN YOU FOUND IS KEEPING SUPERMAN WELL OCCUPIED.
SHE WAS AN EXCELLENT CHOICE FOR THE BLACKROCK.
HER HATRED OF SUPERMAN RIVALS MY OWN...
TELL HER NOT TO STOP. OUR PROJECT IS ALMOST FINISHED...

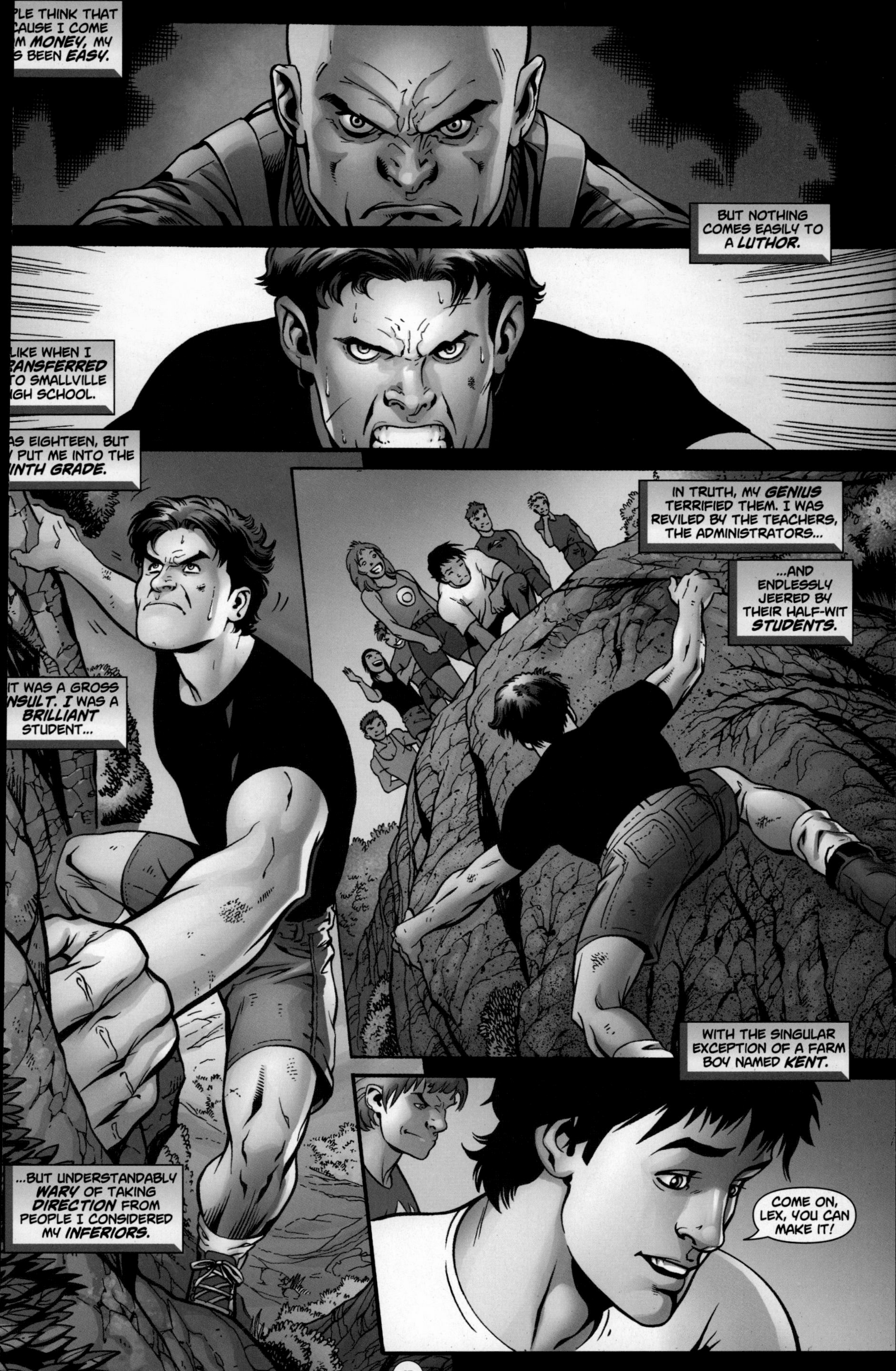
PLE THINK THAT
CAUSE I COME
M MONEY, MY
S BEEN EASY.
BUT NOTHING COMES EASILY TO A LUTHOR.
LIKE WHEN I
RANSFERRED
TO SMALLVILLE
IGH SCHOOL.
AS EIGHTEEN, BUT
PUT ME INTO THE
NINTH GRADE.
IT WAS A GROSS
NSULT. I WAS A
BRILLIANT
STUDENT...
...BUT UNDERSTANDABLY WARY OF TAKING DIRECTION FROM PEOPLE I CONSIDERED MY INFERIORS.
IN TRUTH, MY GENIUS TERRIFIED THEM. I WAS REVILED BY THE TEACHERS, THE ADMINISTRATORS...
...AND ENDLESSLY JEERED BY THEIR HALF-WIT STUDENTS.
WITH THE SINGULAR EXCEPTION OF A FARM BOY NAMED KENT.
COME ON, LEX, YOU CAN MAKE IT!

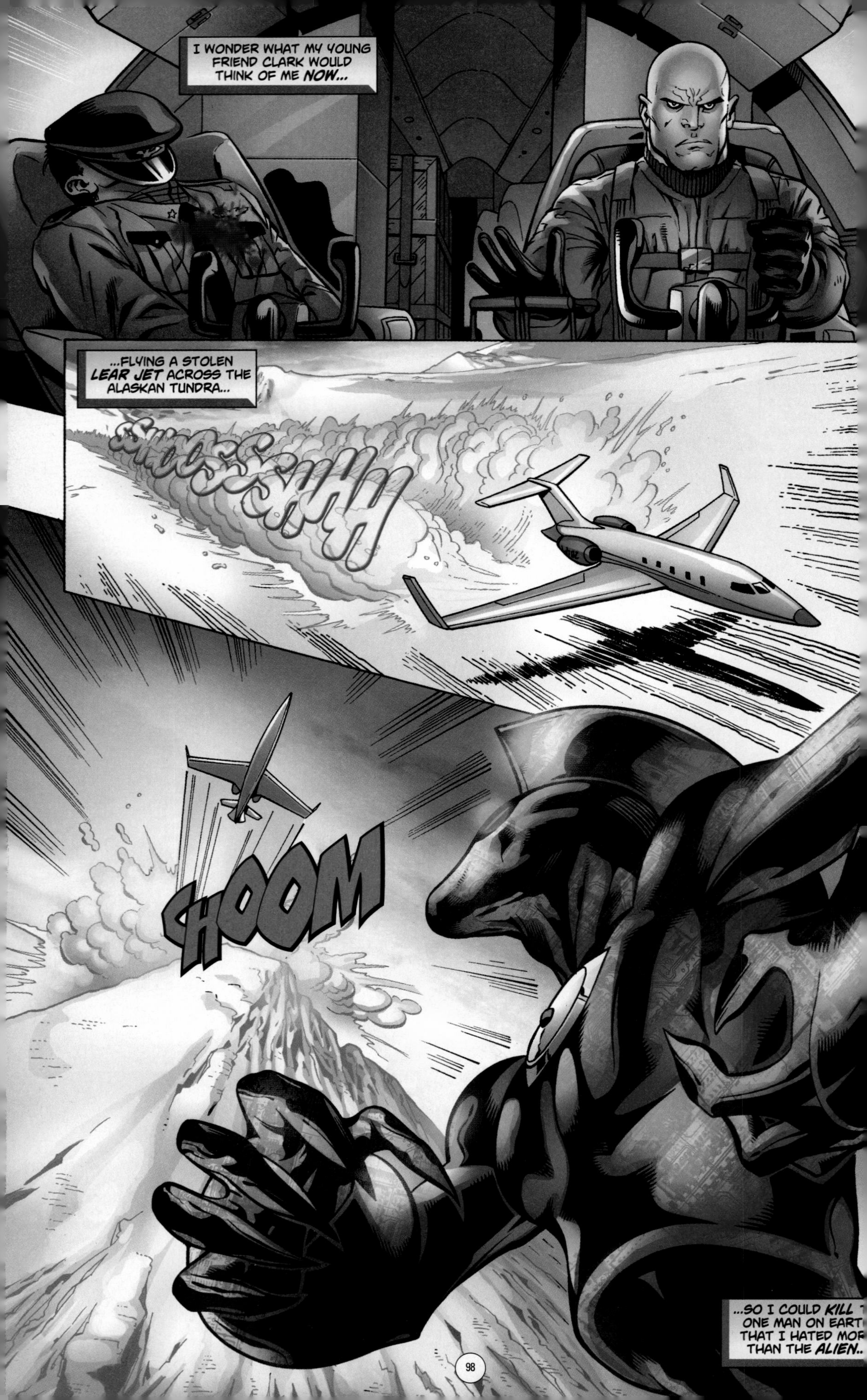
I WONDER WHAT MY YOUNG FRIEND CLARK WOULD THINK OF ME NOW...
...FLYING A STOLEN LEAR JET ACROSS THE ALASKAN TUNDRA...
CHOOM
...SO I COULD KILL T
ONE MAN ON EART
THAT I HATED MOR
THAN THE ALIEN..

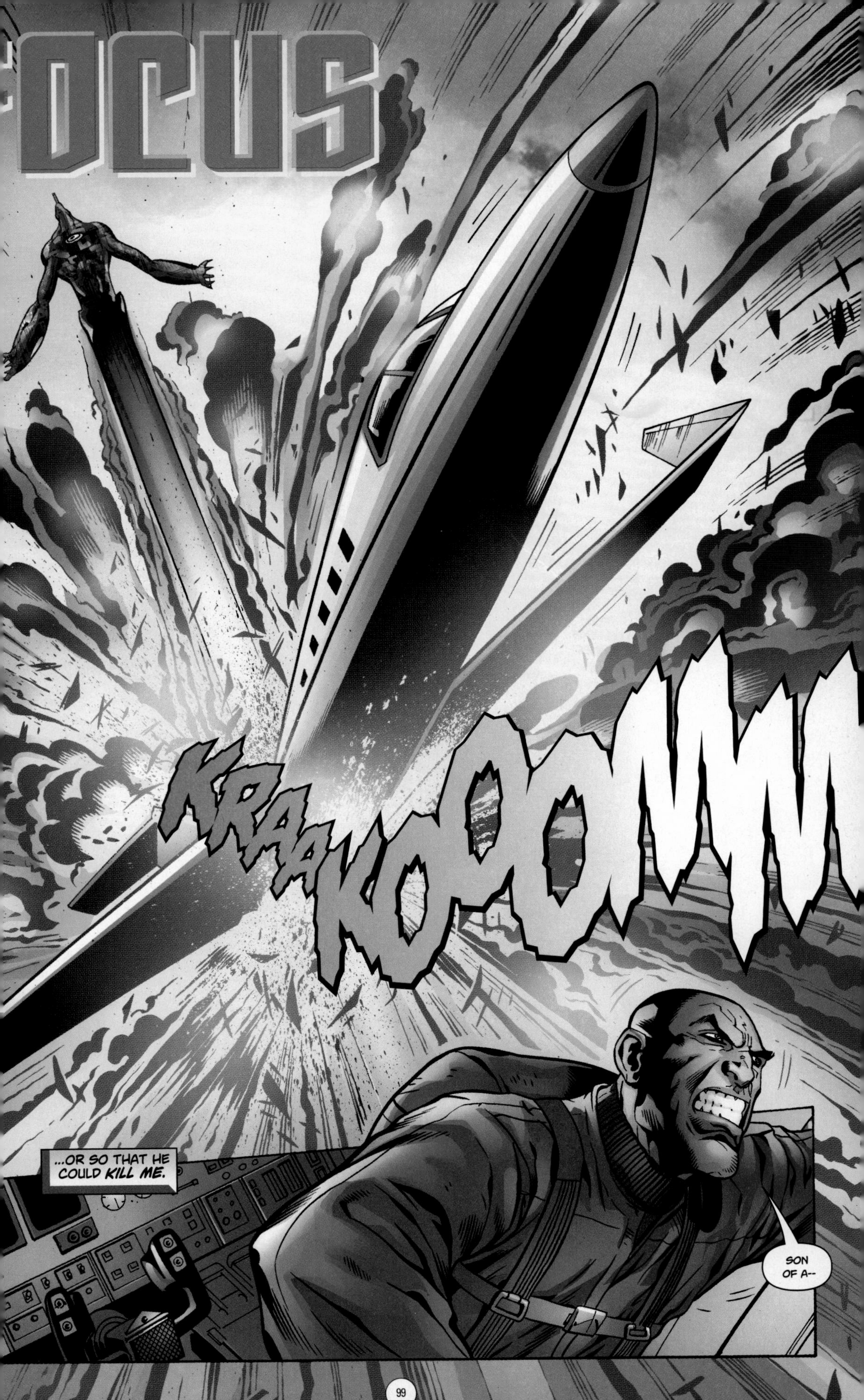
OCUS
KRAAKOOOMM
...OR SO THAT HE COULD KILL ME.
SON OF A--

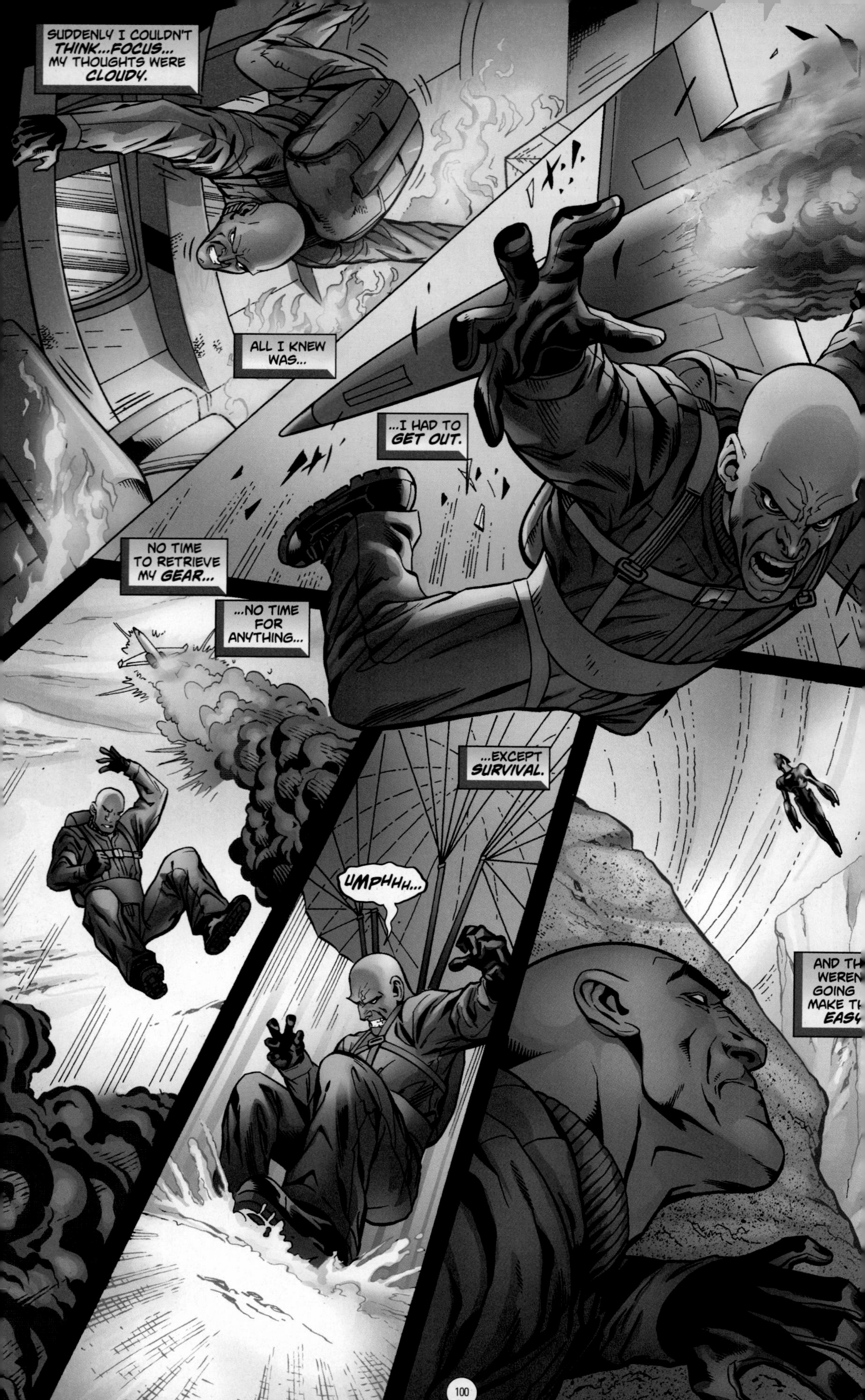
SUDDENLY I COULDN'T THINK...FOCUS... MY THOUGHTS WERE CLOUDY.
ALL I KNEW WAS...
...I HAD TO GET OUT.
NO TIME TO RETRIEVE MY GEAR...
...NO TIME FOR ANYTHING...
...EXCEPT SURVIVAL.
UMPHHH...
AND TH WEREN GOING MAKE TH EAS

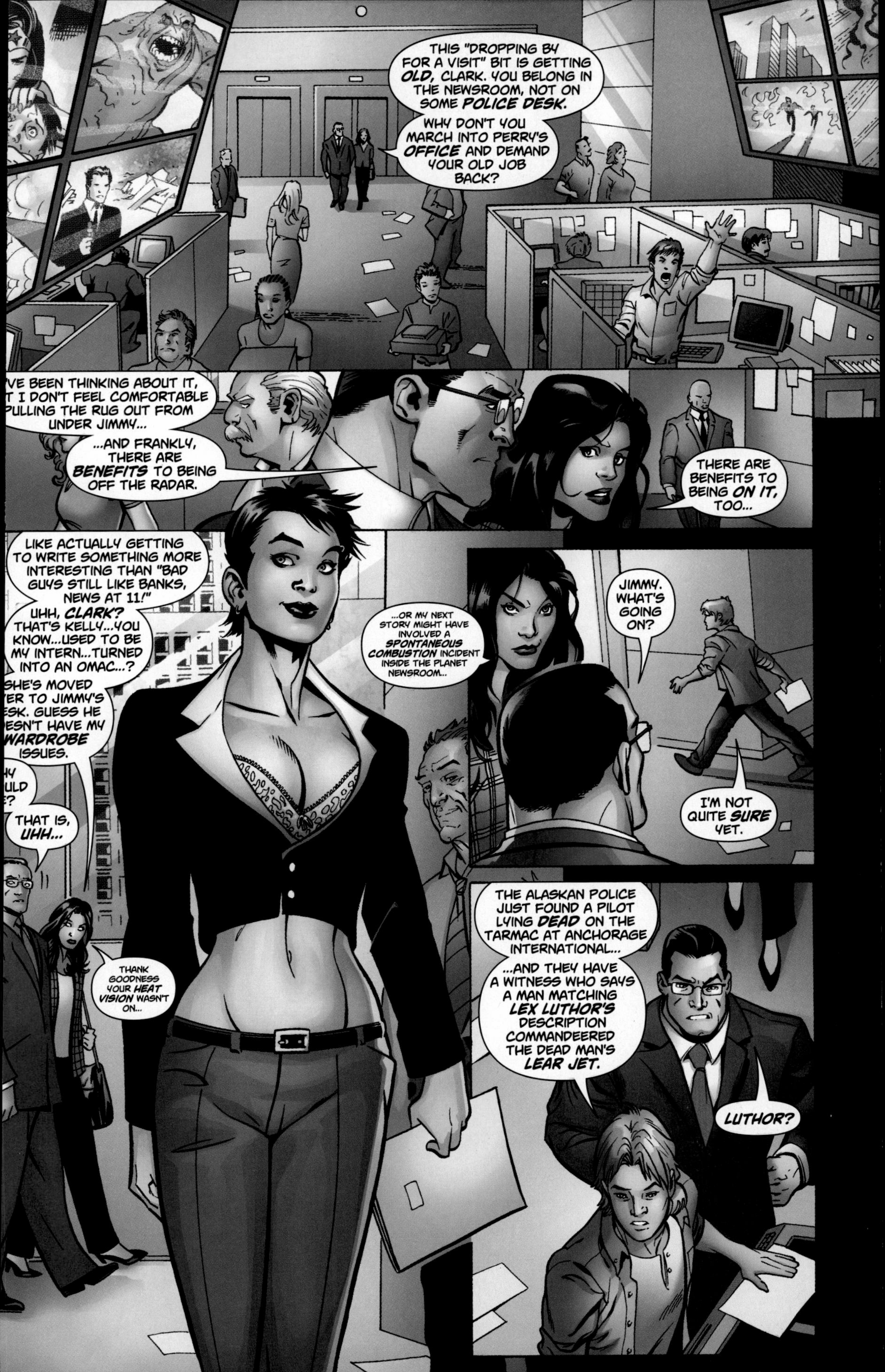
THIS "DROPPING BY FOR A VISIT" BIT IS GETTING OLD, CLARK. YOU BELONG IN THE NEWSROOM, NOT ON SOME POLICE DESK.
WHY DON'T YOU MARCH INTO PERRY'S OFFICE AND DEMAND YOUR OLD JOB BACK?
VE BEEN THINKING ABOUT IT, T I DON'T FEEL COMFORTABLE PULLING THE RUG OUT FROM UNDER JIMMY...
...AND FRANKLY, THERE ARE BENEFITS TO BEING OFF THE RADAR.
THERE ARE BENEFITS TO BEING ON IT, TOO...
LIKE ACTUALLY GETTING TO WRITE SOMETHING MORE INTERESTING THAN "BAD GUYS STILL LIKE BANKS, NEWS AT 11!"
UHH, CLARK? THAT'S KELLY...YOU KNOW...USED TO BE MY INTERN...TURNED INTO AN OMAC...?
HE'S MOVED ER TO JIMMY'S ESK. GUESS HE ESN'T HAVE MY WARDROBE ISSUES.
THAT IS, UHH...
THANK GOODNESS YOUR HEAT VISION WASN'T ON...
...OR MY NEXT STORY MIGHT HAVE INVOLVED A SPONTANEOUS COMBUSTION INCIDENT INSIDE THE PLANET NEWSROOM...
JIMMY. WHAT'S GOING ON?
I'M NOT QUITE SURE YET.
THE ALASKAN POLICE JUST FOUND A PILOT LYING DEAD ON THE TARMAC AT ANCHORAGE INTERNATIONAL...
...AND THEY HAVE A WITNESS WHO SAYS A MAN MATCHING LEX LUTHOR'S DESCRIPTION COMMANDEERED THE DEAD MAN'S LEAR JET.
LUTHOR?

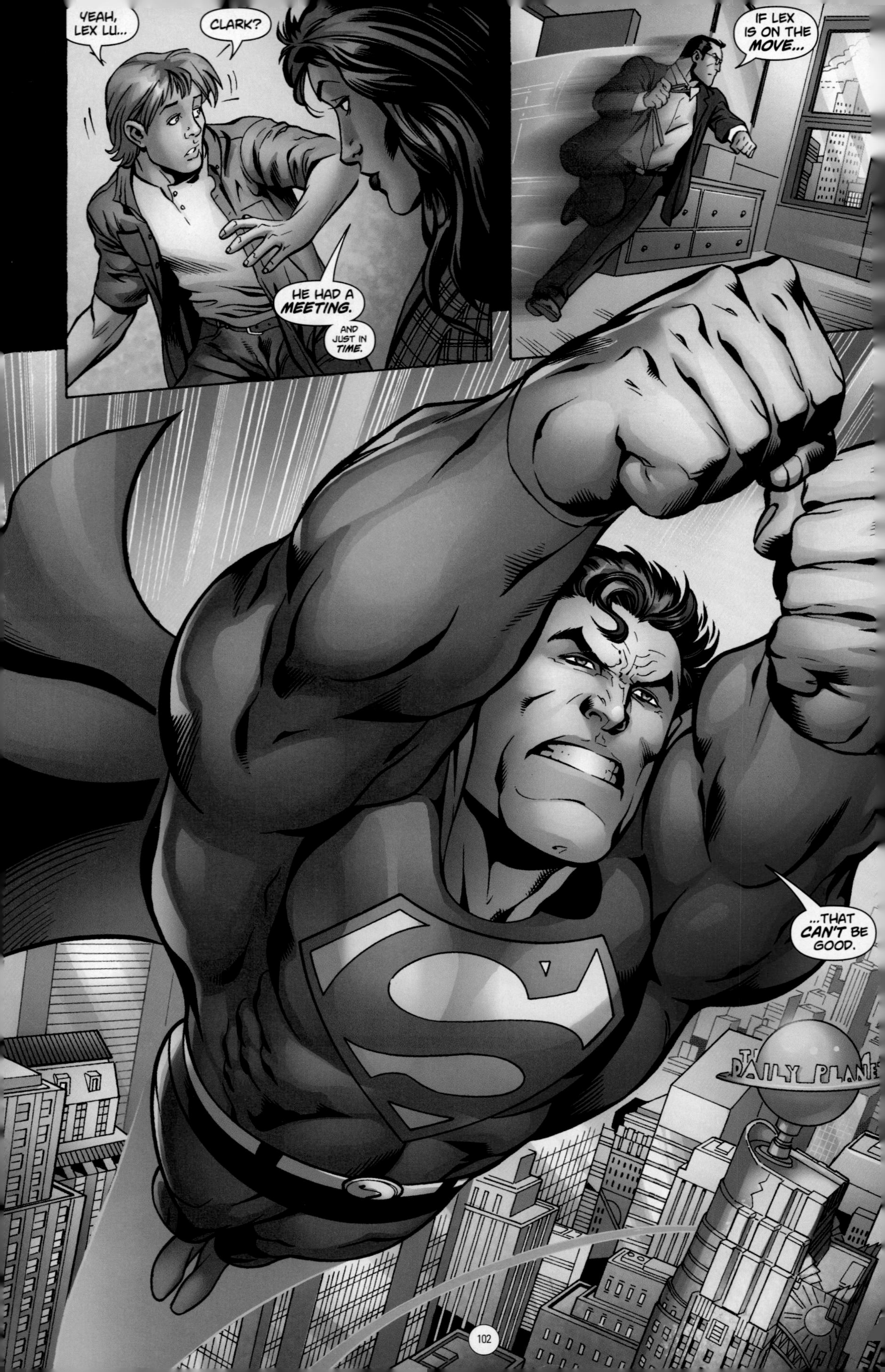
YEAH, LEX LU...
CLARK?
HE HAD A MEETING.
AND JUST IN TIME.
IF LEX IS ON THE MOVE...
...THAT CAN'T BE GOOD.
DAILY PLANE

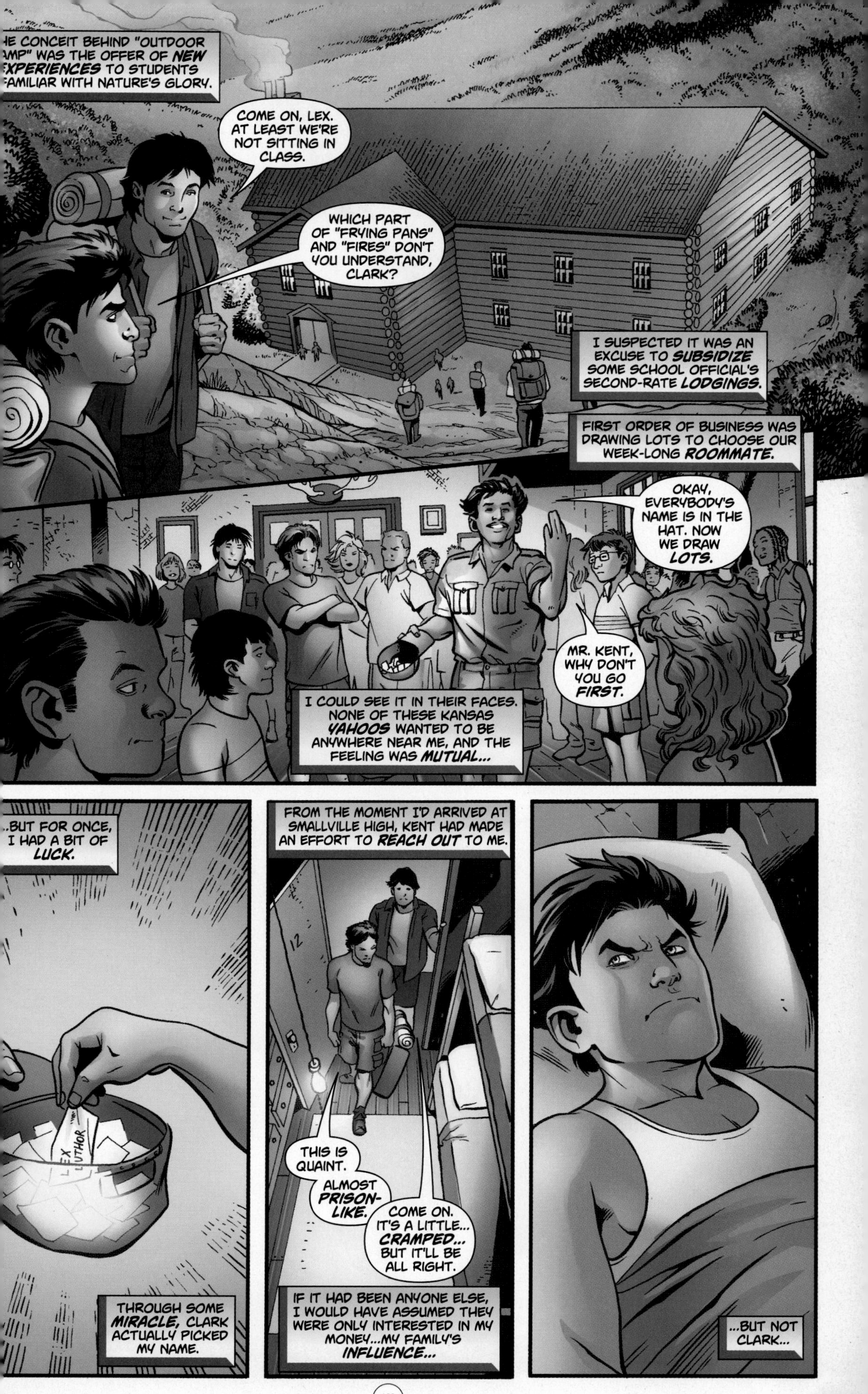

HE CONCEIT BEHIND "OUTDOOR AMP" WAS THE OFFER OF NEW EXPERIENCES TO STUDENTS FAMILIAR WITH NATURE'S GLORY.
COME ON, LEX. AT LEAST WE'RE NOT SITTING IN CLASS.
WHICH PART OF "FRYING PANS" AND "FIRES" DON'T YOU UNDERSTAND, CLARK?
I SUSPECTED IT WAS AN EXCUSE TO SUBSIDIZE SOME SCHOOL OFFICIAL'S SECOND-RATE LODGINGS.
FIRST ORDER OF BUSINESS WAS DRAWING LOTS TO CHOOSE OUR WEEK-LONG ROOMMATE.
OKAY, EVERYBODY'S NAME IS IN THE HAT. NOW WE DRAW LOTS.
MR. KENT, WHY DON'T YOU GO FIRST.
I COULD SEE IT IN THEIR FACES. NONE OF THESE KANSAS YAHOOS WANTED TO BE ANYWHERE NEAR ME, AND THE FEELING WAS MUTUAL...
...BUT FOR ONCE, I HAD A BIT OF LUCK.
LEX LUTHOR
THROUGH SOME MIRACLE, CLARK ACTUALLY PICKED MY NAME.
FROM THE MOMENT I'D ARRIVED AT SMALLVILLE HIGH, KENT HAD MADE AN EFFORT TO REACH OUT TO ME.
THIS IS QUAINT.
ALMOST PRISON-LIKE.
COME ON. IT'S A LITTLE... CRAMPED... BUT IT'LL BE ALL RIGHT.
IF IT HAD BEEN ANYONE ELSE, I WOULD HAVE ASSUMED THEY WERE ONLY INTERESTED IN MY MONEY...MY FAMILY'S INFLUENCE...
...BUT NOT CLARK...

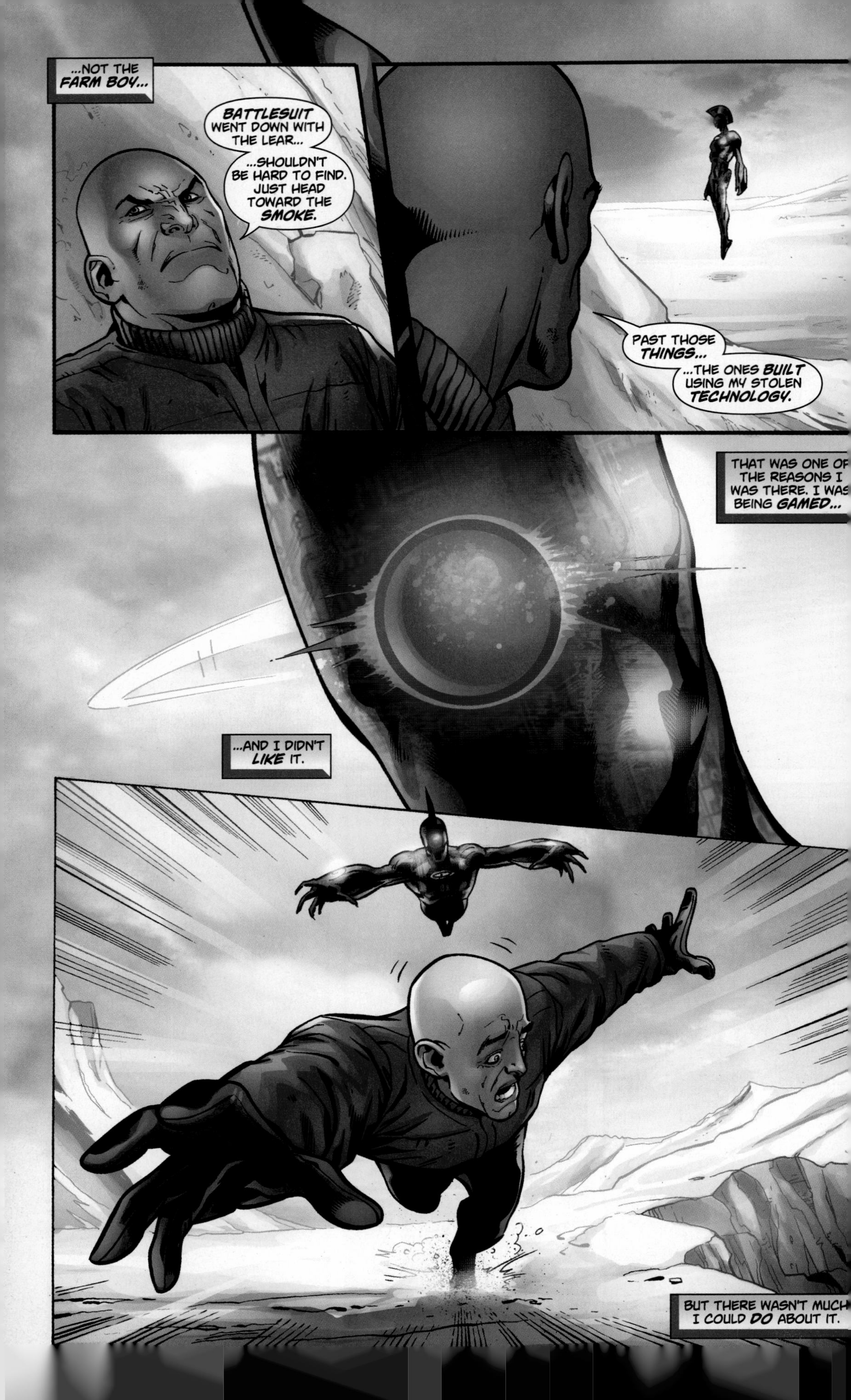
...NOT THE FARM BOY...
BATTLESUIT WENT DOWN WITH THE LEAR...
...SHOULDN'T BE HARD TO FIND. JUST HEAD TOWARD THE SMOKE.
PAST THOSE THINGS...
...THE ONES BUILT USING MY STOLEN TECHNOLOGY.
THAT WAS ONE OF THE REASONS I WAS THERE. I WAS BEING GAMED...
...AND I DIDN'T LIKE IT.
BUT THERE WASN'T MUCH I COULD DO ABOUT IT.

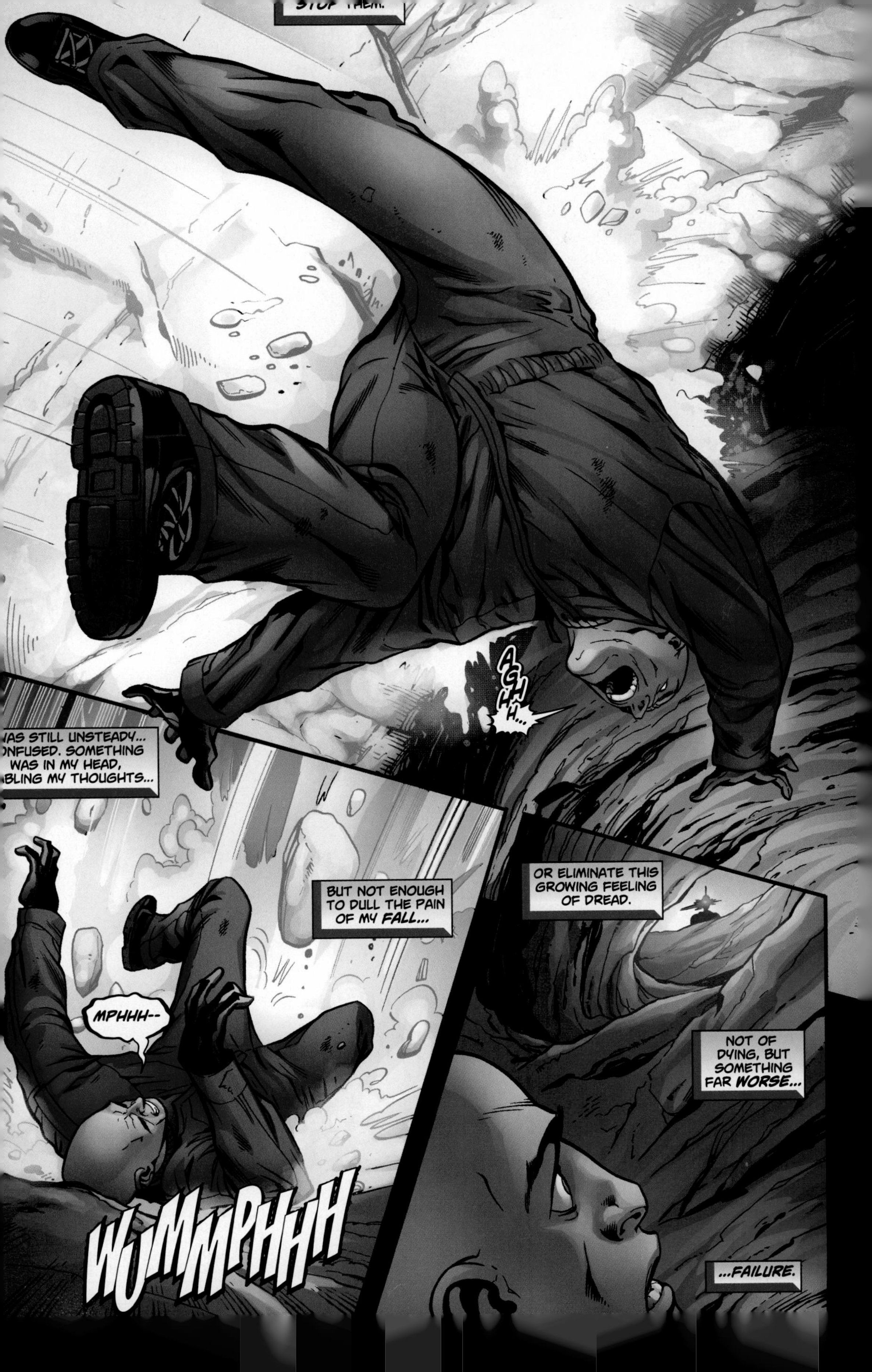

STOP THEM.
AGHHH...
WAS STILL UNSTEADY... ONFUSED. SOMETHING WAS IN MY HEAD, BLING MY THOUGHTS...
BUT NOT ENOUGH TO DULL THE PAIN OF MY FALL...
MPHHH--
WUMMMPHHH
OR ELIMINATE THIS GROWING FEELING OF DREAD.
NOT OF DYING, BUT SOMETHING FAR WORSE...
...FAILURE.

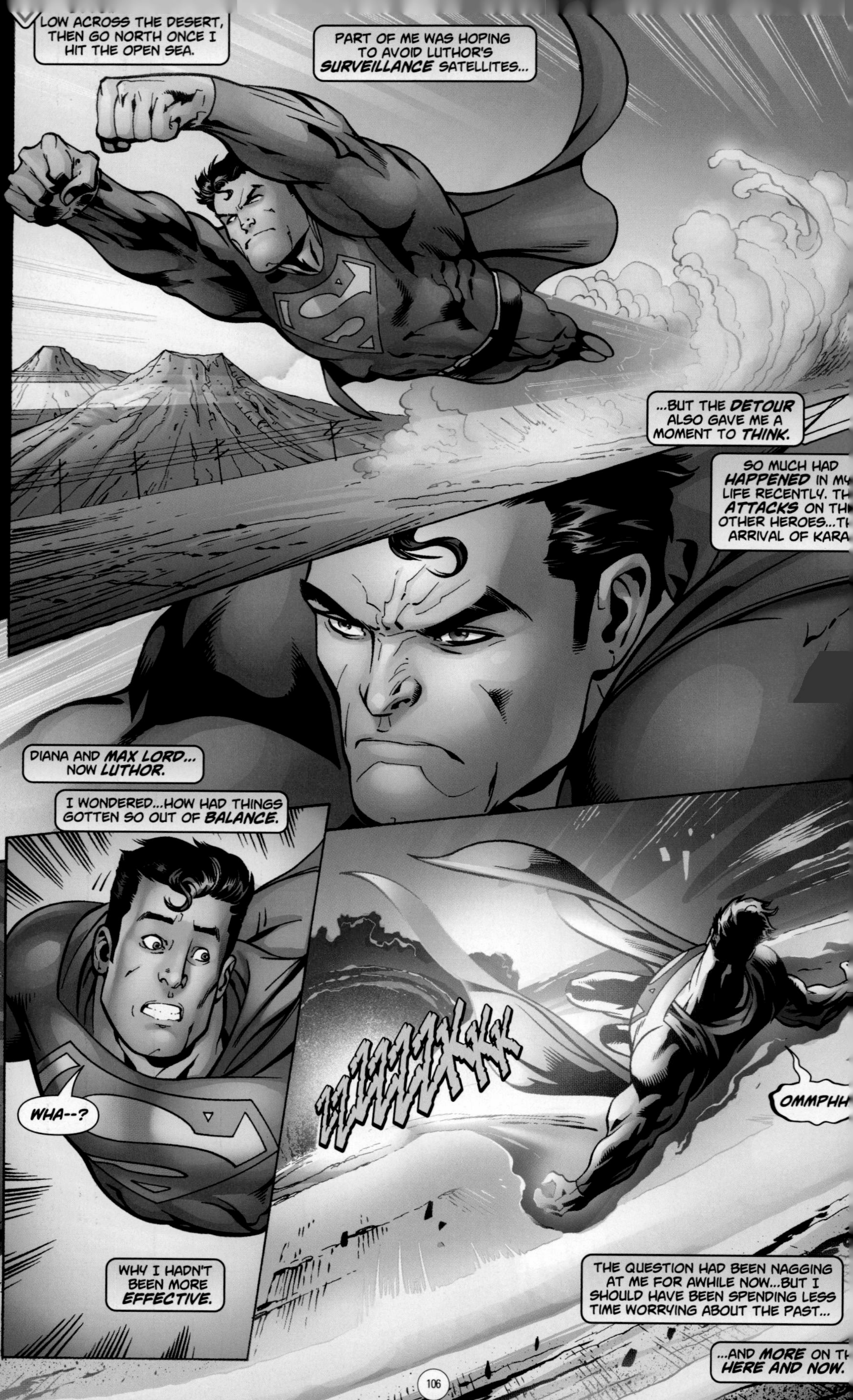
LOW ACROSS THE DESERT, THEN GO NORTH ONCE I HIT THE OPEN SEA.
PART OF ME WAS HOPING TO AVOID LUTHOR'S SURVEILLANCE SATELLITES...
...BUT THE DETOUR ALSO GAVE ME A MOMENT TO THINK.
SO MUCH HAD HAPPENED IN MY LIFE RECENTLY. TH ATTACKS ON TH OTHER HEROES...T ARRIVAL OF KARA
DIANA AND MAX LORD... NOW LUTHOR.
I WONDERED...HOW HAD THINGS GOTTEN SO OUT OF BALANCE.
WHA--?
WHY I HADN'T BEEN MORE EFFECTIVE.
OMMPHH
THE QUESTION HAD BEEN NAGGING AT ME FOR AWHILE NOW...BUT I SHOULD HAVE BEEN SPENDING LESS TIME WORRYING ABOUT THE PAST...
...AND MORE ON T HERE AND NOW.

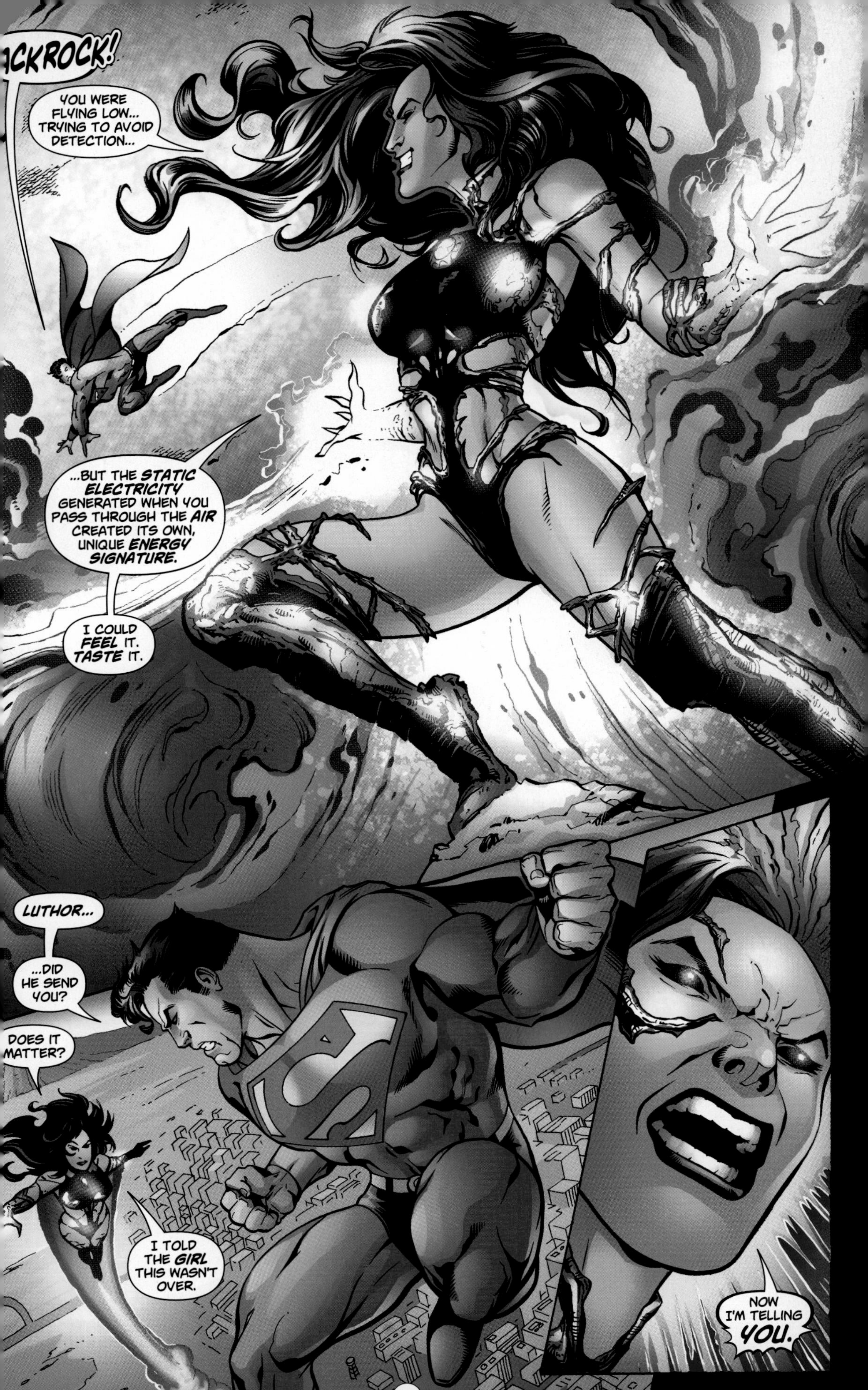
CKROCK!
YOU WERE FLYING LOW... TRYING TO AVOID DETECTION...
...BUT THE STATIC ELECTRICITY GENERATED WHEN YOU PASS THROUGH THE AIR CREATED ITS OWN, UNIQUE ENERGY SIGNATURE.
I COULD FEEL IT. TASTE IT.
LUTHOR...
...DID HE SEND YOU?
DOES IT MATTER?
I TOLD THE GIRL THIS WASN'T OVER.
NOW I'M TELLING YOU.

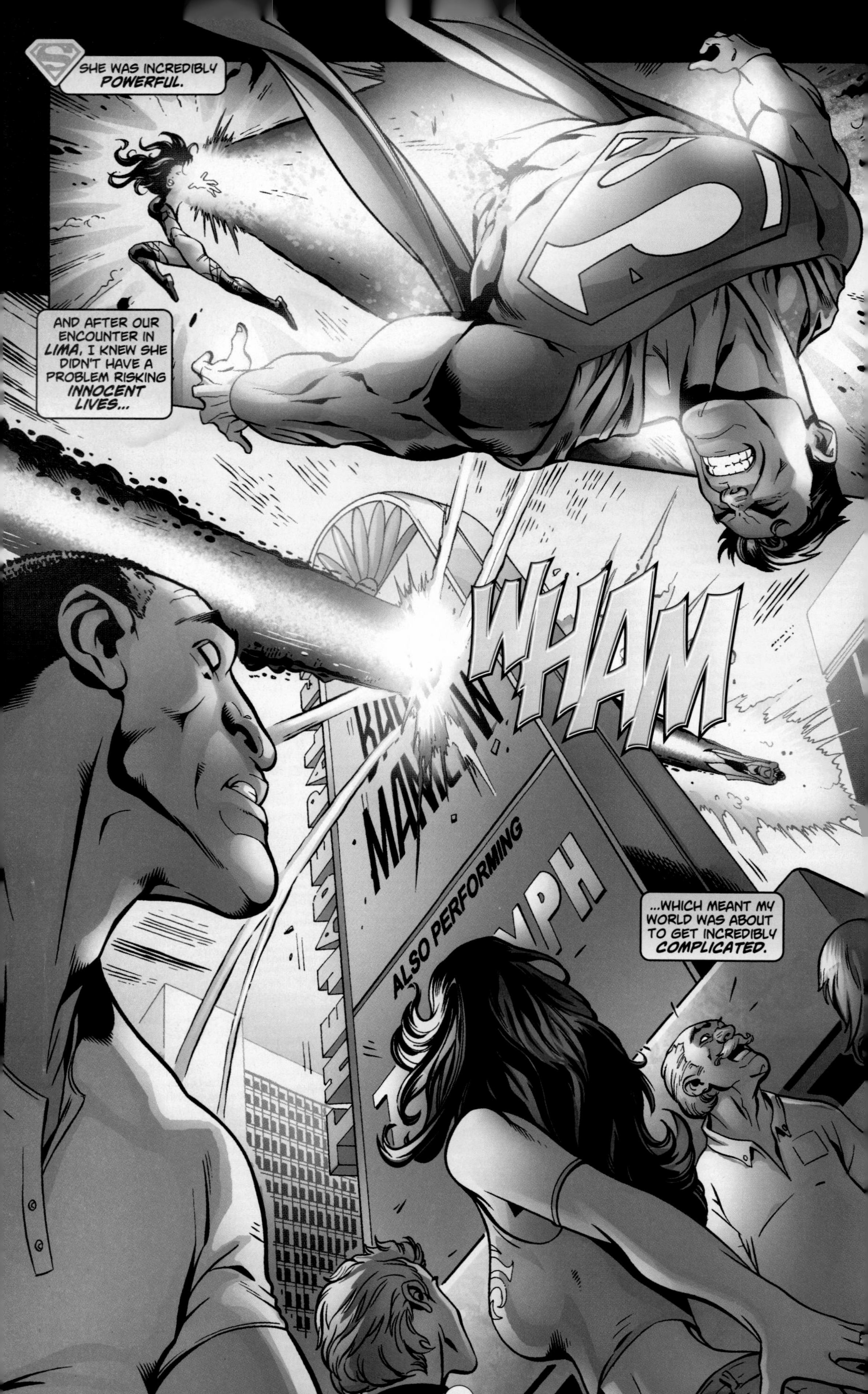

SHE WAS INCREDIBLY POWERFUL.
AND AFTER OUR ENCOUNTER IN LIMA, I KNEW SHE DIDN'T HAVE A PROBLEM RISKING INNOCENT LIVES...
WHAM
ALSO PERFORMING
...WHICH MEANT MY WORLD WAS ABOUT TO GET INCREDIBLY COMPLICATED.

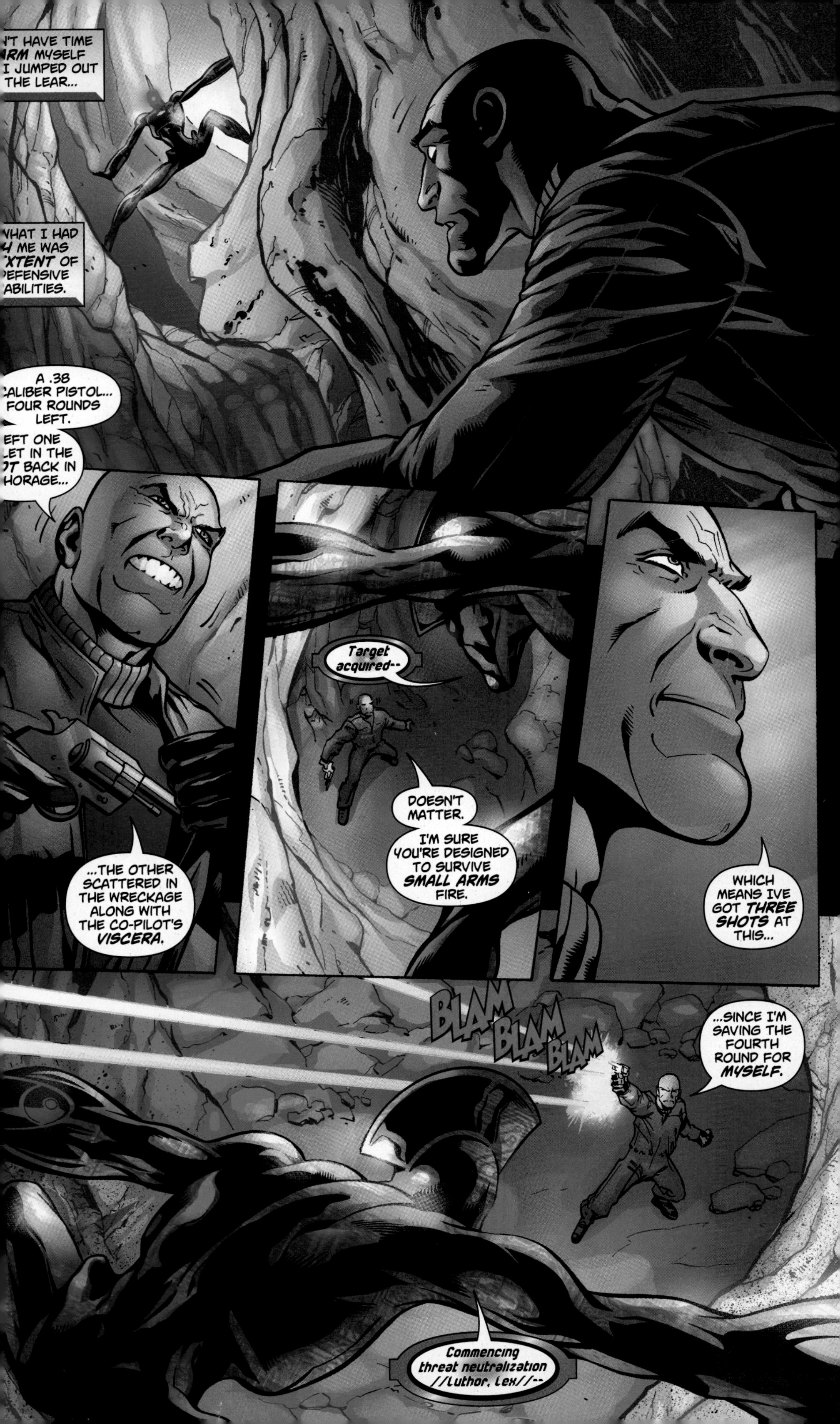

N'T HAVE TIME RM MYSELF I JUMPED OUT THE LEAR...
HAT I HAD ME WAS XTENT OF EFENSIVE ABILITIES.
A .38 CALIBER PISTOL... FOUR ROUNDS LEFT.
EFT ONE LET IN THE T BACK IN HORAGE...
...THE OTHER SCATTERED IN THE WRECKAGE ALONG WITH THE CO-PILOT'S VISCERA.
Target acquired--
DOESN'T MATTER.
I'M SURE YOU'RE DESIGNED TO SURVIVE SMALL ARMS FIRE.
WHICH MEANS IVE GOT THREE SHOTS AT THIS...
BLAM BLAM BLAM
...SINCE I'M SAVING THE FOURTH ROUND FOR MYSELF.
Commencing threat neutralization //Luthor, Lex//--

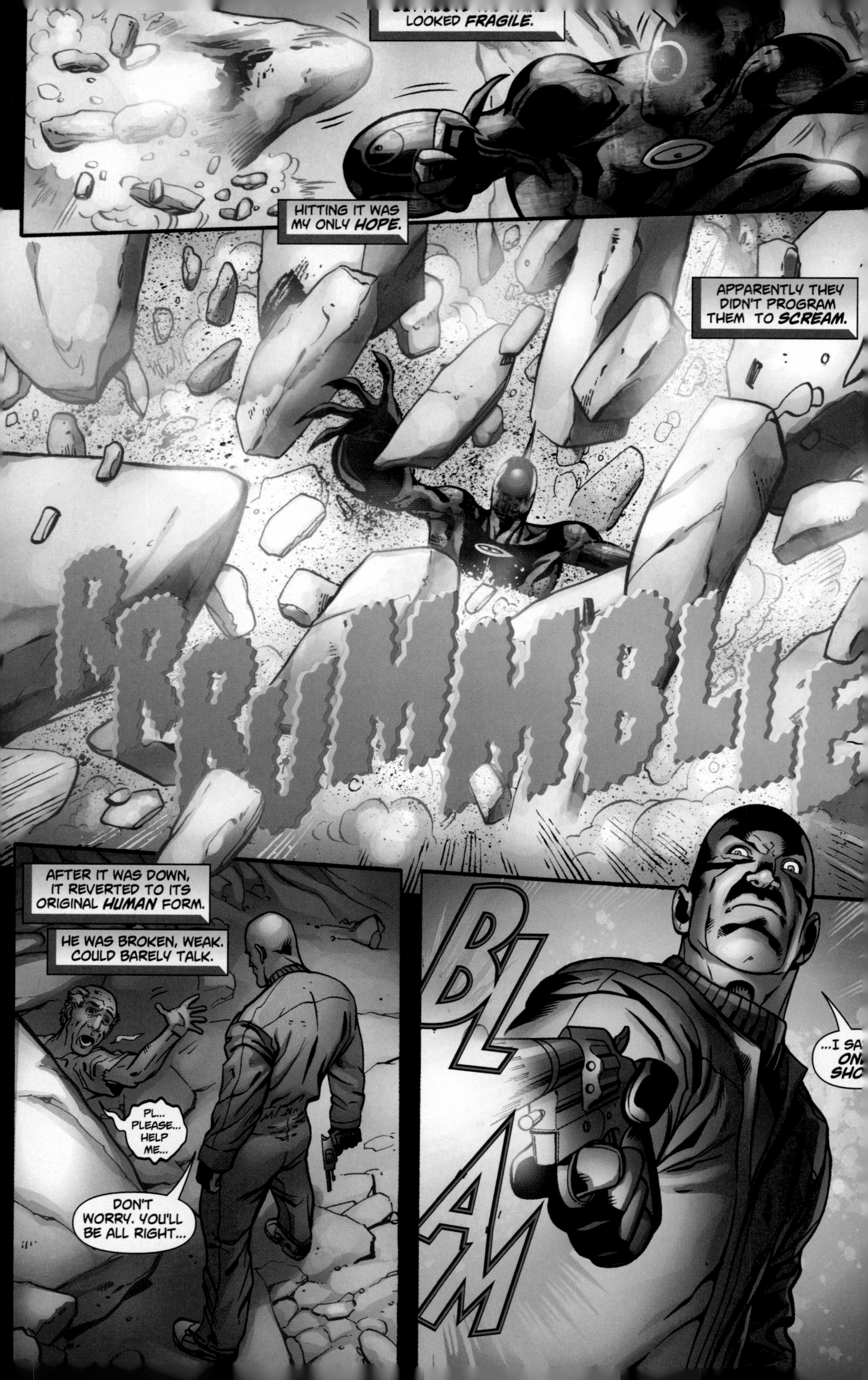
LOOKED FRAGILE.
HITTING IT WAS MY ONLY HOPE.
APPARENTLY THEY DIDN'T PROGRAM THEM TO SCREAM.
RRUMMBLE
AFTER IT WAS DOWN, IT REVERTED TO ITS ORIGINAL HUMAN FORM.
HE WAS BROKEN, WEAK. COULD BARELY TALK.
PL... PLEASE... HELP ME...
DON'T WORRY. YOU'LL BE ALL RIGHT...
BLAM
...I SA
ON
SHO

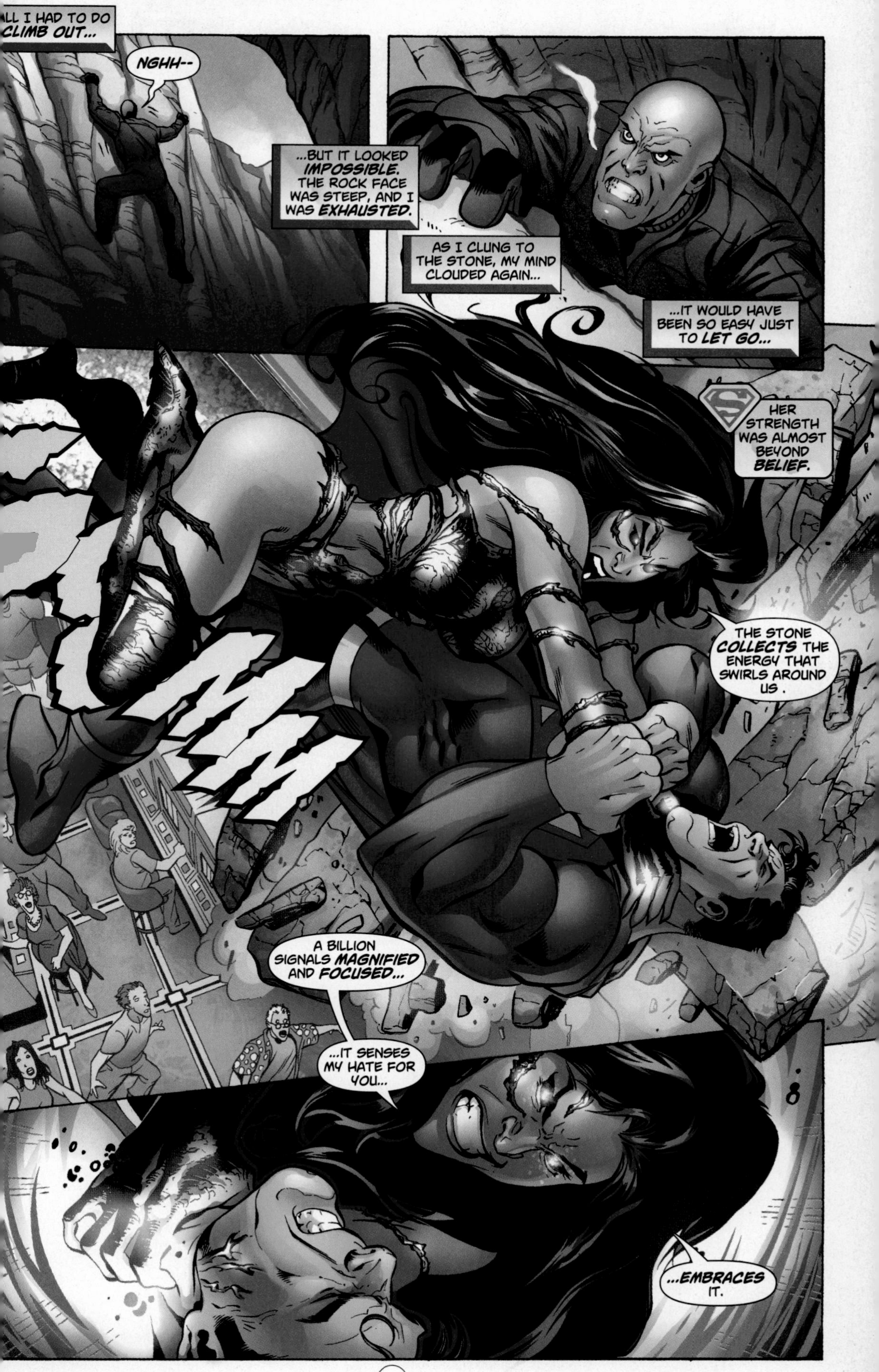

ALL I HAD TO DO CLIMB OUT...
NGHH--
...BUT IT LOOKED IMPOSSIBLE. THE ROCK FACE WAS STEEP, AND I WAS EXHAUSTED.
AS I CLUNG TO THE STONE, MY MIND CLOUDED AGAIN...
...IT WOULD HAVE BEEN SO EASY JUST TO LET GO...
HER STRENGTH WAS ALMOST BEYOND BELIEF.
THE STONE COLLECTS THE ENERGY THAT SWIRLS AROUND US.
A BILLION SIGNALS MAGNIFIED AND FOCUSED...
...IT SENSES MY HATE FOR YOU...
...EMBRACES IT.

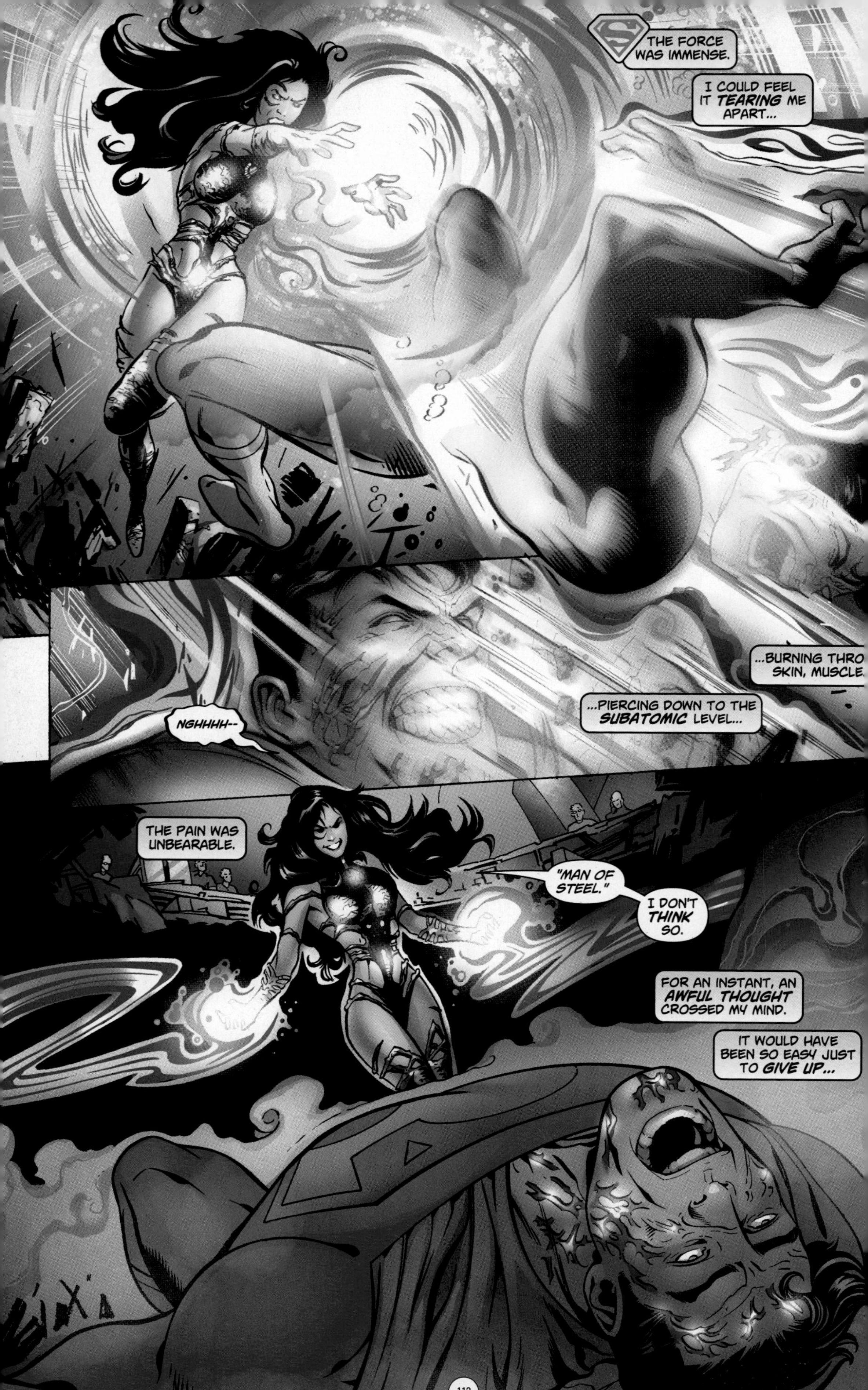
THE FORCE WAS IMMENSE.
I COULD FEEL IT TEARING ME APART...
...BURNING THRO SKIN, MUSCLE.
...PIERCING DOWN TO THE SUBATOMIC LEVEL...
NGHHHH--
THE PAIN WAS UNBEARABLE.
"MAN OF STEEL."
I DON'T THINK SO.
FOR AN INSTANT, AN AWFUL THOUGHT CROSSED MY MIND.
IT WOULD HAVE BEEN SO EASY JUST TO GIVE UP...

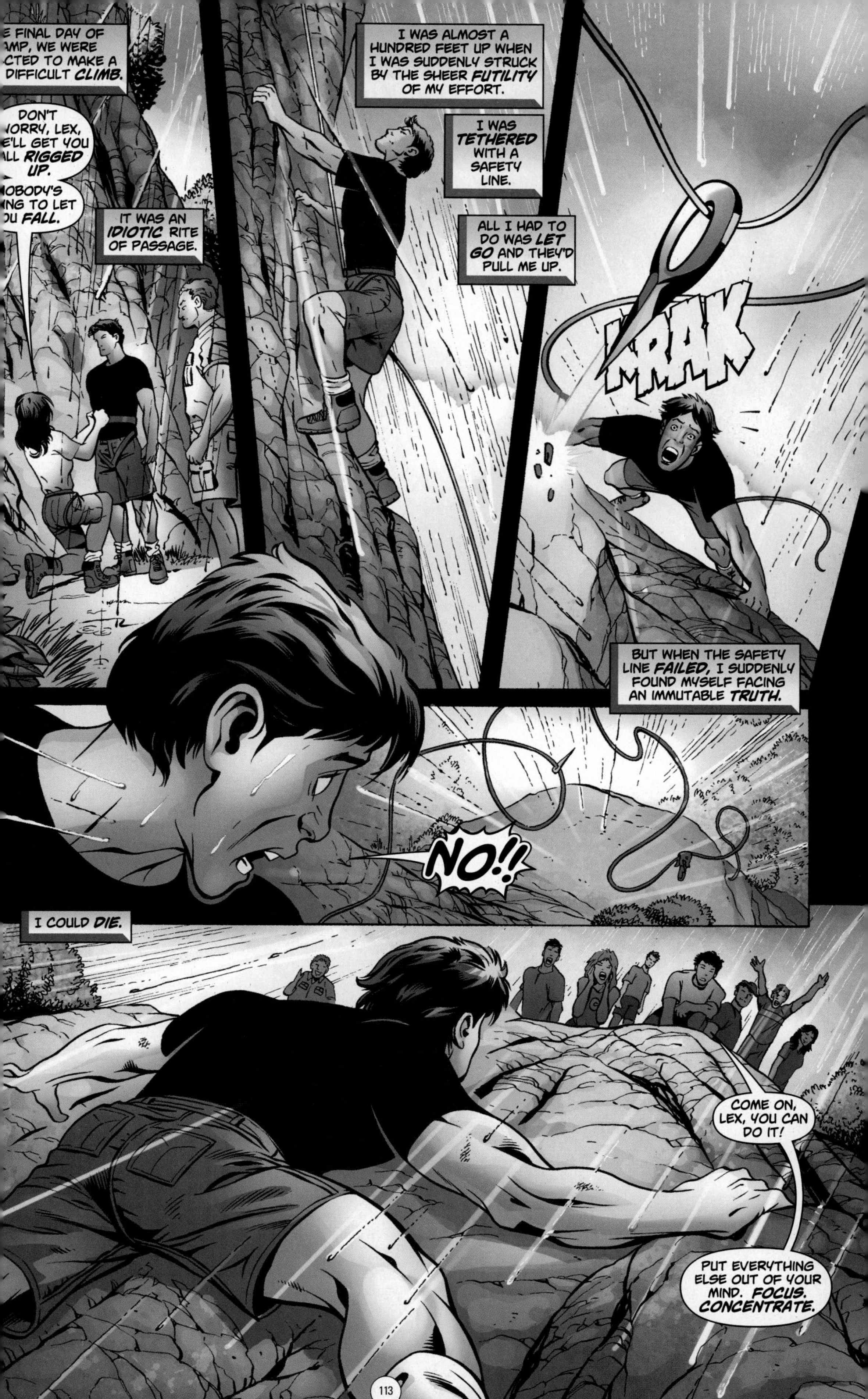
E FINAL DAY OF AMP, WE WERE CTED TO MAKE A DIFFICULT CLIMB.
DON'T ORRY, LEX, E'LL GET YOU ALL RIGGED UP.
OBODY'S NG TO LET OU FALL.
IT WAS AN IDIOTIC RITE OF PASSAGE.
I WAS ALMOST A HUNDRED FEET UP WHEN I WAS SUDDENLY STRUCK BY THE SHEER FUTILITY OF MY EFFORT.
I WAS TETHERED WITH A SAFETY LINE.
ALL I HAD TO DO WAS LET GO AND THEY'D PULL ME UP.
KRAK
BUT WHEN THE SAFETY LINE FAILED, I SUDDENLY FOUND MYSELF FACING AN IMMUTABLE TRUTH.
NO!!
I COULD DIE.
COME ON, LEX, YOU CAN DO IT!
PUT EVERYTHING ELSE OUT OF YOUR MIND. FOCUS. CONCENTRATE.

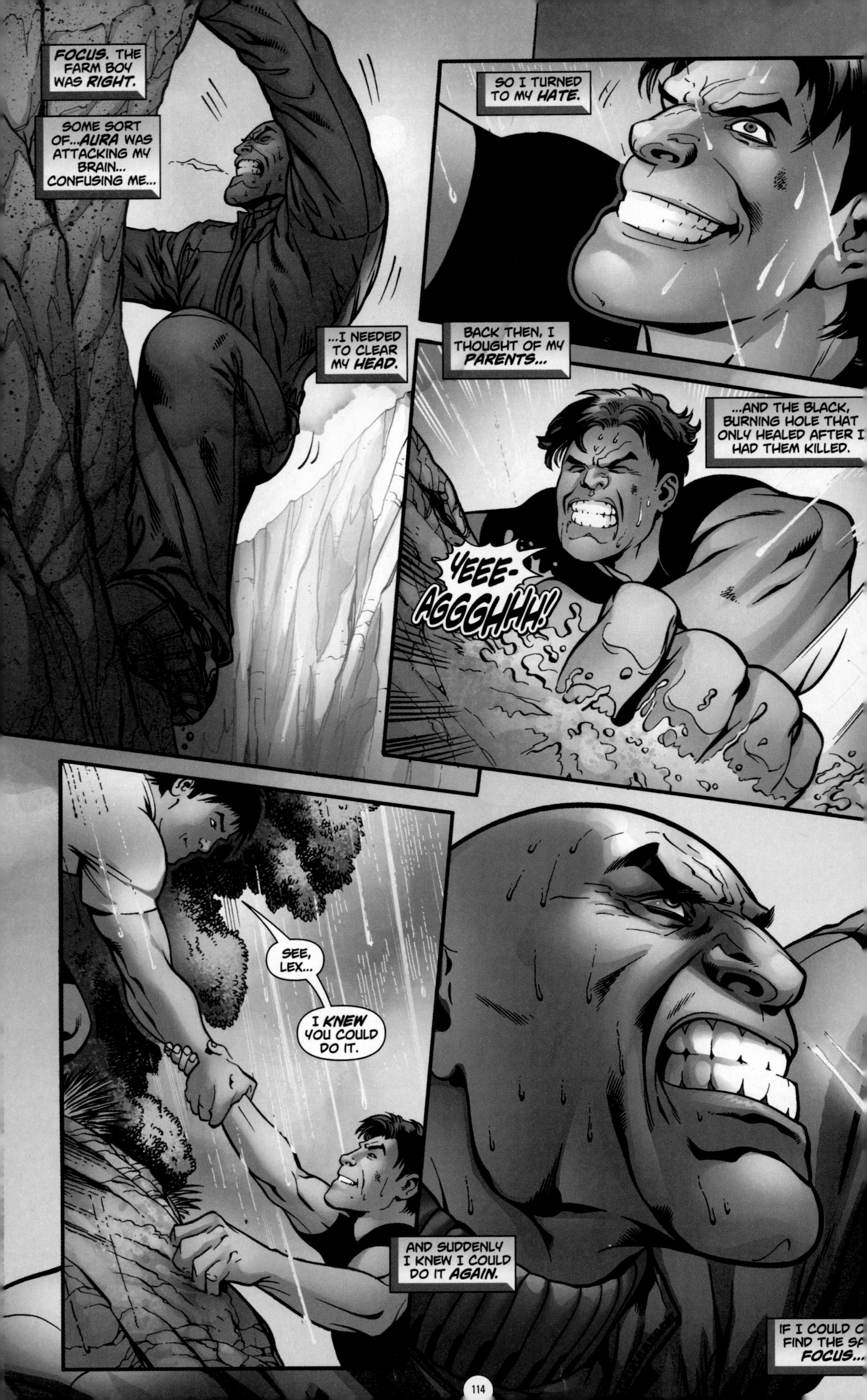

FOCUS. THE FARM BOY WAS RIGHT.
SOME SORT OF...AURA WAS ATTACKING MY BRAIN... CONFUSING ME...
SO I TURNED TO MY HATE.
...I NEEDED TO CLEAR MY HEAD.
BACK THEN, I THOUGHT OF MY PARENTS...
...AND THE BLACK, BURNING HOLE THAT ONLY HEALED AFTER I HAD THEM KILLED.
YEEE-AGGGHHH!
SEE, LEX...
I KNEW YOU COULD DO IT.
AND SUDDENLY I KNEW I COULD DO IT AGAIN.
IF I COULD
FIND THE SA
FOCUS...

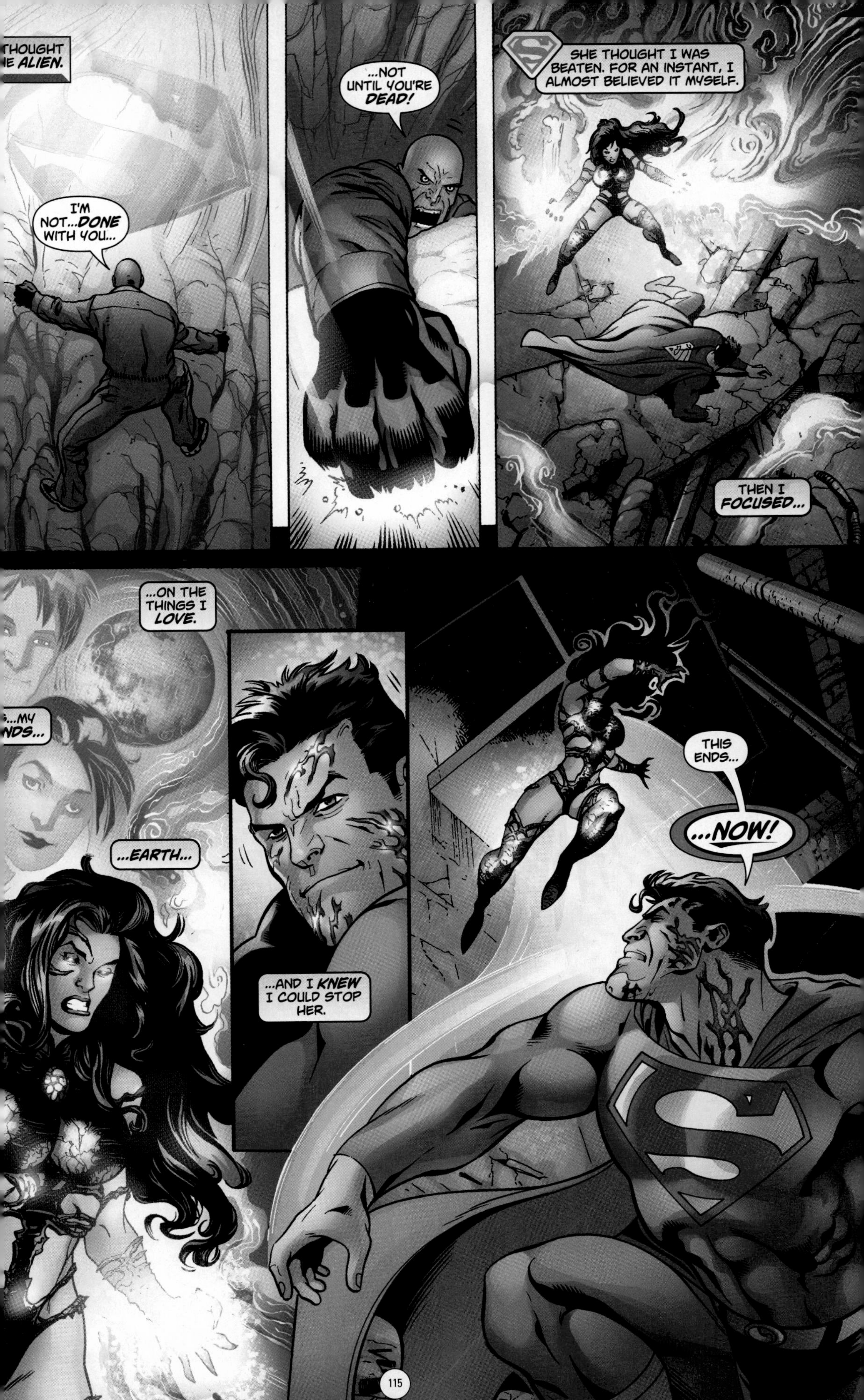

THOUGHT
E ALIEN.
I'M NOT...DONE WITH YOU...
...NOT UNTIL YOU'RE DEAD!
SHE THOUGHT I WAS BEATEN. FOR AN INSTANT, I ALMOST BELIEVED IT MYSELF.
THEN I FOCUSED...
...ON THE THINGS I LOVE.
...MY
NDS...
...EARTH...
...AND I KNEW I COULD STOP HER.
THIS ENDS...
...NOW!

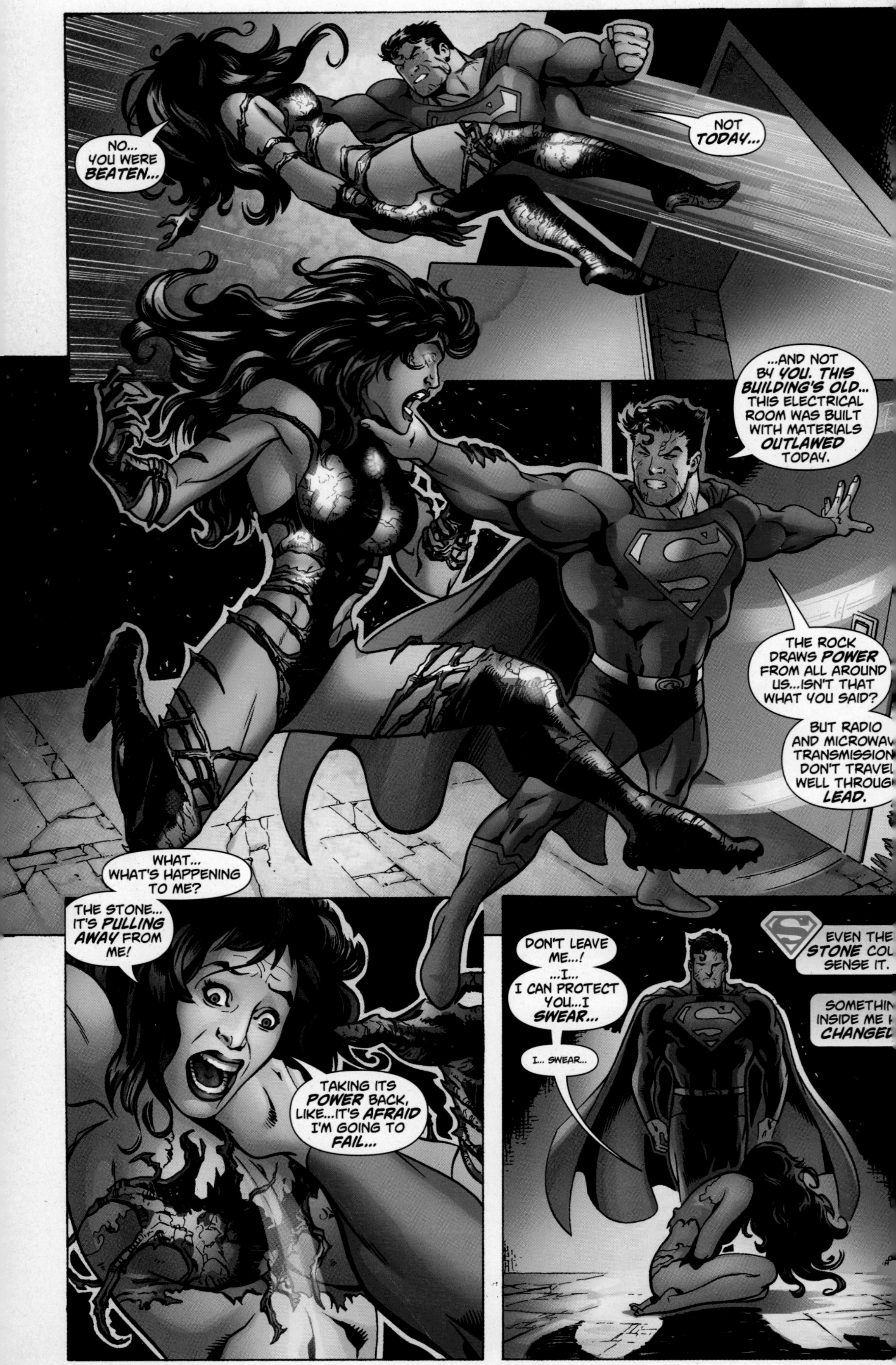
NO... YOU WERE BEATEN...
NOT TODAY...
...AND NOT BY YOU. THIS BUILDING'S OLD... THIS ELECTRICAL ROOM WAS BUILT WITH MATERIALS OUTLAWED TODAY.
THE ROCK DRAWS POWER FROM ALL AROUND US...ISN'T THAT WHAT YOU SAID?
BUT RADIO AND MICROWAV TRANSMISSION DON'T TRAVEL WELL THROUG LEAD.
WHAT... WHAT'S HAPPENING TO ME?
THE STONE... IT'S PULLING AWAY FROM ME!
TAKING ITS POWER BACK, LIKE...IT'S AFRAID I'M GOING TO FAIL...
DON'T LEAVE ME...!
...I... I CAN PROTECT YOU...I SWEAR...
I... SWEAR...
EVEN THE STONE CO SENSE IT.
SOMETHIN INSIDE ME H CHANGED

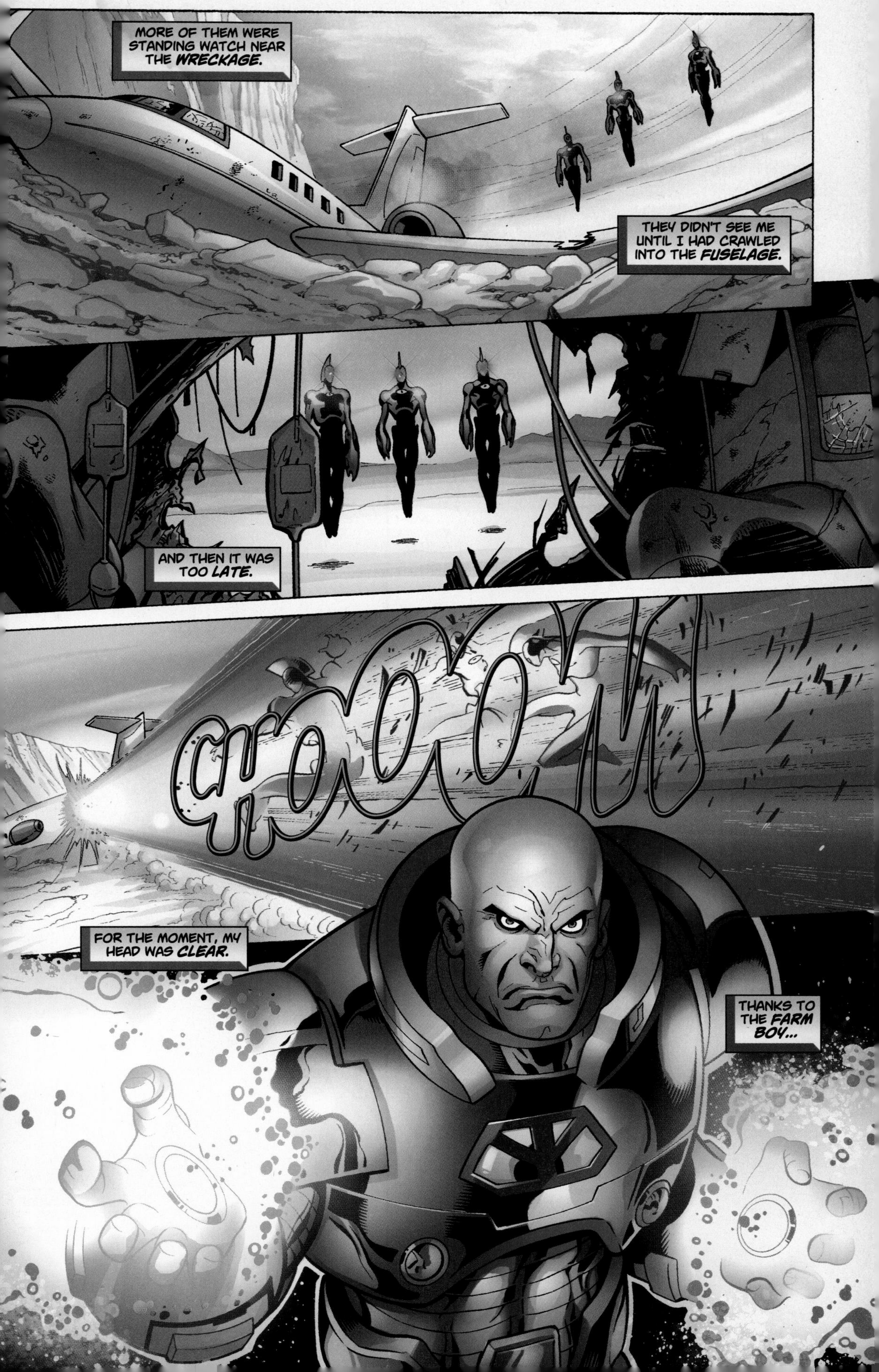
MORE OF THEM WERE STANDING WATCH NEAR THE WRECKAGE.
THEY DIDN'T SEE ME UNTIL I HAD CRAWLED INTO THE FUSELAGE.
AND THEN IT WAS TOO LATE.
GROOOM
FOR THE MOMENT, MY HEAD WAS CLEAR.
THANKS TO THE FARM BOY...

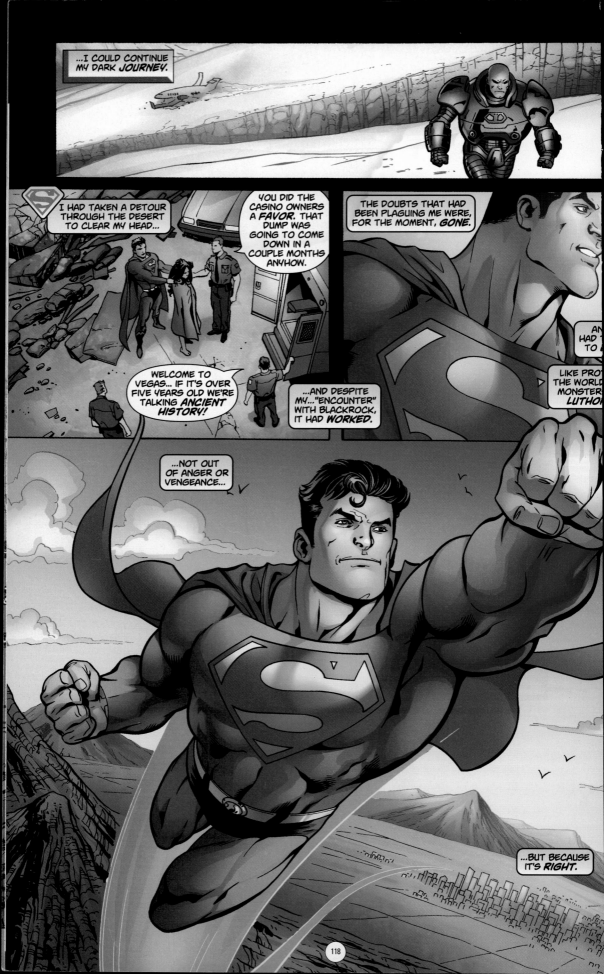

...I COULD CONTINUE MY DARK *JOURNEY*.

I HAD TAKEN A DETOUR THROUGH THE DESERT TO CLEAR MY HEAD...

YOU DID THE CASINO OWNERS A *FAVOR*. THAT DUMP WAS GOING TO COME DOWN IN A COUPLE MONTHS ANYHOW.

THE DOUBTS THAT HAD BEEN PLAGUING ME WERE, FOR THE MOMENT, *GONE*.

WELCOME TO VEGAS... IF IT'S OVER FIVE YEARS OLD WE'RE TALKING *ANCIENT HISTORY!*

...AND DESPITE MY..."ENCOUNTER" WITH BLACKROCK, IT HAD *WORKED*.

AN HAD TO TO

LIKE PRO THE WORLD MONSTER LUTHO

...NOT OUT OF ANGER OR VENGEANCE...

...BUT BECAUSE IT'S *RIGHT*.

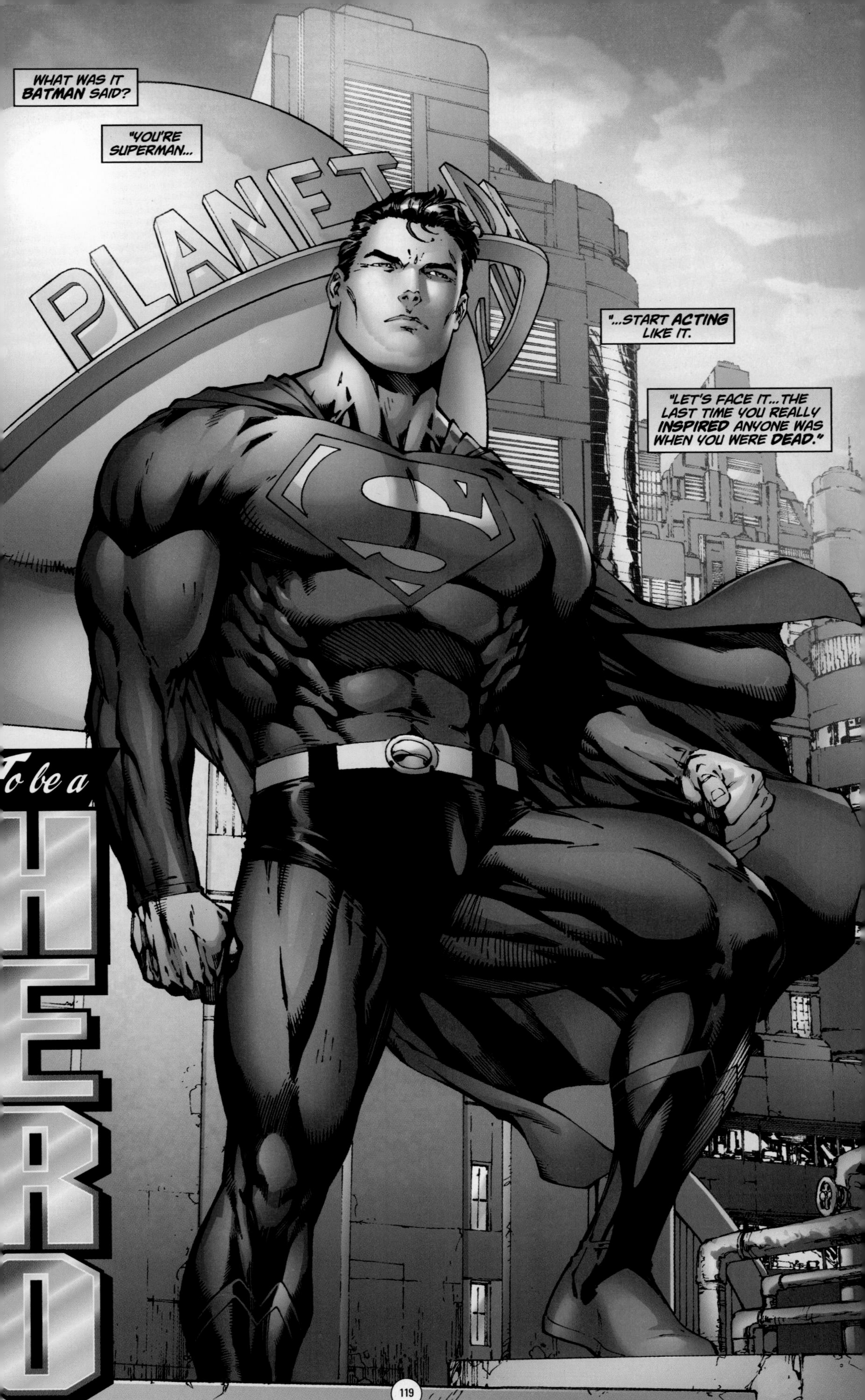
WHAT WAS IT BATMAN SAID?
"YOU'RE SUPERMAN...
PLANET
"...START ACTING LIKE IT.
"LET'S FACE IT...THE LAST TIME YOU REALLY INSPIRED ANYONE WAS WHEN YOU WERE DEAD."
To be a HERO

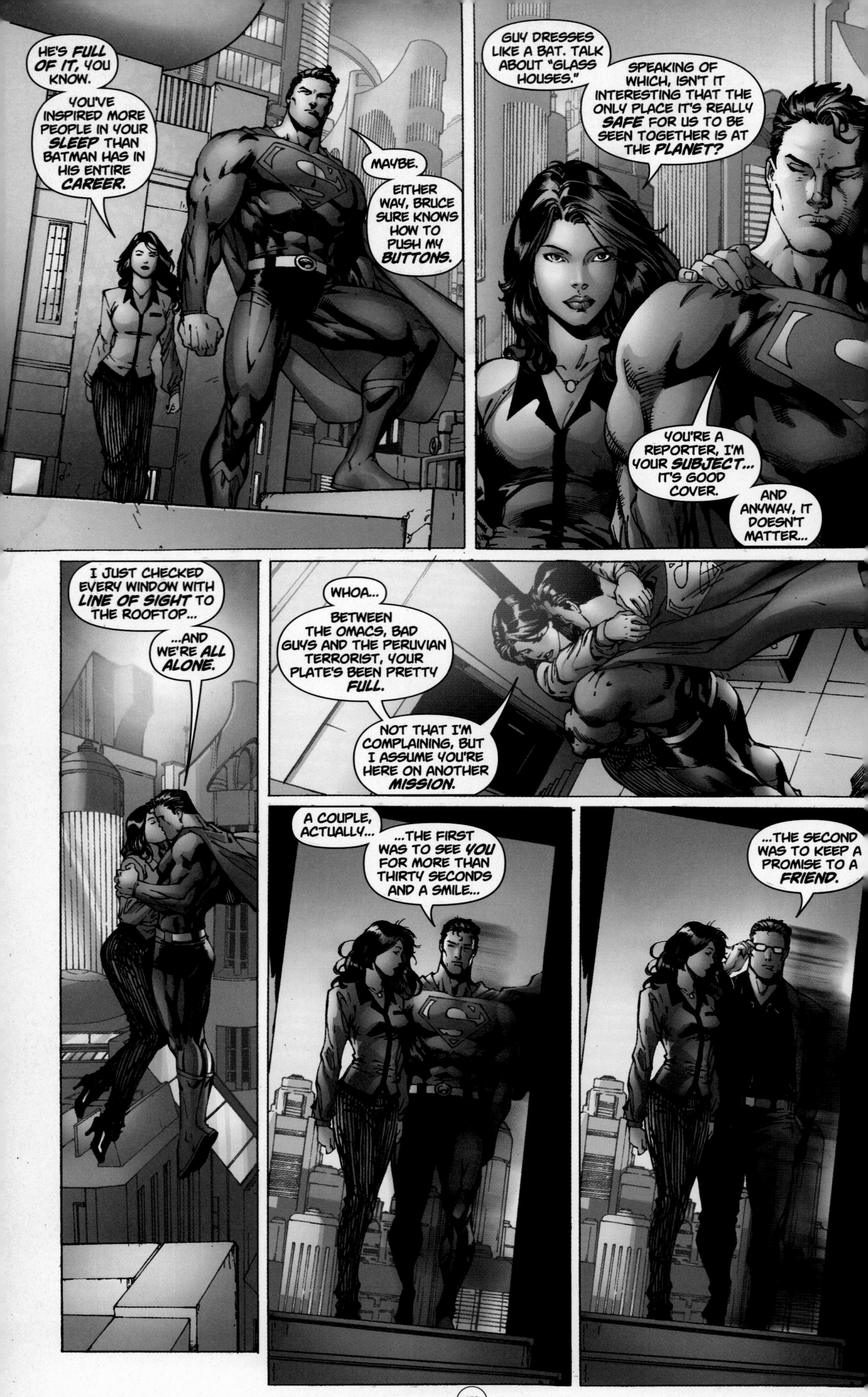
HE'S FULL OF IT, YOU KNOW.
YOU'VE INSPIRED MORE PEOPLE IN YOUR SLEEP THAN BATMAN HAS IN HIS ENTIRE CAREER.
MAYBE.
EITHER WAY, BRUCE SURE KNOWS HOW TO PUSH MY BUTTONS.
GUY DRESSES LIKE A BAT. TALK ABOUT "GLASS HOUSES."
SPEAKING OF WHICH, ISN'T IT INTERESTING THAT THE ONLY PLACE IT'S REALLY SAFE FOR US TO BE SEEN TOGETHER IS AT THE PLANET?
YOU'RE A REPORTER, I'M YOUR SUBJECT... IT'S GOOD COVER.
AND ANYWAY, IT DOESN'T MATTER...
I JUST CHECKED EVERY WINDOW WITH LINE OF SIGHT TO THE ROOFTOP...
...AND WE'RE ALL ALONE.
WHOA...
BETWEEN THE OMACS, BAD GUYS AND THE PERUVIAN TERRORIST, YOUR PLATE'S BEEN PRETTY FULL.
NOT THAT I'M COMPLAINING, BUT I ASSUME YOU'RE HERE ON ANOTHER MISSION.
A COUPLE, ACTUALLY...
...THE FIRST WAS TO SEE YOU FOR MORE THAN THIRTY SECONDS AND A SMILE...
...THE SECOND WAS TO KEEP A PROMISE TO A FRIEND.

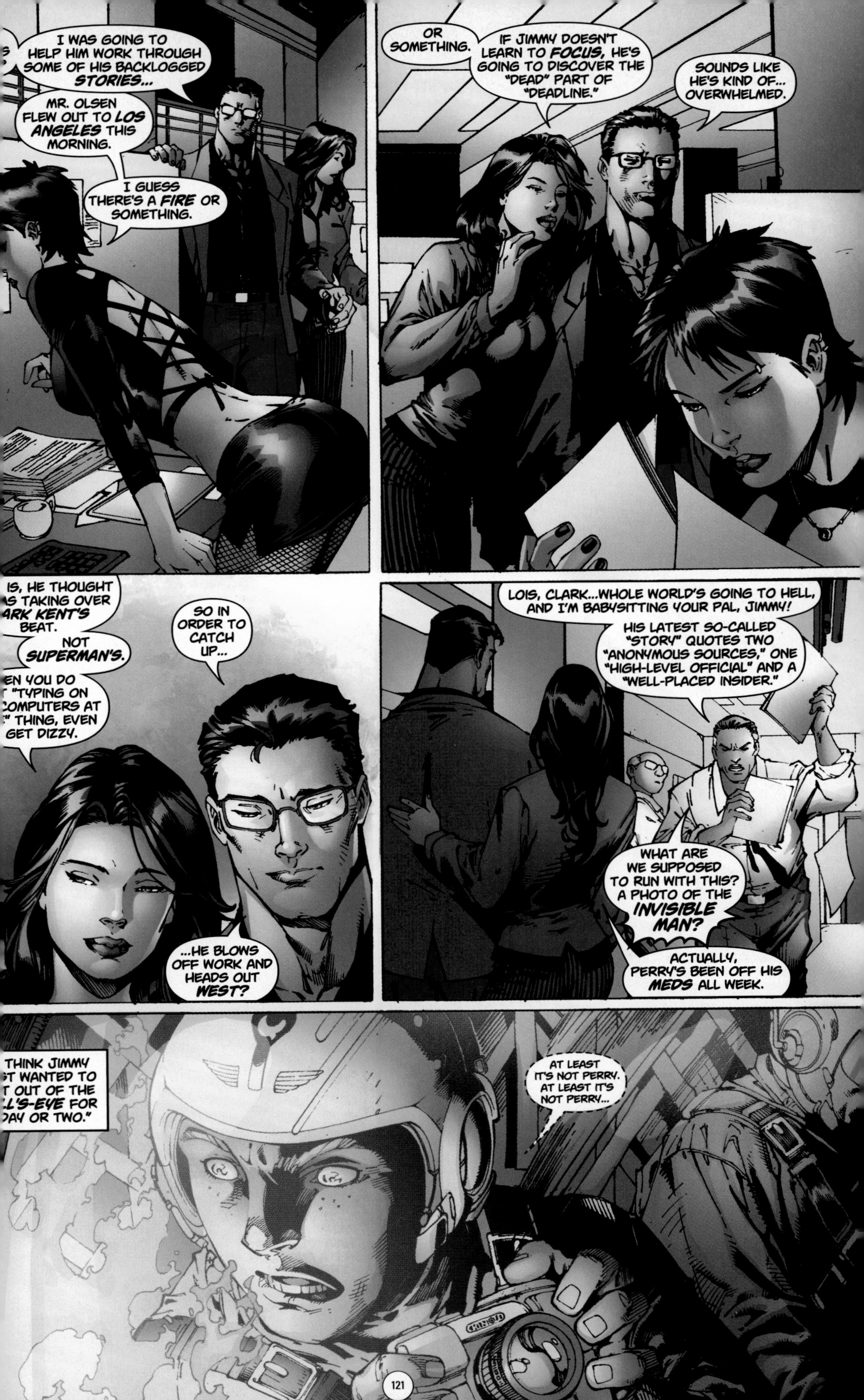

I WAS GOING TO HELP HIM WORK THROUGH SOME OF HIS BACKLOGGED STORIES...
MR. OLSEN FLEW OUT TO LOS ANGELES THIS MORNING.
I GUESS THERE'S A FIRE OR SOMETHING.
OR SOMETHING.
IF JIMMY DOESN'T LEARN TO FOCUS, HE'S GOING TO DISCOVER THE "DEAD" PART OF "DEADLINE."
SOUNDS LIKE HE'S KIND OF... OVERWHELMED.
IS, HE THOUGHT
S TAKING OVER
ARK KENT'S
BEAT.
NOT SUPERMAN'S.
EN YOU DO
"TYPING ON
COMPUTERS AT
" THING, EVEN
GET DIZZY.
SO IN ORDER TO CATCH UP...
...HE BLOWS OFF WORK AND HEADS OUT WEST?
LOIS, CLARK...WHOLE WORLD'S GOING TO HELL, AND I'M BABYSITTING YOUR PAL, JIMMY!
HIS LATEST SO-CALLED "STORY" QUOTES TWO "ANONYMOUS SOURCES," ONE "HIGH-LEVEL OFFICIAL" AND A "WELL-PLACED INSIDER."
WHAT ARE WE SUPPOSED TO RUN WITH THIS? A PHOTO OF THE INVISIBLE MAN?
ACTUALLY, PERRY'S BEEN OFF HIS MEDS ALL WEEK.
THINK JIMMY
ST WANTED TO
T OUT OF THE
L'S-EYE FOR
DAY OR TWO."
AT LEAST IT'S NOT PERRY. AT LEAST IT'S NOT PERRY...

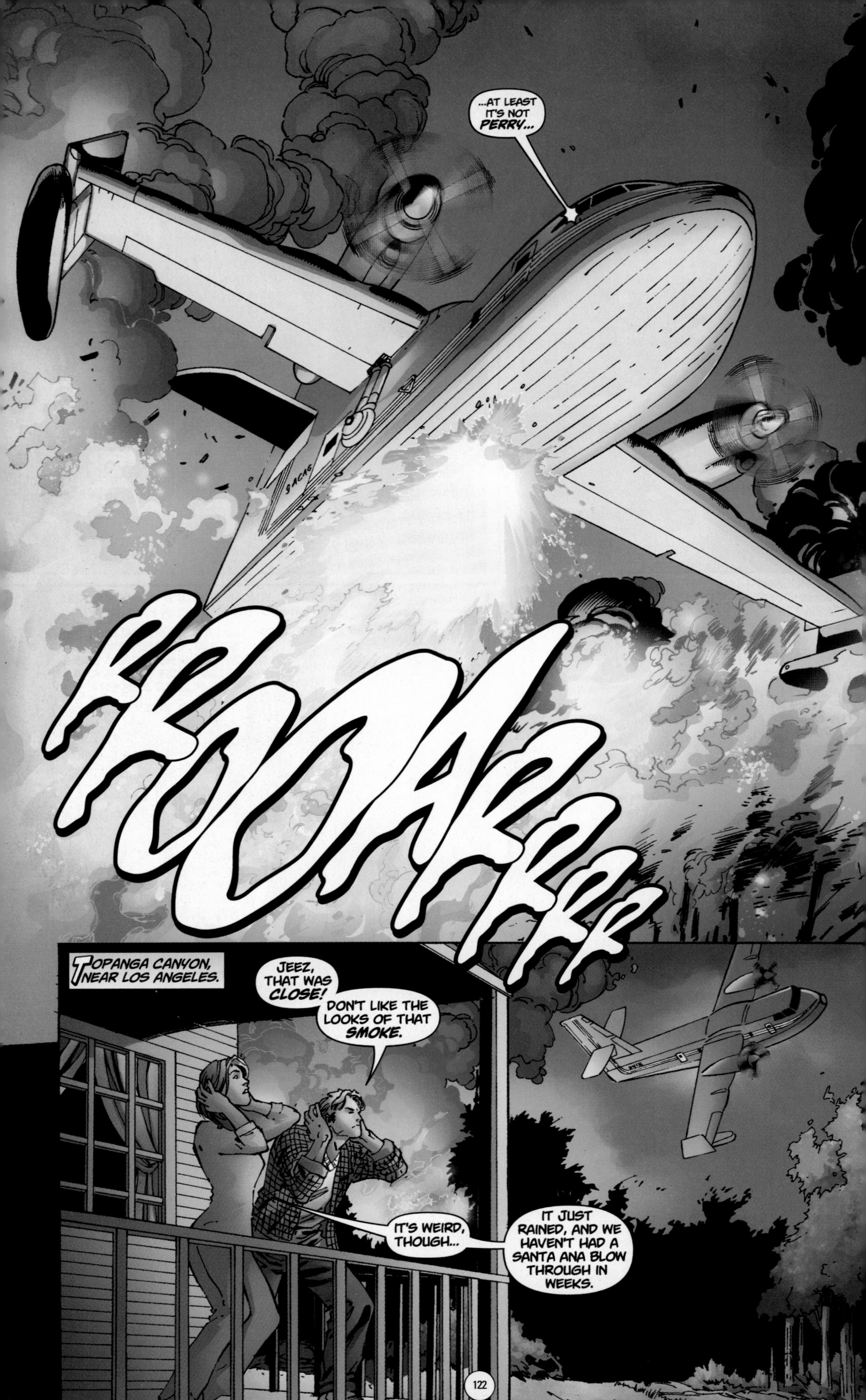

...AT LEAST IT'S NOT PERRY...
ROOARRRR
TOPANGA CANYON, NEAR LOS ANGELES.
JEEZ, THAT WAS CLOSE!
DON'T LIKE THE LOOKS OF THAT SMOKE.
IT'S WEIRD, THOUGH...
IT JUST RAINED, AND WE HAVEN'T HAD A SANTA ANA BLOW THROUGH IN WEEKS.

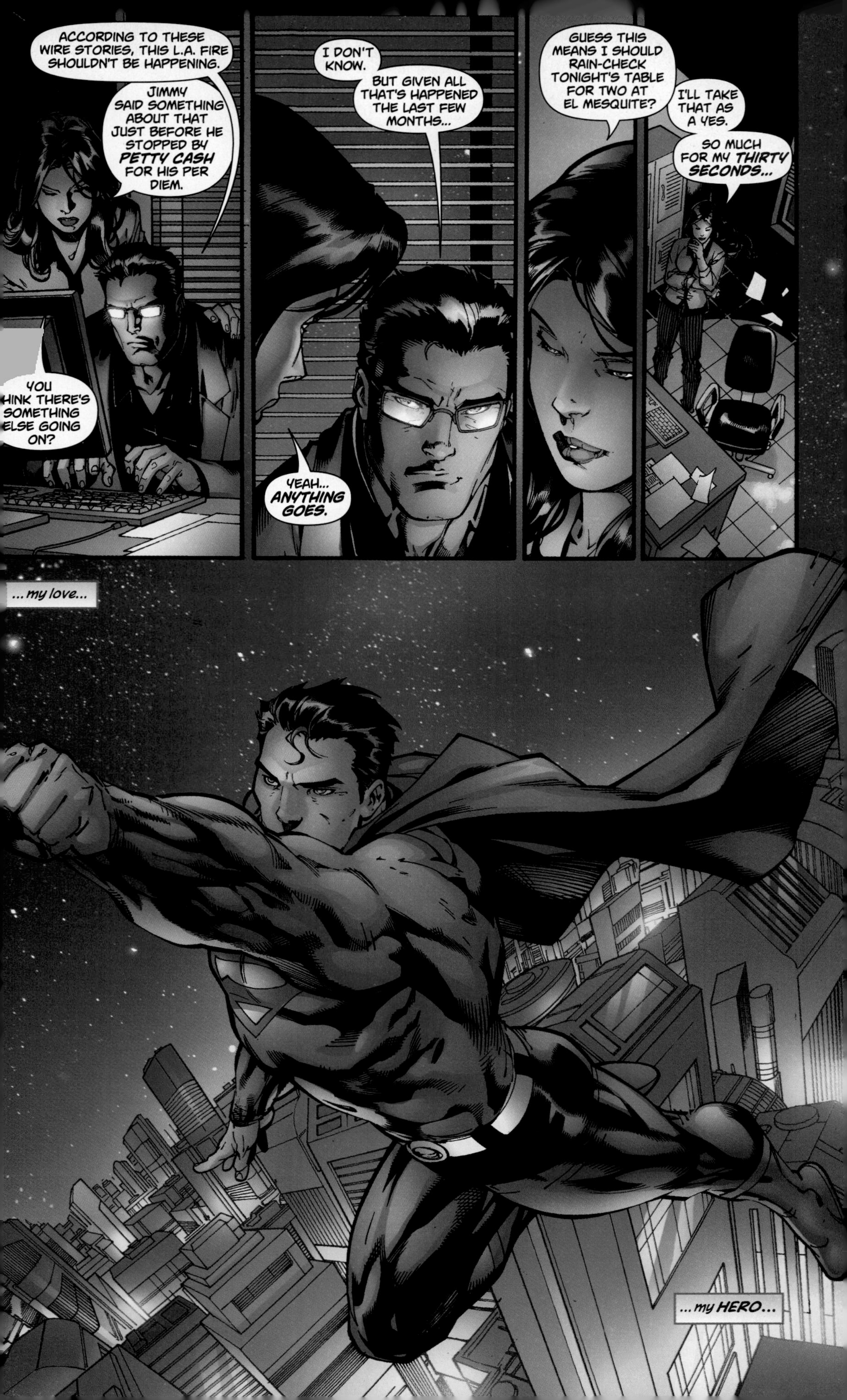
ACCORDING TO THESE WIRE STORIES, THIS L.A. FIRE SHOULDN'T BE HAPPENING.
JIMMY SAID SOMETHING ABOUT THAT JUST BEFORE HE STOPPED BY **PETTY CASH** FOR HIS PER DIEM.
YOU HINK THERE'S SOMETHING ELSE GOING ON?
I DON'T KNOW.
BUT GIVEN ALL THAT'S HAPPENED THE LAST FEW MONTHS...
YEAH... **ANYTHING GOES.**
GUESS THIS MEANS I SHOULD RAIN-CHECK TONIGHT'S TABLE FOR TWO AT EL MESQUITE?
I'LL TAKE THAT AS A YES.
SO MUCH FOR MY **THIRTY SECONDS...**
...my love...
...my **HERO**...

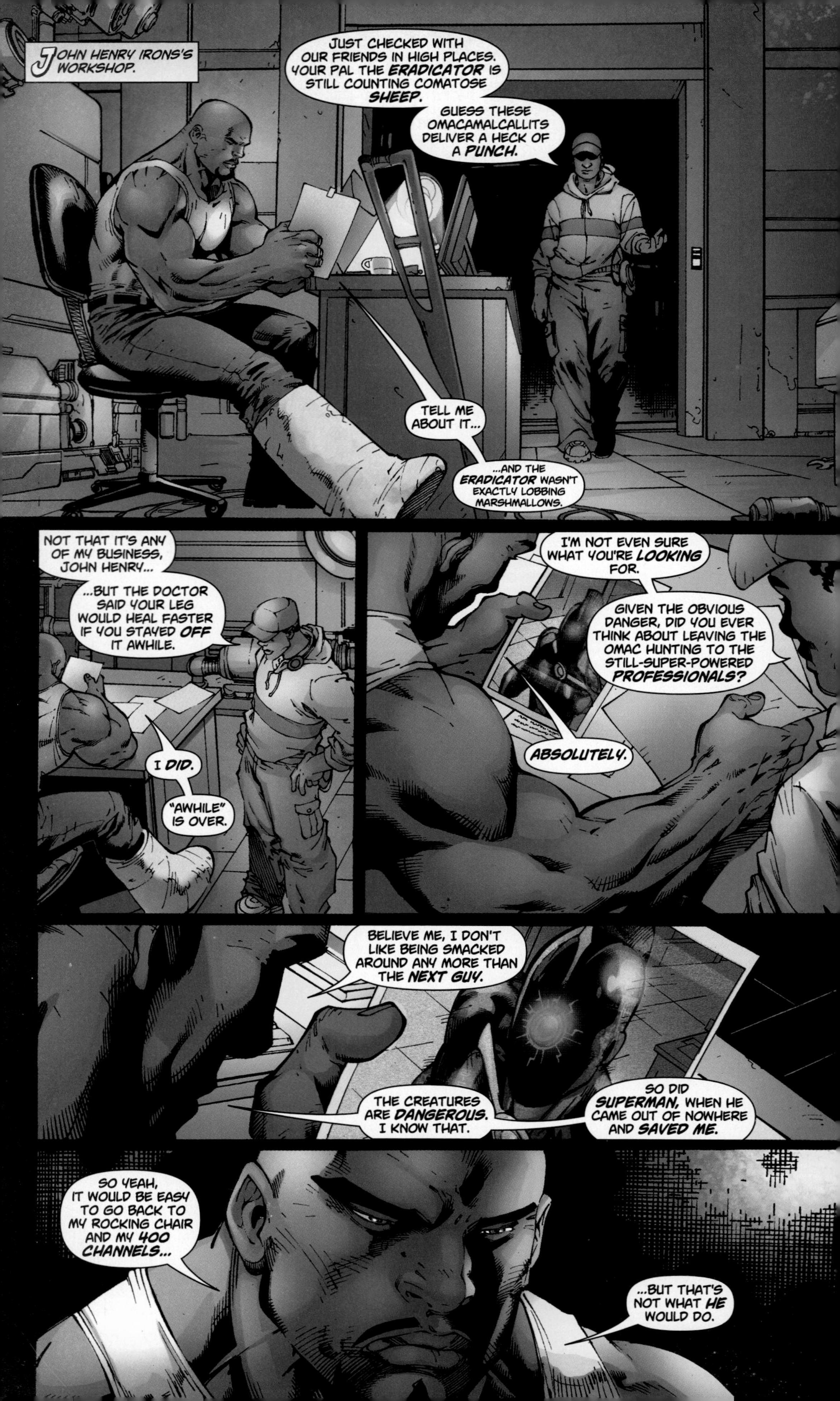
JOHN HENRY IRONS'S WORKSHOP.
JUST CHECKED WITH OUR FRIENDS IN HIGH PLACES. YOUR PAL THE ERADICATOR IS STILL COUNTING COMATOSE SHEEP.
GUESS THESE OMACAMALCALLITS DELIVER A HECK OF A PUNCH.
TELL ME ABOUT IT...
...AND THE ERADICATOR WASN'T EXACTLY LOBBING MARSHMALLOWS.
NOT THAT IT'S ANY OF MY BUSINESS, JOHN HENRY...
...BUT THE DOCTOR SAID YOUR LEG WOULD HEAL FASTER IF YOU STAYED OFF IT AWHILE.
I DID.
"AWHILE" IS OVER.
I'M NOT EVEN SURE WHAT YOU'RE LOOKING FOR.
GIVEN THE OBVIOUS DANGER, DID YOU EVER THINK ABOUT LEAVING THE OMAC HUNTING TO THE STILL-SUPER-POWERED PROFESSIONALS?
ABSOLUTELY.
BELIEVE ME, I DON'T LIKE BEING SMACKED AROUND ANY MORE THAN THE NEXT GUY.
THE CREATURES ARE DANGEROUS. I KNOW THAT.
SO DID SUPERMAN, WHEN HE CAME OUT OF NOWHERE AND SAVED ME.
SO YEAH, IT WOULD BE EASY TO GO BACK TO MY ROCKING CHAIR AND MY 400 CHANNELS...
...BUT THAT'S NOT WHAT HE WOULD DO.

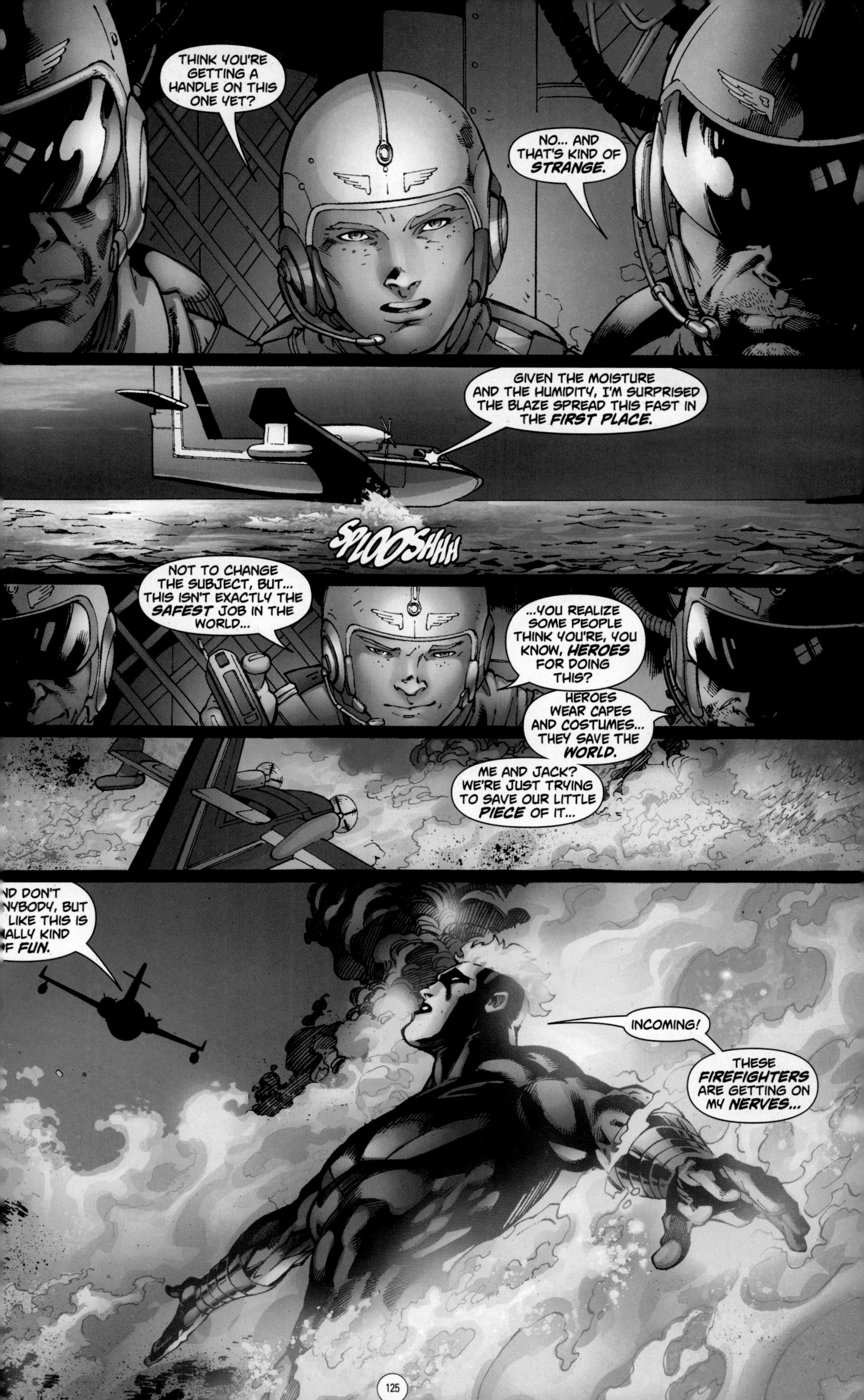
THINK YOU'RE GETTING A HANDLE ON THIS ONE YET?
NO... AND THAT'S KIND OF STRANGE.
GIVEN THE MOISTURE AND THE HUMIDITY, I'M SURPRISED THE BLAZE SPREAD THIS FAST IN THE FIRST PLACE.
SPLOOSHHH
NOT TO CHANGE THE SUBJECT, BUT... THIS ISN'T EXACTLY THE SAFEST JOB IN THE WORLD...
...YOU REALIZE SOME PEOPLE THINK YOU'RE, YOU KNOW, HEROES FOR DOING THIS?
HEROES WEAR CAPES AND COSTUMES... THEY SAVE THE WORLD.
ME AND JACK? WE'RE JUST TRYING TO SAVE OUR LITTLE PIECE OF IT...
ND DON'T NYBODY, BUT LIKE THIS IS ALLY KIND F FUN.
INCOMING!
THESE FIREFIGHTERS ARE GETTING ON MY NERVES...

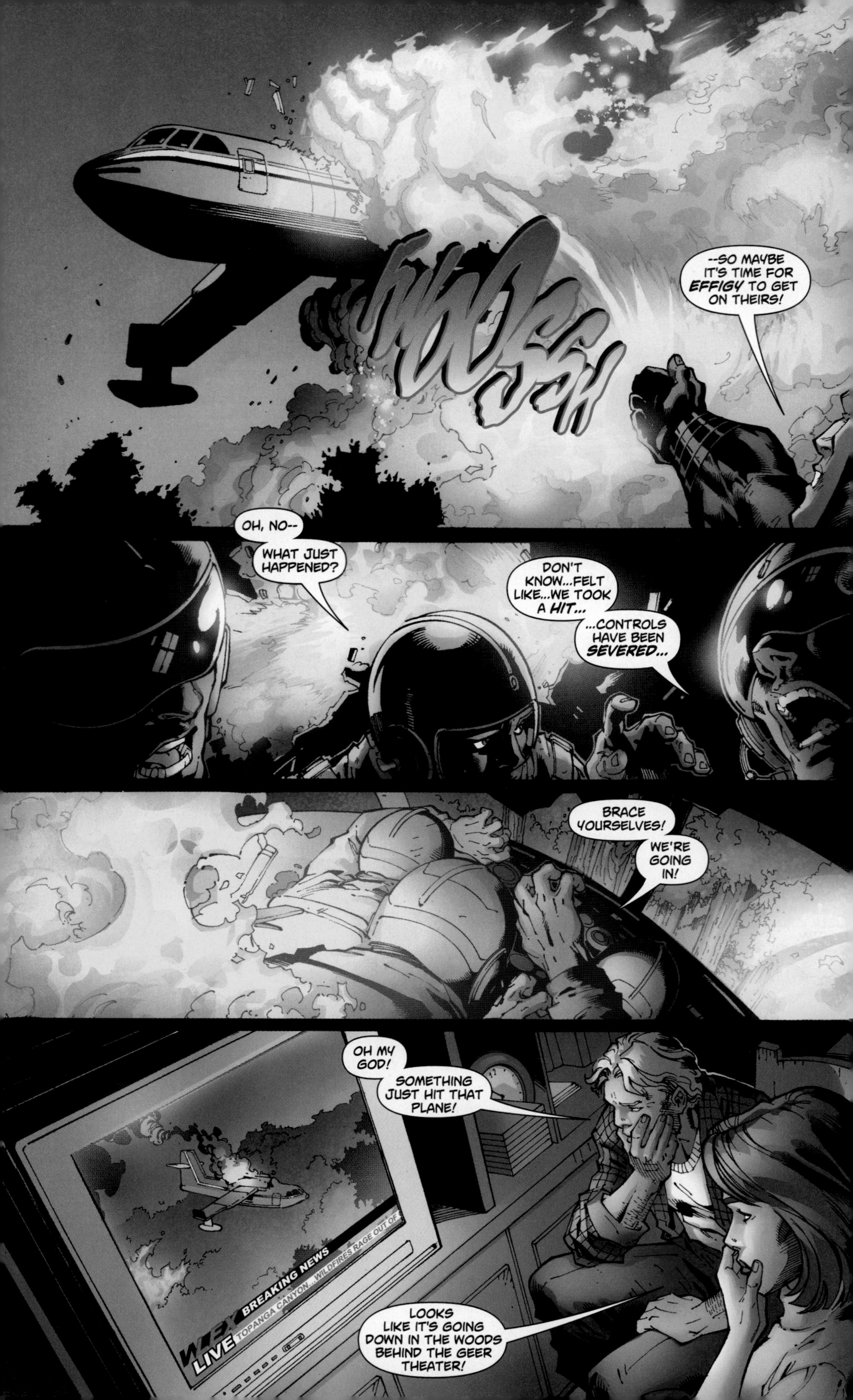

--SO MAYBE IT'S TIME FOR EFFIGY TO GET ON THEIRS!
OH, NO--
WHAT JUST HAPPENED?
DON'T KNOW...FELT LIKE...WE TOOK A HIT...
...CONTROLS HAVE BEEN SEVERED...
BRACE YOURSELVES!
WE'RE GOING IN!
OH MY GOD!
SOMETHING JUST HIT THAT PLANE!
BREAKING NEWS
LIVE
TOPANGA CANYON...WILDFIRES RAGE OUT OF
LOOKS LIKE IT'S GOING DOWN IN THE WOODS BEHIND THE GEER THEATER!

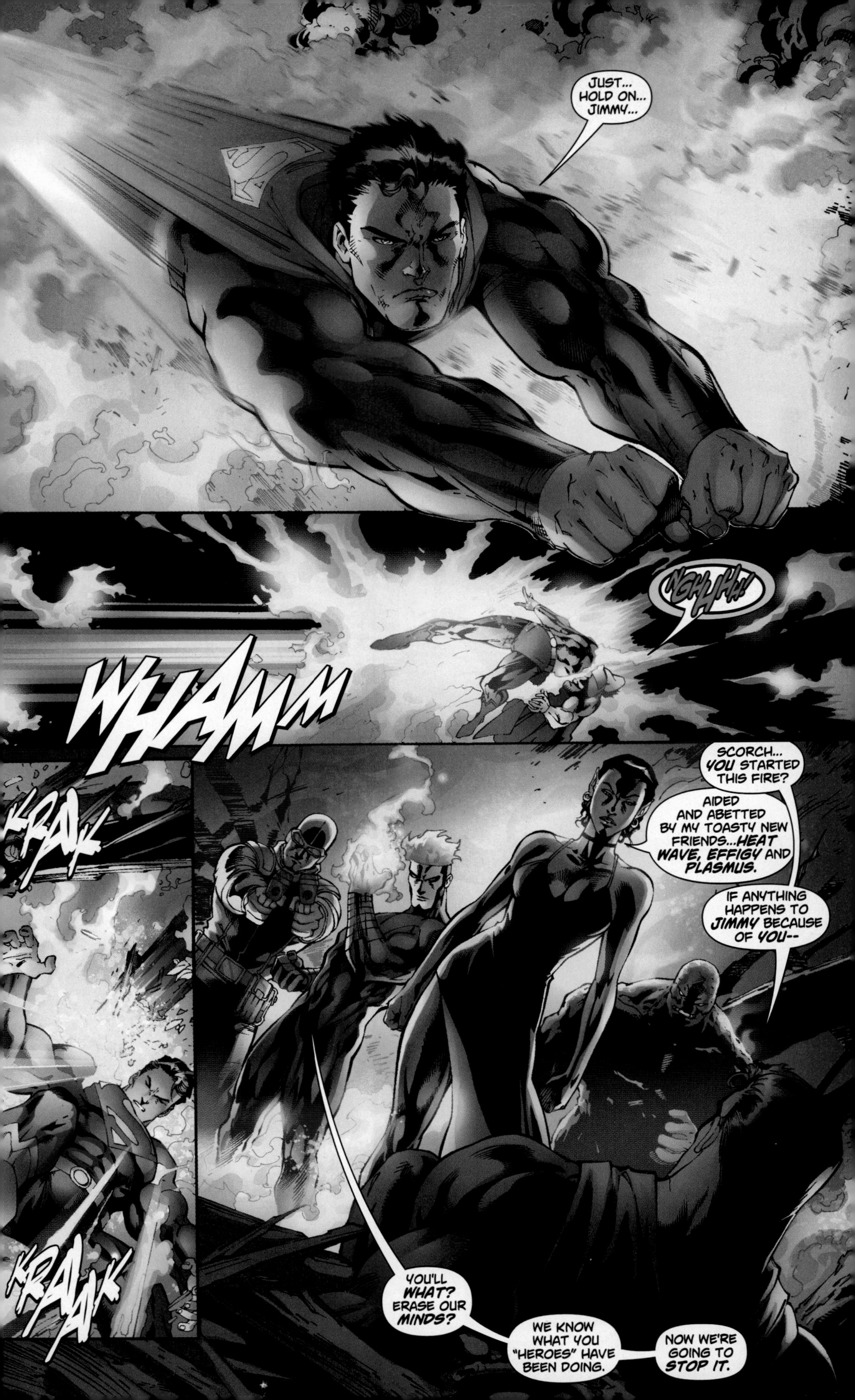
JUST... HOLD ON... JIMMY...
NGHHH!
WHAMM
KRAK
KRAAK
SCORCH... YOU STARTED THIS FIRE?
AIDED AND ABETTED BY MY TOASTY NEW FRIENDS...HEAT WAVE, EFFIGY AND PLASMUS.
IF ANYTHING HAPPENS TO JIMMY BECAUSE OF YOU--
YOU'LL WHAT? ERASE OUR MINDS?
WE KNOW WHAT YOU "HEROES" HAVE BEEN DOING.
NOW WE'RE GOING TO STOP IT.

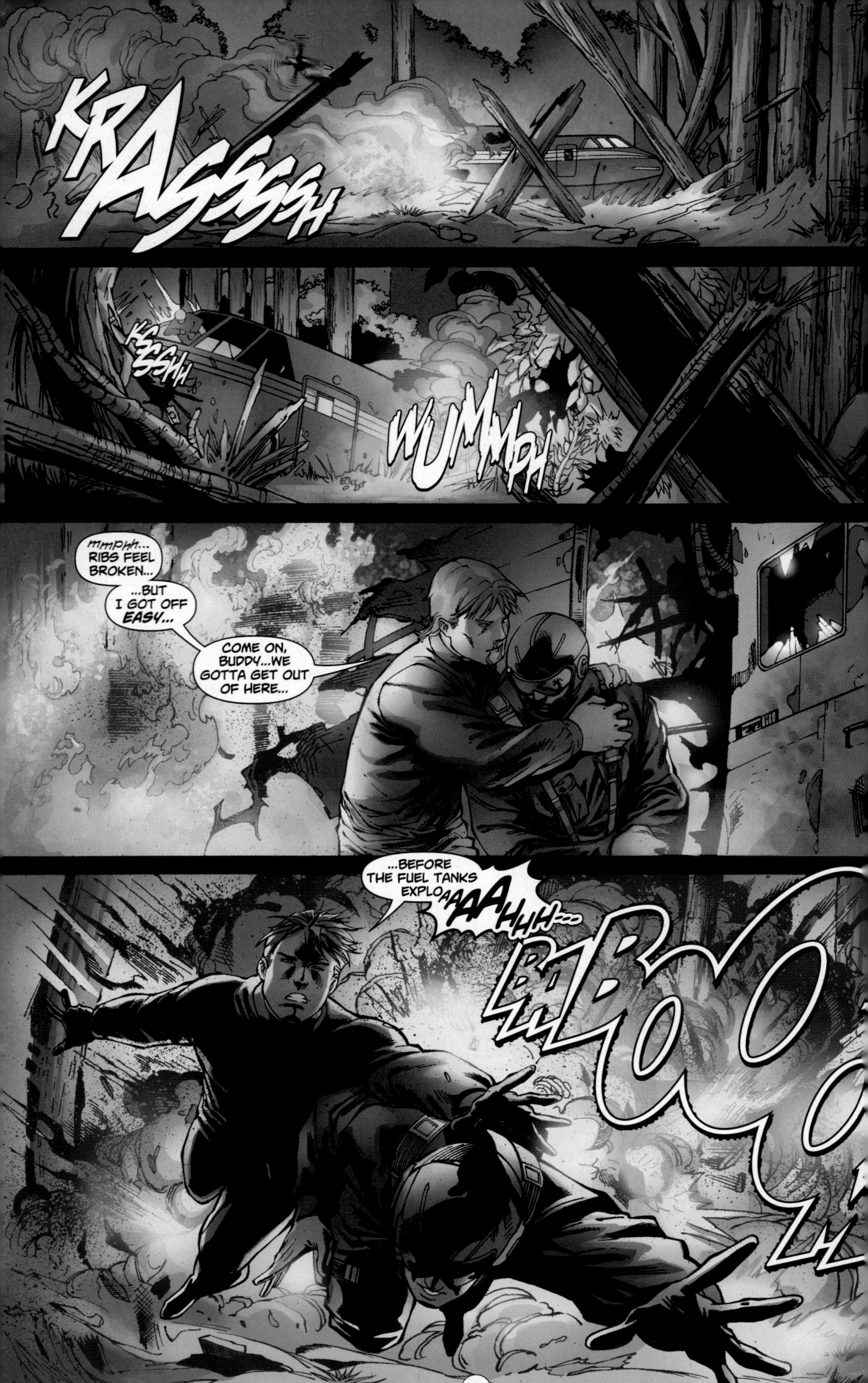
KRASSSSH
KSSSHH
WUMMPH
mmphh... RIBS FEEL BROKEN...
...BUT I GOT OFF EASY...
COME ON, BUDDY...WE GOTTA GET OUT OF HERE...
...BEFORE THE FUEL TANKS EXPLOAAAAHHH--

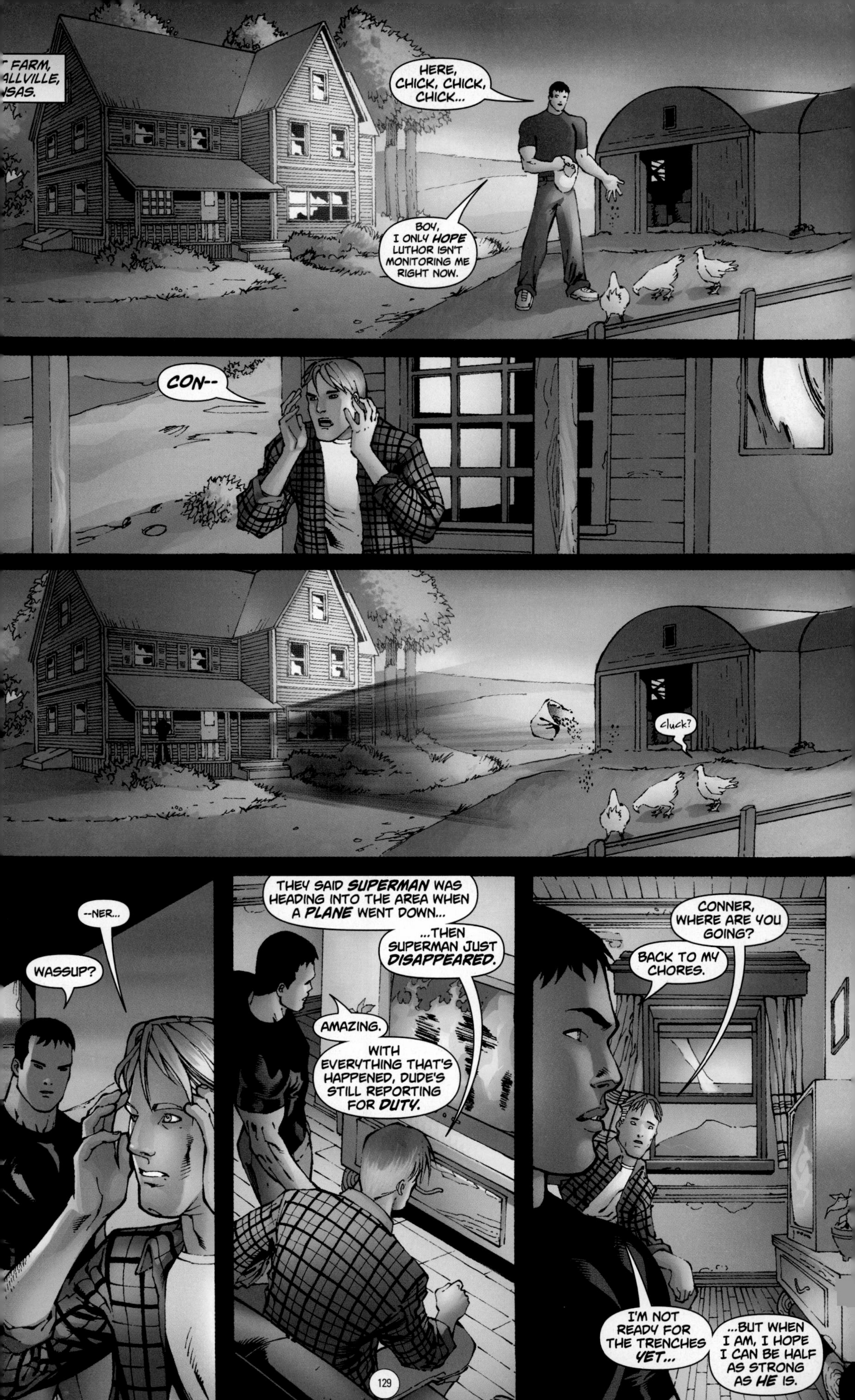
FARM,
ALLVILLE,
NSAS.
HERE, CHICK, CHICK, CHICK...
BOY, I ONLY HOPE LUTHOR ISN'T MONITORING ME RIGHT NOW.
CON--
cluck?
--NER...
WASSUP?
THEY SAID SUPERMAN WAS HEADING INTO THE AREA WHEN A PLANE WENT DOWN...
...THEN SUPERMAN JUST DISAPPEARED.
AMAZING.
WITH EVERYTHING THAT'S HAPPENED, DUDE'S STILL REPORTING FOR DUTY.
CONNER, WHERE ARE YOU GOING?
BACK TO MY CHORES.
I'M NOT READY FOR THE TRENCHES YET...
...BUT WHEN I AM, I HOPE I CAN BE HALF AS STRONG AS HE IS.

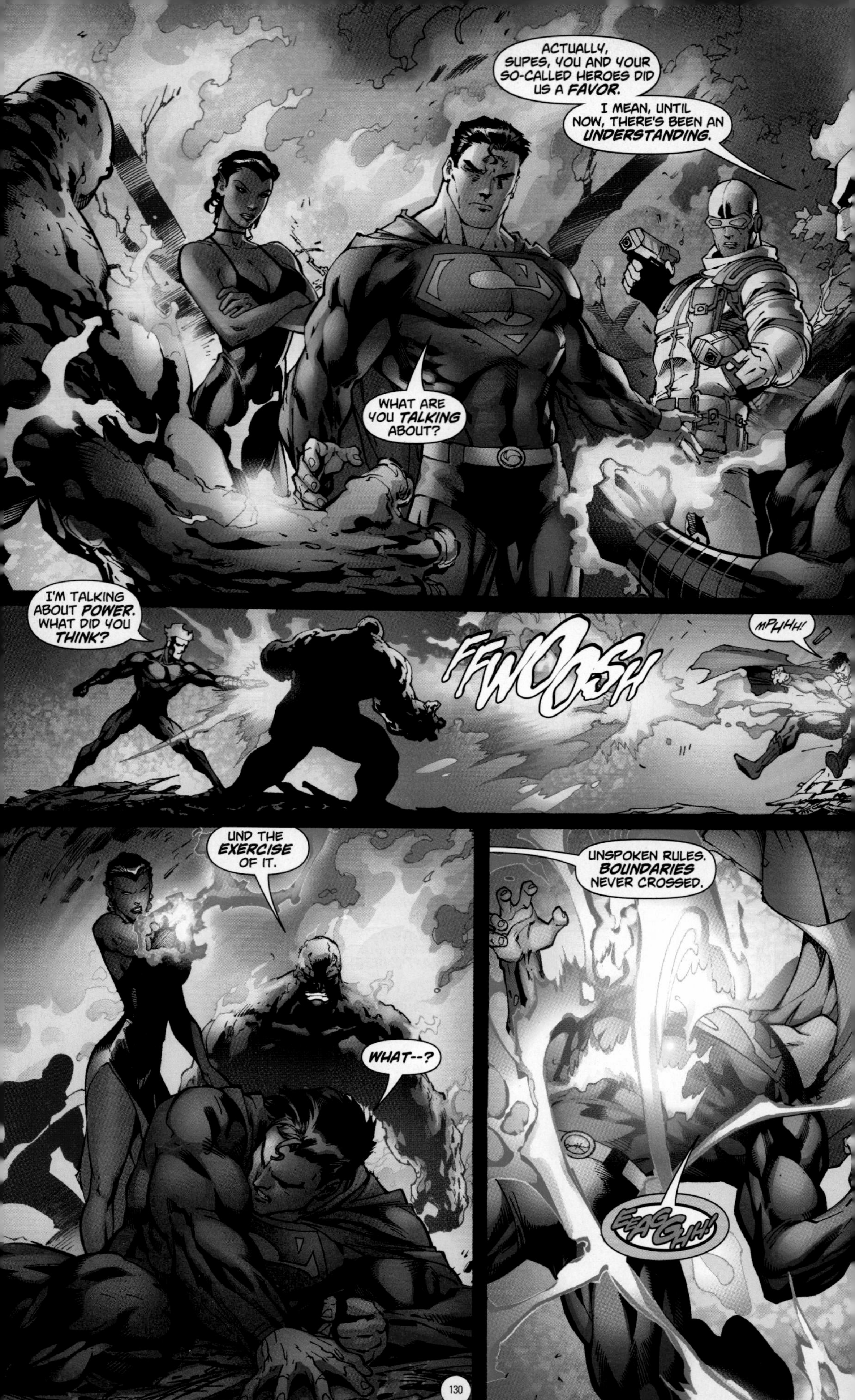
ACTUALLY, SUPES, YOU AND YOUR SO-CALLED HEROES DID US A FAVOR.
I MEAN, UNTIL NOW, THERE'S BEEN AN UNDERSTANDING.
WHAT ARE YOU TALKING ABOUT?
I'M TALKING ABOUT POWER. WHAT DID YOU THINK?
FFWOOSH
MPHHH!
UND THE EXERCISE OF IT.
WHAT--?
UNSPOKEN RULES. BOUNDARIES NEVER CROSSED.
EEAGGHH!

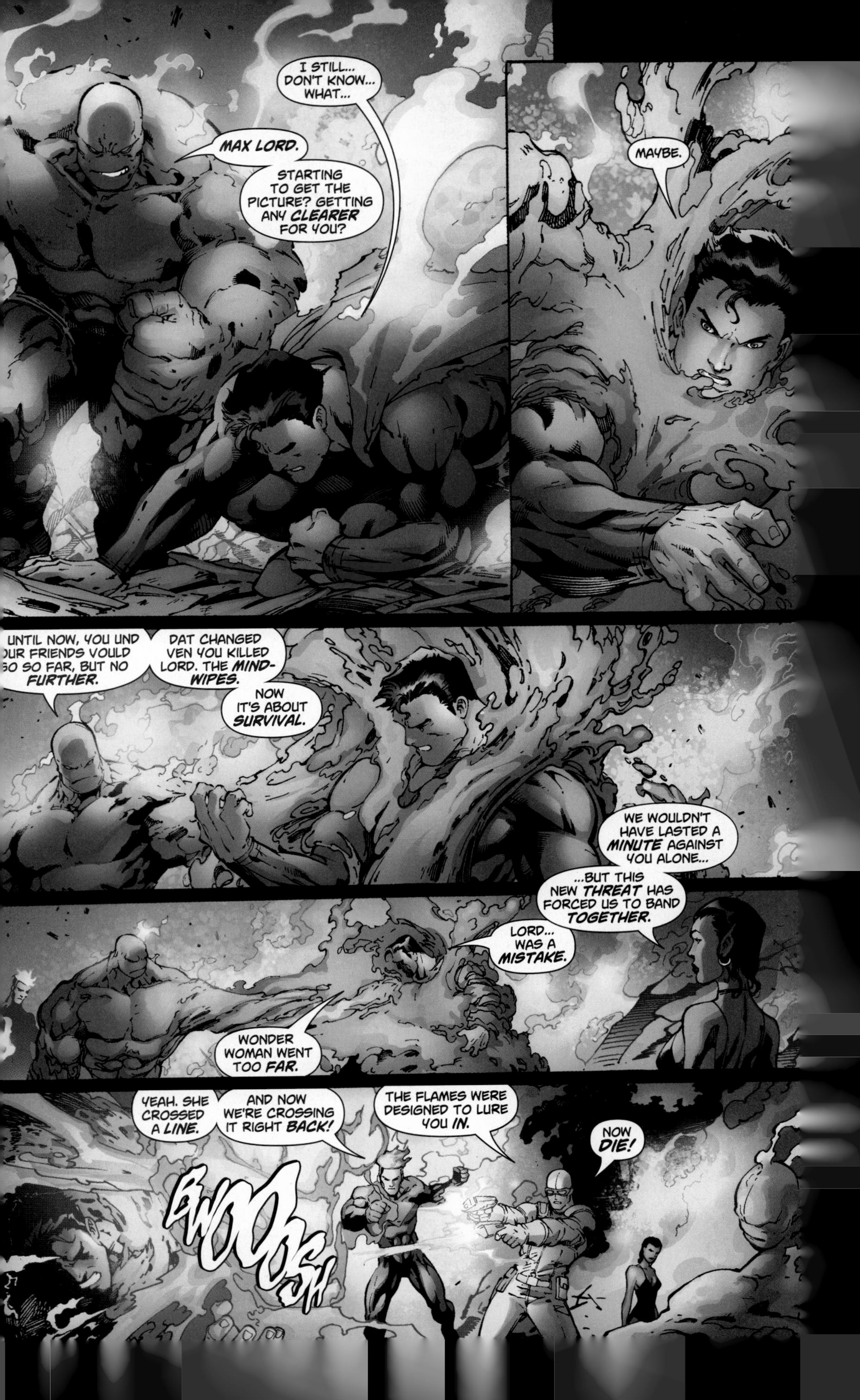

I STILL... DON'T KNOW... WHAT...
MAX LORD.
STARTING TO GET THE PICTURE? GETTING ANY CLEARER FOR YOU?
MAYBE.
UNTIL NOW, YOU UND OUR FRIENDS VOULD GO SO FAR, BUT NO FURTHER.
DAT CHANGED VEN YOU KILLED LORD. THE MIND-WIPES.
NOW IT'S ABOUT SURVIVAL.
WE WOULDN'T HAVE LASTED A MINUTE AGAINST YOU ALONE...
...BUT THIS NEW THREAT HAS FORCED US TO BAND TOGETHER.
LORD... WAS A MISTAKE.
WONDER WOMAN WENT TOO FAR.
YEAH. SHE CROSSED A LINE.
AND NOW WE'RE CROSSING IT RIGHT BACK!
THE FLAMES WERE DESIGNED TO LURE YOU IN.
NOW DIE!
FWOOOOSH

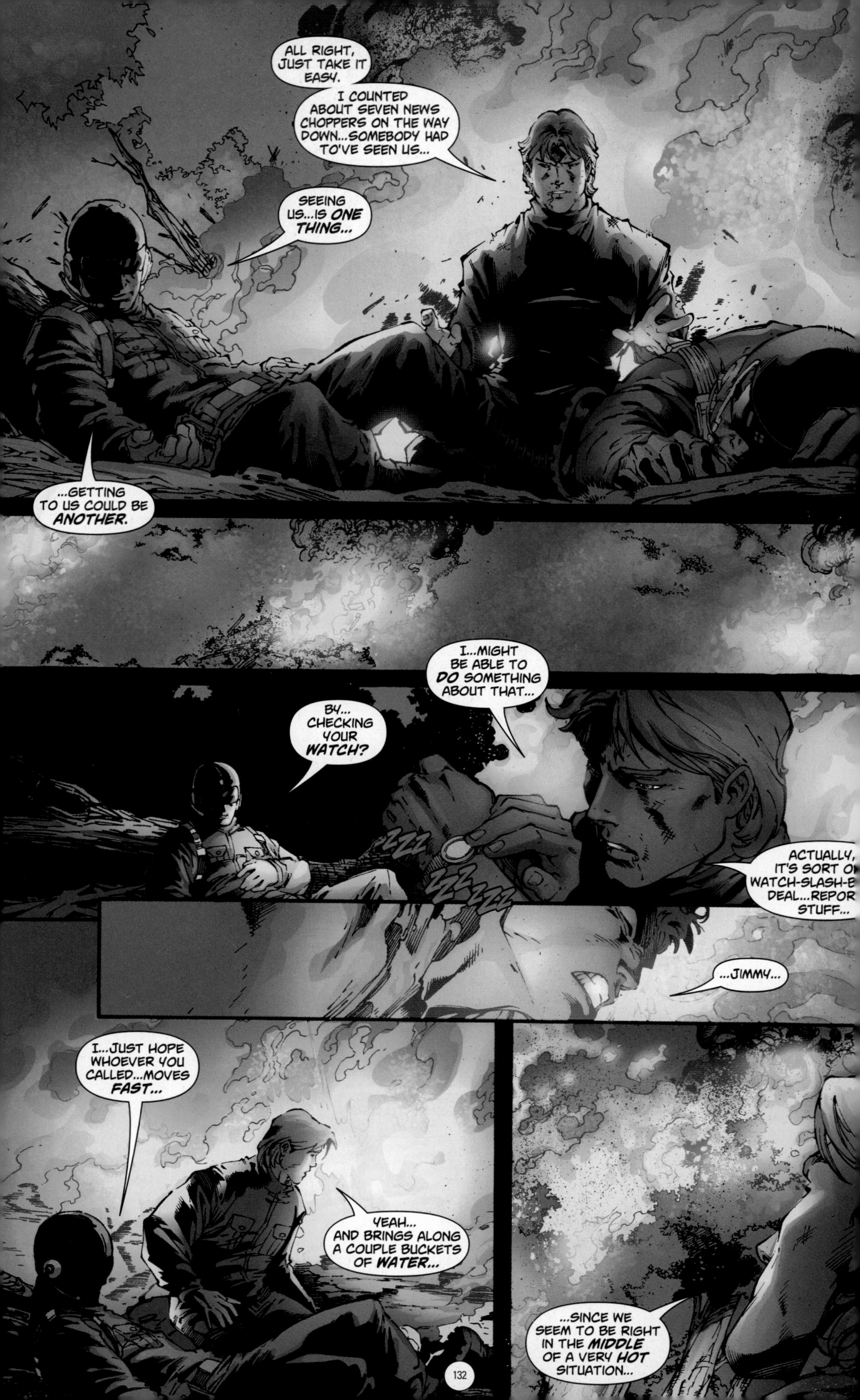
ALL RIGHT, JUST TAKE IT EASY.
I COUNTED ABOUT SEVEN NEWS CHOPPERS ON THE WAY DOWN...SOMEBODY HAD TO'VE SEEN US...
SEEING US...IS ONE THING...
...GETTING TO US COULD BE ANOTHER.
I...MIGHT BE ABLE TO DO SOMETHING ABOUT THAT...
BY... CHECKING YOUR WATCH?
ACTUALLY, IT'S SORT O WATCH-SLASH-B DEAL...REPOR STUFF...
...JIMMY...
I...JUST HOPE WHOEVER YOU CALLED...MOVES FAST...
YEAH... AND BRINGS ALONG A COUPLE BUCKETS OF WATER...
...SINCE WE SEEM TO BE RIGHT IN THE MIDDLE OF A VERY HOT SITUATION...

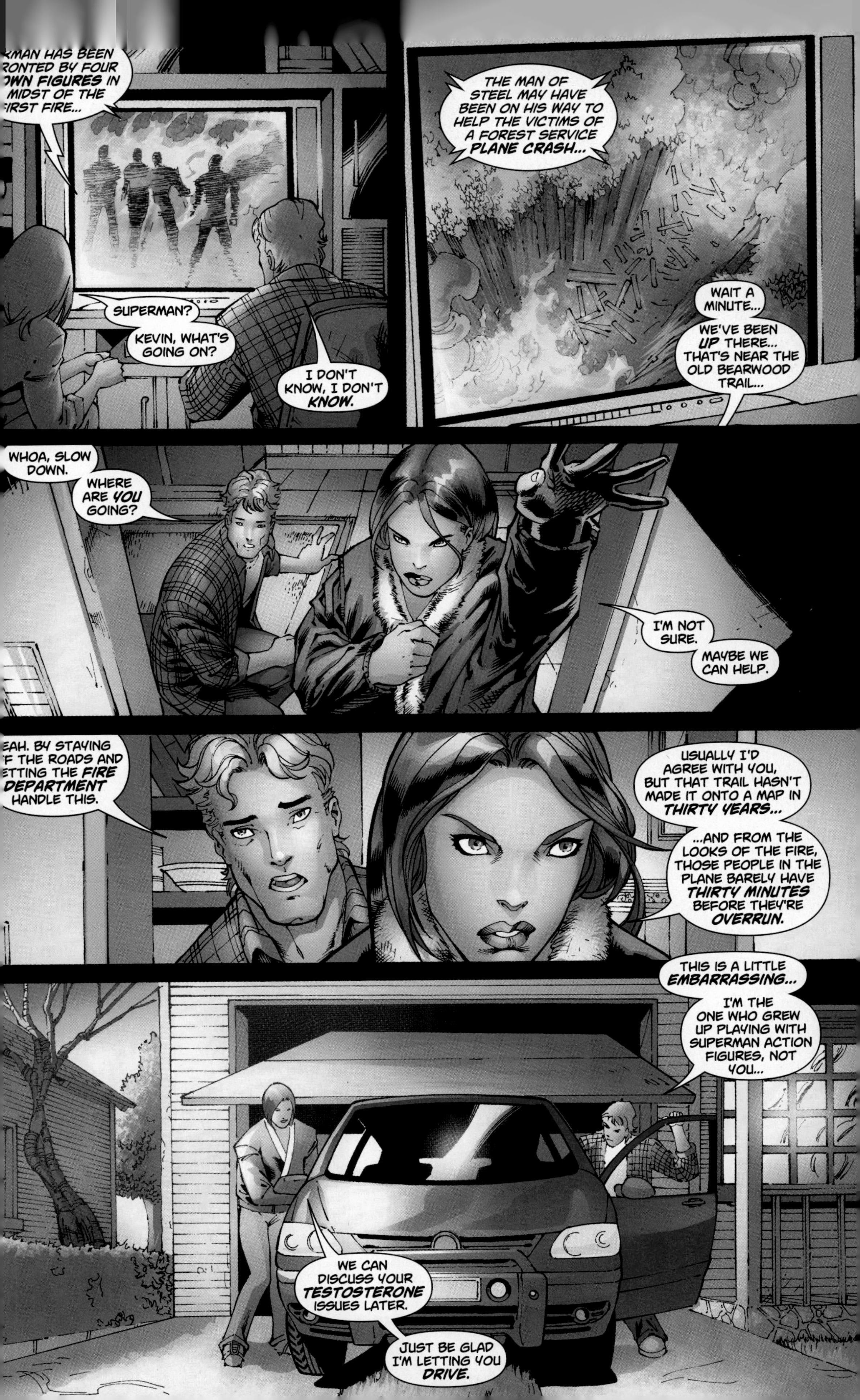

RMAN HAS BEEN RONTED BY FOUR OWN FIGURES IN MIDST OF THE FIRST FIRE...
SUPERMAN?
KEVIN, WHAT'S GOING ON?
I DON'T KNOW, I DON'T KNOW.
THE MAN OF STEEL MAY HAVE BEEN ON HIS WAY TO HELP THE VICTIMS OF A FOREST SERVICE PLANE CRASH...
WAIT A MINUTE...
WE'VE BEEN UP THERE... THAT'S NEAR THE OLD BEARWOOD TRAIL...
WHOA, SLOW DOWN.
WHERE ARE YOU GOING?
I'M NOT SURE.
MAYBE WE CAN HELP.
EAH. BY STAYING F THE ROADS AND ETTING THE FIRE DEPARTMENT HANDLE THIS.
USUALLY I'D AGREE WITH YOU, BUT THAT TRAIL HASN'T MADE IT ONTO A MAP IN THIRTY YEARS...
...AND FROM THE LOOKS OF THE FIRE, THOSE PEOPLE IN THE PLANE BARELY HAVE THIRTY MINUTES BEFORE THEY'RE OVERRUN.
THIS IS A LITTLE EMBARRASSING...
I'M THE ONE WHO GREW UP PLAYING WITH SUPERMAN ACTION FIGURES, NOT YOU...
WE CAN DISCUSS YOUR TESTOSTERONE ISSUES LATER.
JUST BE GLAD I'M LETTING YOU DRIVE.

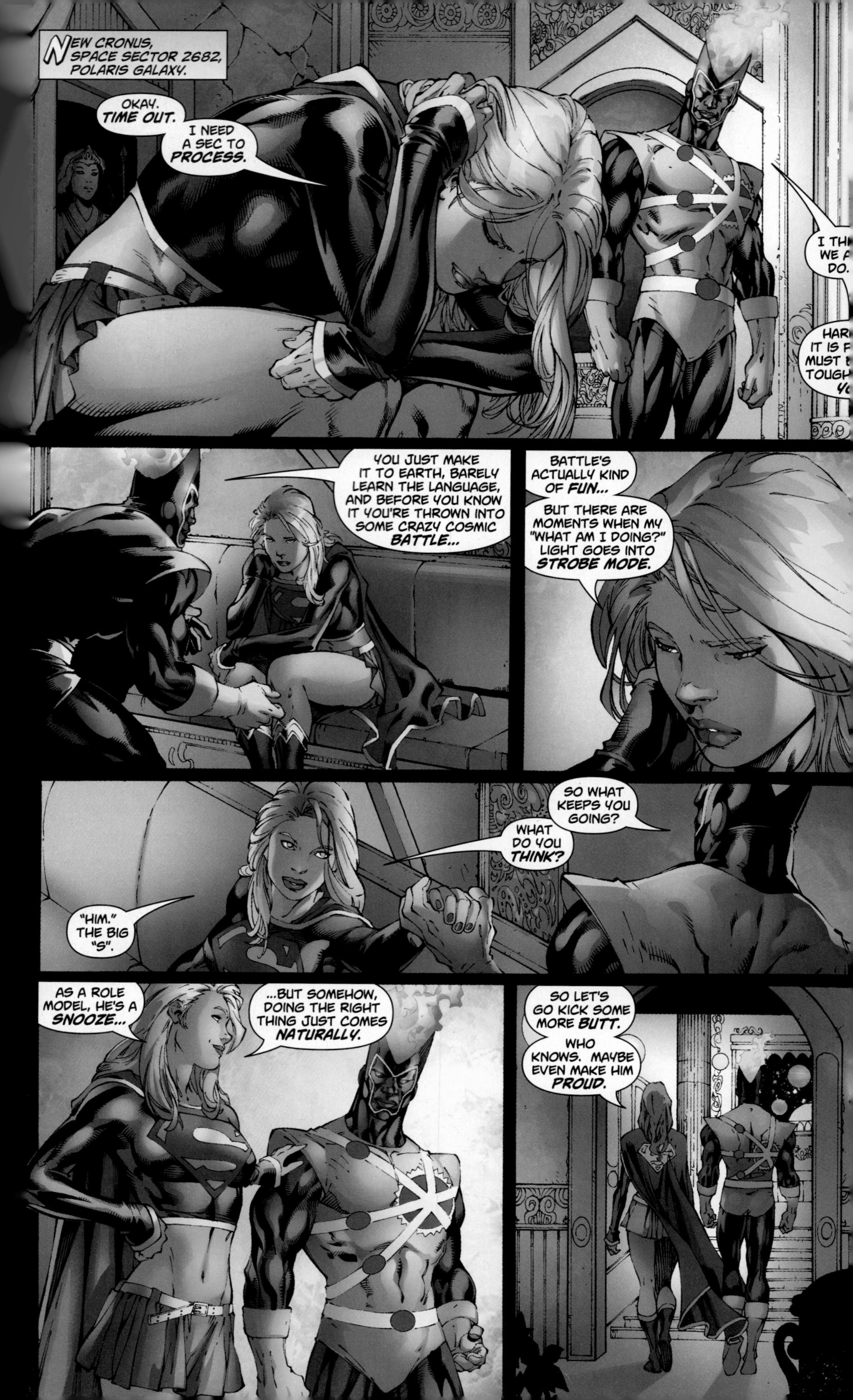
NEW CRONUS, SPACE SECTOR 2682, POLARIS GALAXY.
OKAY. TIME OUT.
I NEED A SEC TO PROCESS.
YOU JUST MAKE IT TO EARTH, BARELY LEARN THE LANGUAGE, AND BEFORE YOU KNOW IT YOU'RE THROWN INTO SOME CRAZY COSMIC BATTLE...
BATTLE'S ACTUALLY KIND OF FUN...
BUT THERE ARE MOMENTS WHEN MY "WHAT AM I DOING?" LIGHT GOES INTO STROBE MODE.
SO WHAT KEEPS YOU GOING?
WHAT DO YOU THINK?
"HIM." THE BIG "S".
AS A ROLE MODEL, HE'S A SNOOZE...
...BUT SOMEHOW, DOING THE RIGHT THING JUST COMES NATURALLY.
SO LET'S GO KICK SOME MORE BUTT.
WHO KNOWS. MAYBE EVEN MAKE HIM PROUD.

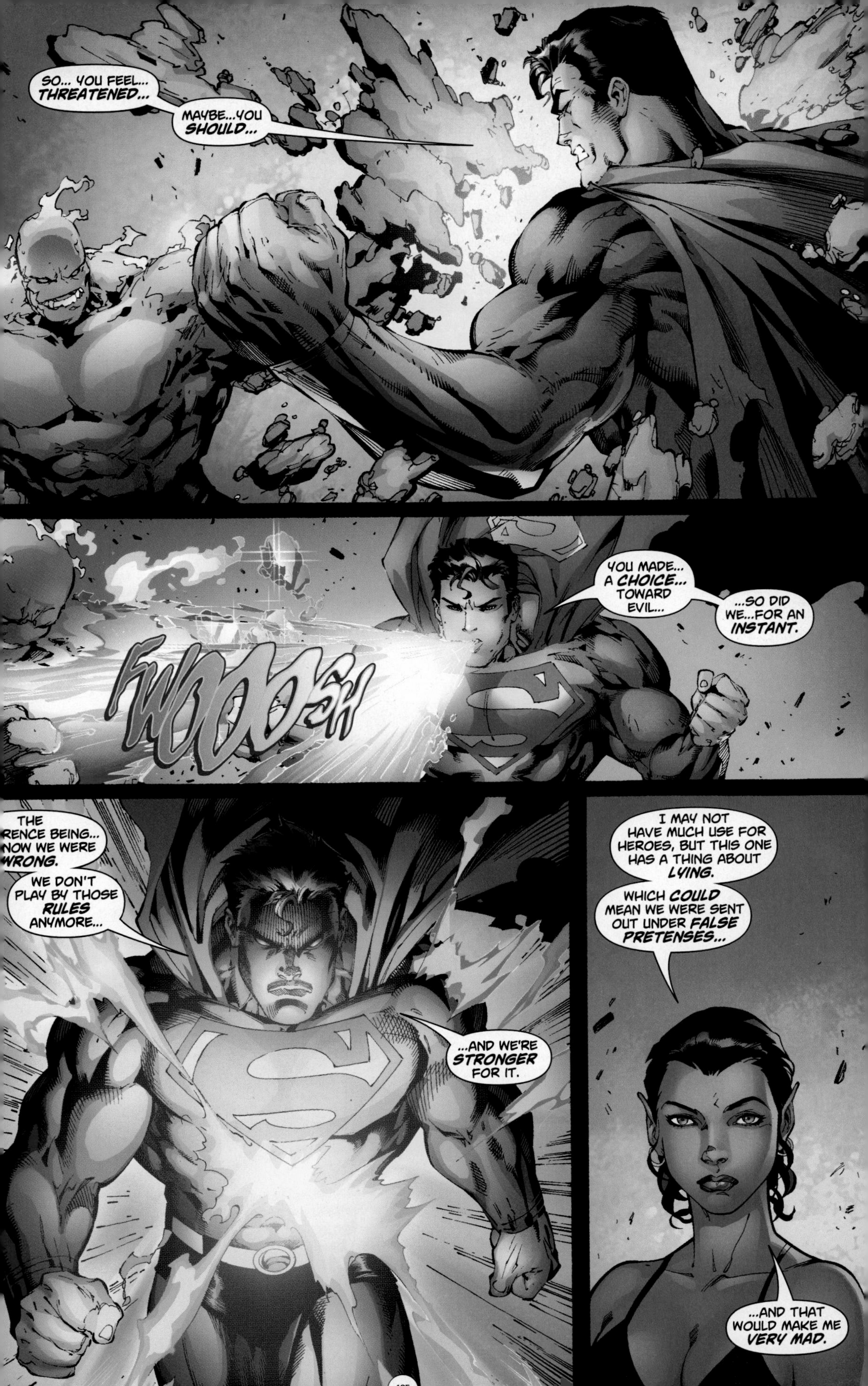
SO... YOU FEEL... THREATENED...
MAYBE...YOU SHOULD...
YOU MADE... A CHOICE... TOWARD EVIL...
...SO DID WE...FOR AN INSTANT.
FWOOOSH
THE RENCE BEING... NOW WE WERE WRONG.
WE DON'T PLAY BY THOSE RULES ANYMORE...
...AND WE'RE STRONGER FOR IT.
I MAY NOT HAVE MUCH USE FOR HEROES, BUT THIS ONE HAS A THING ABOUT LYING.
WHICH COULD MEAN WE WERE SENT OUT UNDER FALSE PRETENSES...
...AND THAT WOULD MAKE ME VERY MAD.

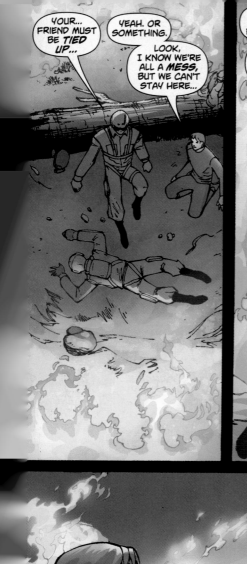

YOUR... FRIEND MUST BE *TIED UP...*

YEAH. OR SOMETHING. LOOK, I KNOW WE'RE ALL A *MESS*, BUT WE CAN'T STAY HERE...

nghh... FEELS *BROKEN...* YOU BETTER *GO...* I'LL RIDE IT OUT WITH JACK...

NO...WE'LL RIDE IT OUT *TOGETHER...*

AND HOPE FOR A MIRA--

HEY! YOU GUYS NEED A LIFT?

ROOOAARR

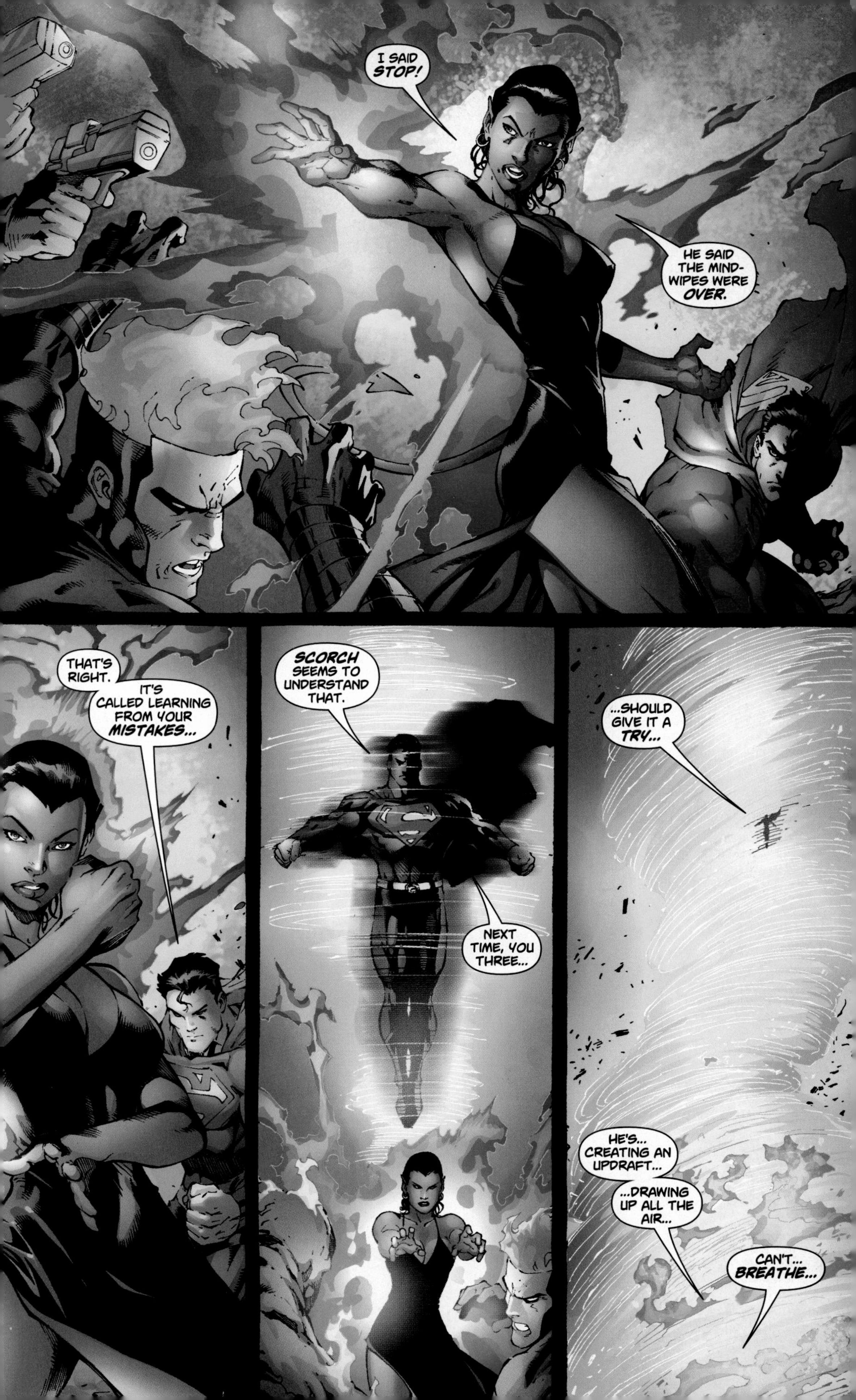
I SAID STOP!
HE SAID THE MIND-WIPES WERE OVER.
THAT'S RIGHT.
IT'S CALLED LEARNING FROM YOUR MISTAKES...
SCORCH SEEMS TO UNDERSTAND THAT.
NEXT TIME, YOU THREE...
...SHOULD GIVE IT A TRY...
HE'S... CREATING AN UPDRAFT...
...DRAWING UP ALL THE AIR...
CAN'T... BREATHE...

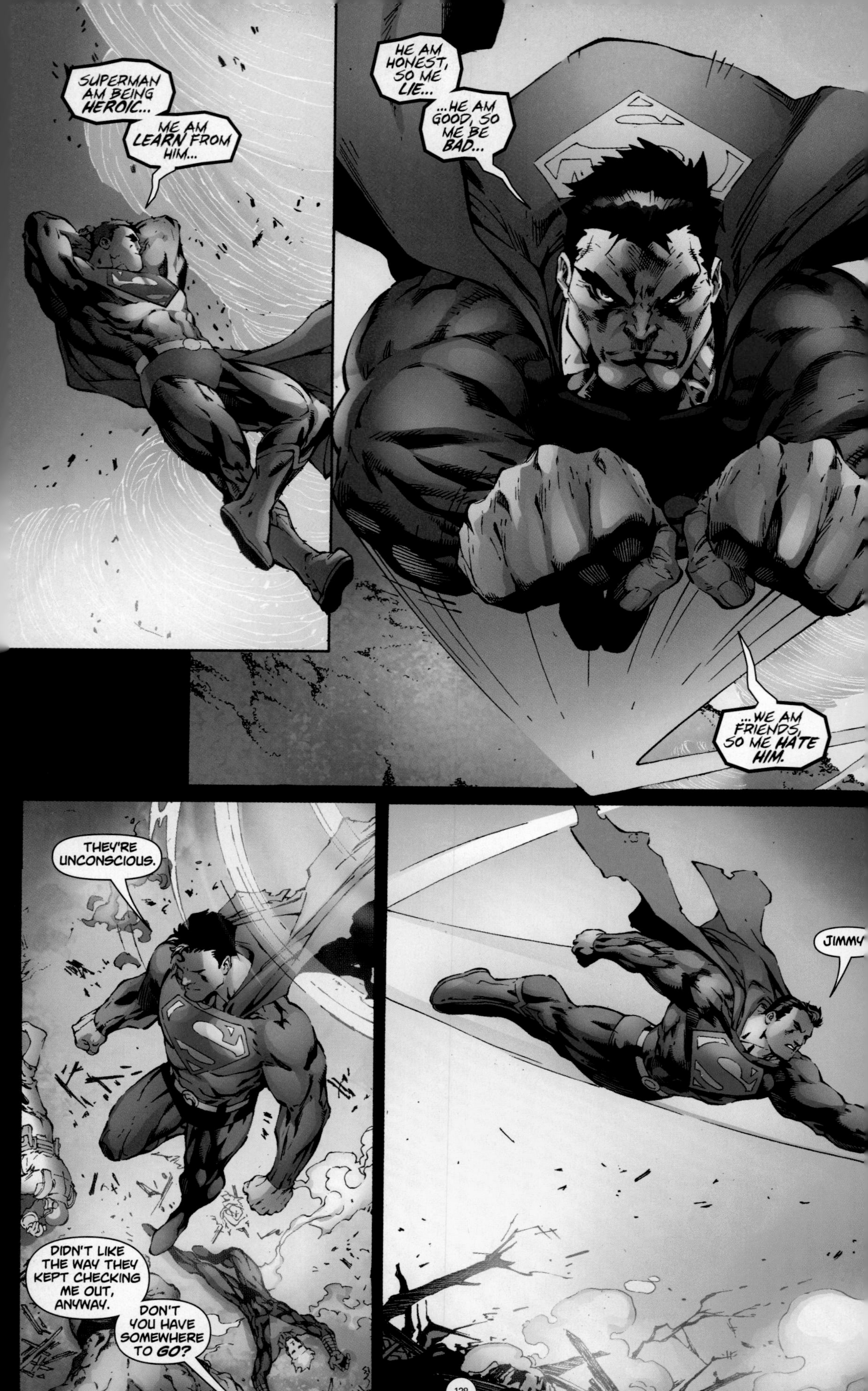
SUPERMAN AM BEING HEROIC...
ME AM LEARN FROM HIM...
HE AM HONEST, SO ME LIE...
...HE AM GOOD, SO ME BE BAD...
...WE AM FRIENDS, SO ME HATE HIM.
THEY'RE UNCONSCIOUS.
DIDN'T LIKE THE WAY THEY KEPT CHECKING ME OUT, ANYWAY.
DON'T YOU HAVE SOMEWHERE TO GO?
JIMMY

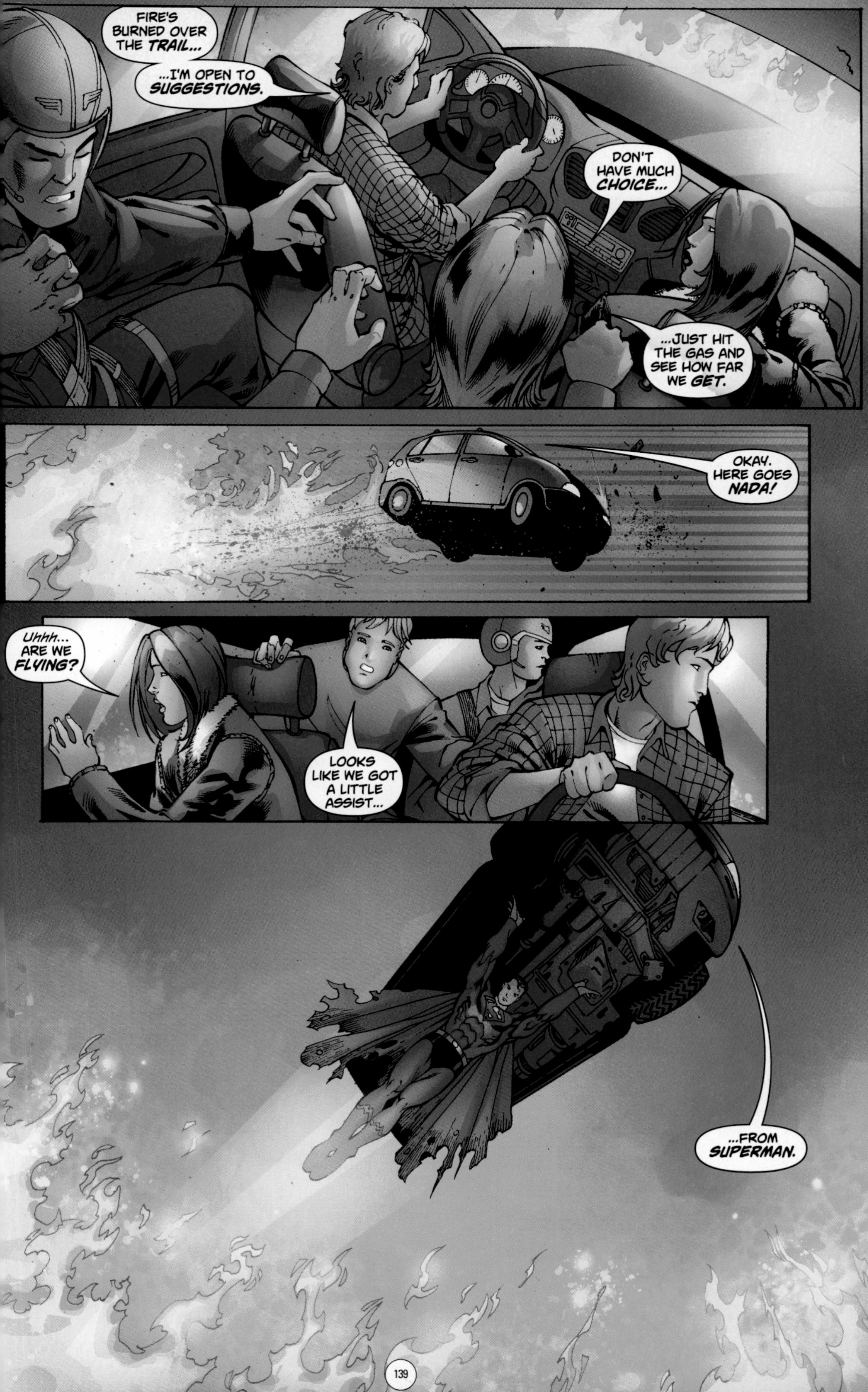
FIRE'S BURNED OVER THE TRAIL...
...I'M OPEN TO SUGGESTIONS.
DON'T HAVE MUCH CHOICE...
...JUST HIT THE GAS AND SEE HOW FAR WE GET.
OKAY. HERE GOES NADA!
Uhhh... ARE WE FLYING?
LOOKS LIKE WE GOT A LITTLE ASSIST...
...FROM SUPERMAN.

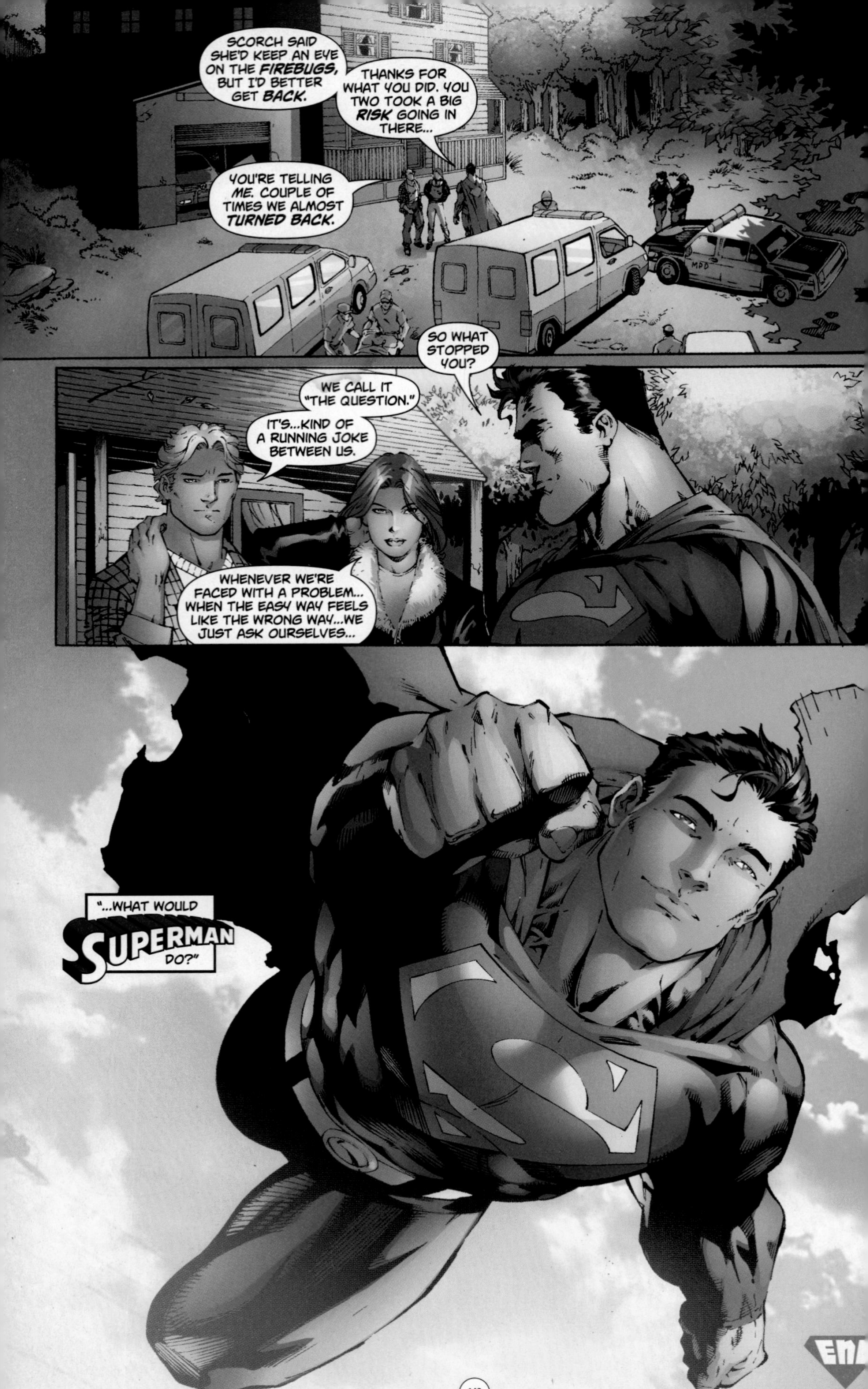
SCORCH SAID SHE'D KEEP AN EYE ON THE FIREBUGS, BUT I'D BETTER GET BACK.
THANKS FOR WHAT YOU DID. YOU TWO TOOK A BIG RISK GOING IN THERE...
YOU'RE TELLING ME. COUPLE OF TIMES WE ALMOST TURNED BACK.
MPD
SO WHAT STOPPED YOU?
WE CALL IT "THE QUESTION."
IT'S...KIND OF A RUNNING JOKE BETWEEN US.
WHENEVER WE'RE FACED WITH A PROBLEM... WHEN THE EASY WAY FEELS LIKE THE WRONG WAY...WE JUST ASK OURSELVES...
"...WHAT WOULD SUPERMAN DO?"
END

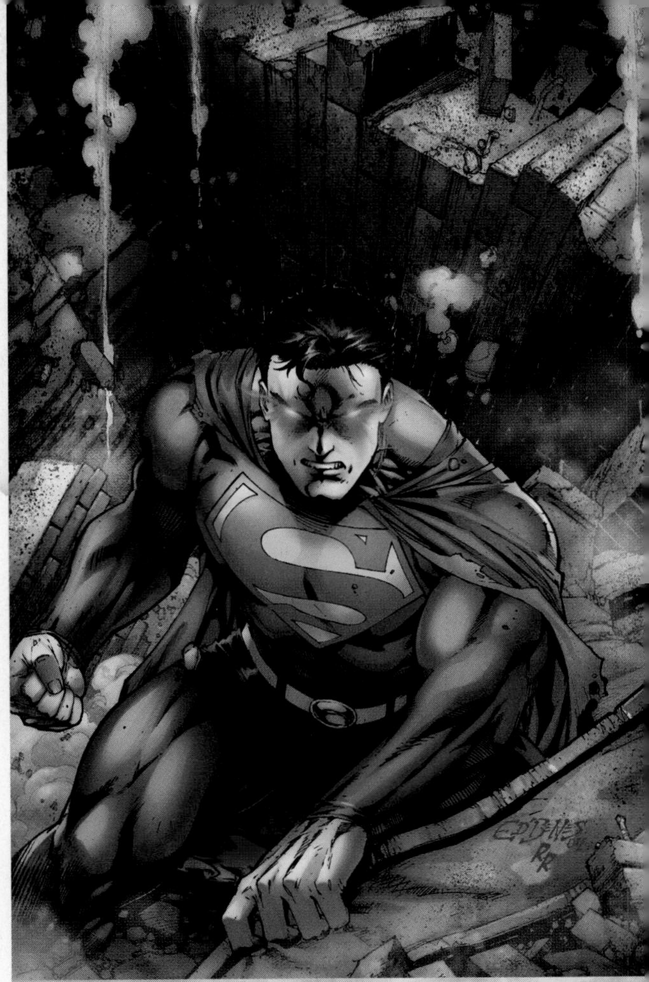

Superman #217
Art by Ed Benes
Color by Rod Reis

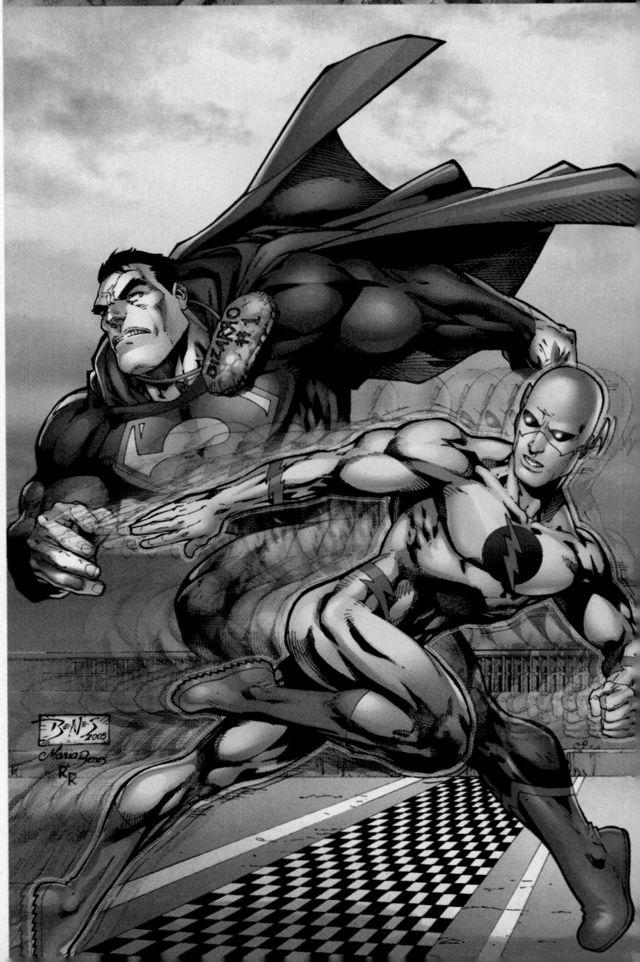
BIZARRO #1

Superman #221
Art by Ed Benes & Mariah Benes
Color by Rod Reis

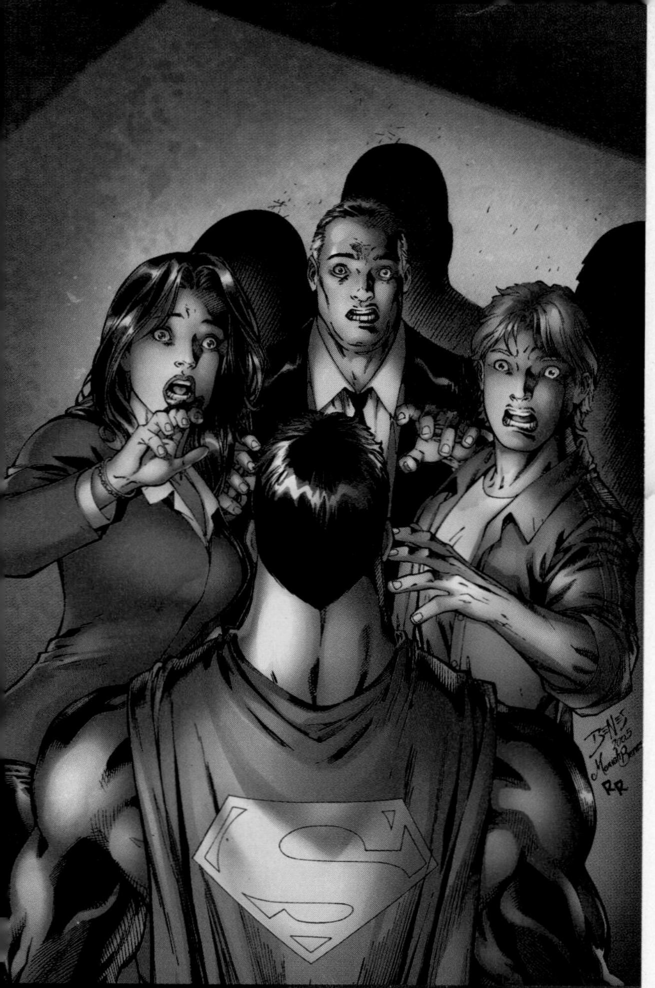

Superman #222
Art by Ed Benes & Mariah Benes
Color by Rod Reis

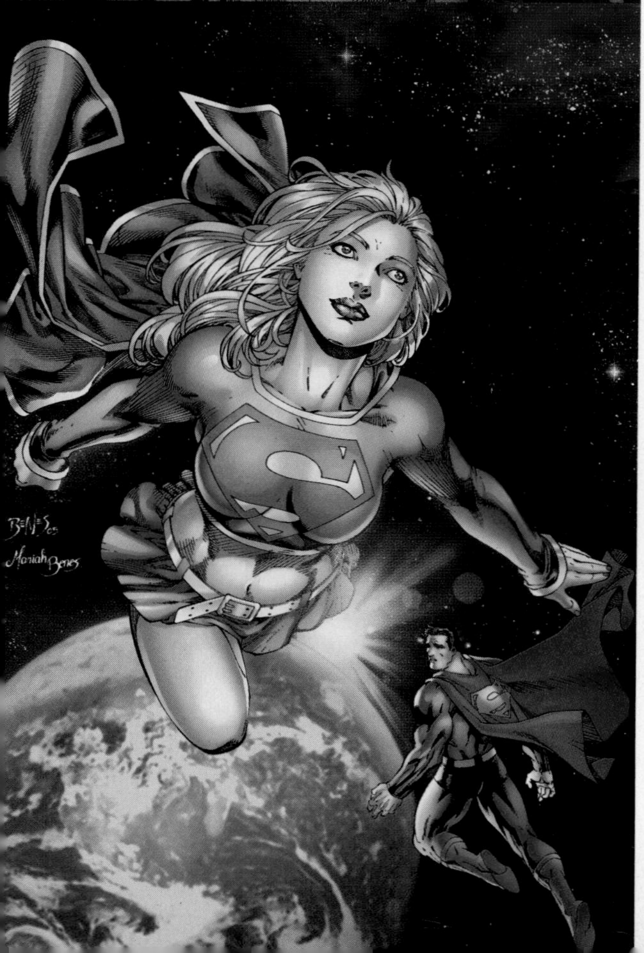

Superman #223
Art by Ed Benes & Mariah Benes
Color by Rod Reis

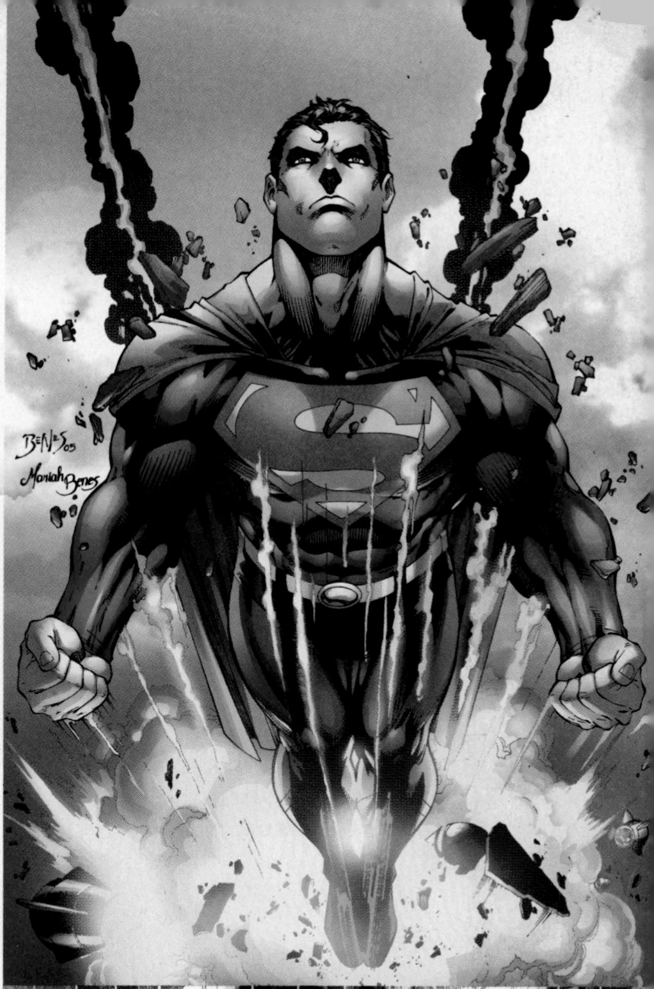

Superman #224
Art by Ed Benes & Mariah Benes
Color by Rod Reis

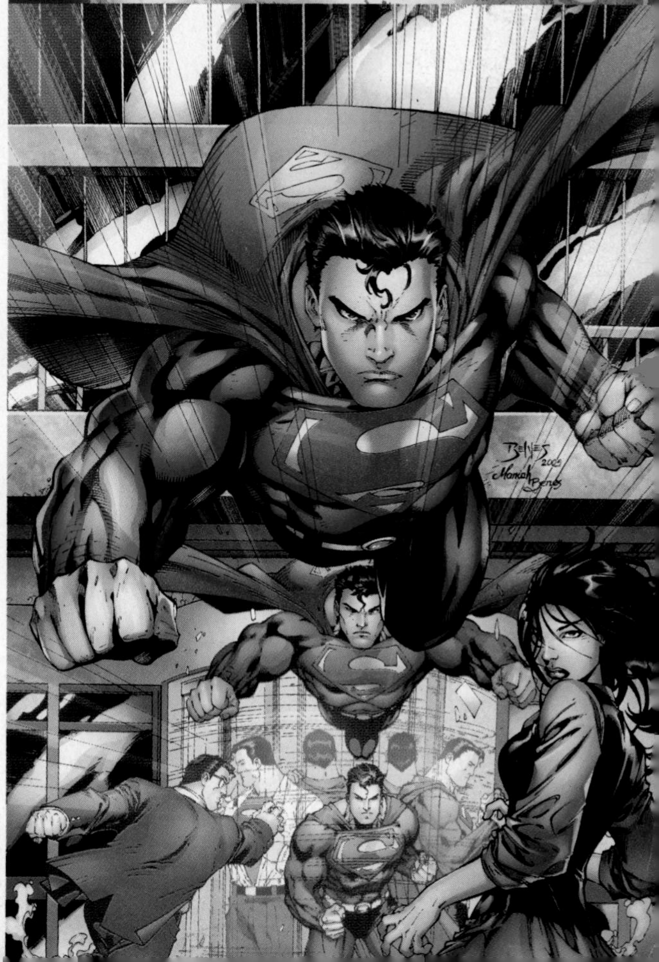

Superman #225
Art by Ed Benes & Mariah Benes
Color by Rod Reis

SUPERMAN

READ MORE OF THE
MAN OF STEEL'S
ADVENTURES IN THESE
COLLECTIONS FROM
DC COMICS:

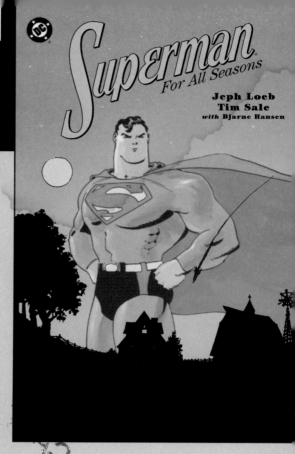

Superman
For All Seasons

Jeph Loeb
Tim Sale
with Bjarne Hansen

SUPERMAN FOR ALL SEASONS

A tale of Superman's
earliest adventures told
on a mythic scale by the
award-winning creative
team of **Jeph Loeb** and
Tim Sale, with spectacular
colors by **Bjarne Hansen**.

SUPERMAN: SECRET IDENTITY

**KURT BUSIEK
STUART IMMONEN**

SUPERMAN: THE MAN OF STEEL

**JOHN BYRNE
DICK GIORDANO**

SUPERMAN: RED SON

**MARK MILLAR
DAVE JOHNSON
VARIOUS**

SEARCH THE GRAPHIC NOVELS SECTION OF
WWW.DCCOMICS.COM

FOR ART AND INFORMATION ON ALL OF OUR BOOKS